VIRGIN LAND

VIRGIN LAND

THE AMERICAN WEST AS SYMBOL AND MYTH

Henry Nash Smith

HARVARD UNIVERSITY PRESS
Cambridge, Massachusetts

FOR ELINOR

PREFACE TO THE TWENTIETH ANNIVERSARY PRINTING

This reissue of a book first published in 1950 reproduces the original printing with only minor revisions to remove some ineptitudes of style and correct a few errors of fact. Much good work has been done during the past twenty years on topics dealt with in *Virgin Land,* but none of it seems to me to cast doubt on my conclusions, and I have decided to let the book stand substantially unchanged.

Nevertheless, one problem does demand comment. It grows out of the following statements about "symbol" and "myth" in the original preface: "I do not mean to raise the question whether such products of the imagination accurately reflect empirical fact. They exist on a different plane. But as I have tried to show, they sometimes exert a decided influence on practical affairs." Several critics, beginning with my former student Barry Marks,[1] have pointed out that these sentences are not borne out in the book itself, which deals repeatedly with the relation of symbols and myths to empirical fact. What then did my disclaimer mean? Although the phrasing was clumsy, I was trying to make a valid point: I wanted to protest against the common usage of the term "myth" to mean simply an erroneous belief, and to insist that the relation between the imaginative constructions I was dealing with and the history of the West in the nineteenth century was a more complicated affair.

My idea was sounder than I realized. For on rereading the book now I am forced to the chastening realization that I was guilty of the same kind of oversimplification I ascribed to others. Although I had gained some theoretical perspective on the nature of fictions from Bergson, Lévy-Bruhl, and Vaihinger, my attitude toward popular beliefs about the West was in practice often reductionist. I tended to conceive of them simply as distortions of empirical fact and to regard this as their most interesting characteristic. As Alan Trachtenberg recently observed, the analytic model implied by my metaphor of distinct planes is "too severely fixed and dualistic." [2] It encourages an unduly rigid distinction between symbols and myths on the one hand, and on the other a supposed extramental historical reality discoverable by means of conventional scholarly procedures. The vestiges of dualism in my assumptions made it difficult for me to recognize that there is a continuous dialectic interplay between the mind and its environment, and that our perceptions of objects and events are no less a part of consciousness than are our fantasies.

Yet it might be argued that the materials presented in *Virgin Land* are abundant and various enough to compensate for this inadequacy of method. They provide a basis for developing my original statements about symbol and myth into a more elaborate scheme. For one thing, because such images tend to be timeless, their relation to historical events is always changing. Thus (1) the discussion of the Lewis and Clark expedition in Chapters I and II shows that although these explorers failed to discover a feasible route for trade with the Orient (as Jefferson had hoped), the notion of a northwest passage to India was not entirely illusory. It helped to motivate further exploration, and an Oregon Trail was eventually found along which emigrants could travel overland from the Missouri frontier to the Pacific Coast. Again, (2) although the myth of the Garden of the World (discussed in Chapters XIII-XV) was of course never realized in all its details, and was eventually outmoded by the industrial development of the Mississippi Valley, it embodied the partial truth that the yeoman ideal of an agri-

cultural economy based on free labor had greater imaginative appeal for voters than did the myth of the Southern
plantation and the slave system. This fact contributed significantly to the Republican victory of 1860 and therefore
to the defeat of the Southern program of secession.

An even more complex relation between faith and material
circumstances appears in Chapter XVI, "The Garden and
the Desert," which presents evidence to show that (3) the
myth of the Great American Desert was partially supplanted
by a competing version of the myth of the Garden as agricultural settlement moved out upon the subhumid plains
following the Civil War. The fanciful belief that "rain follows the plow" was both effect and cause of social and economic pressures toward settlement of the plains. On the
other hand, Chapter XIX advances the thesis that (4) the
application of the myth of the Garden to vast areas in the
trans-Mississippi West having very low rainfall prevented
desirable reform of the public land system by masking the
facts about the climate. To mention only one further example
of interaction between collective representations and historical processes, (5) the elements of the myth of the Garden
embodied in Frederick Jackson Turner's "frontier hypothesis" (discussed in Chapter XXII) give to that theory an
imaginative power transcending its denotative function as
an explanation of economic, social, and political changes.

These illustrations point to the conclusion that history cannot happen — that is, men cannot engage in purposive
group behavior — without images which simultaneously express collective desires and impose coherence on the infinitely numerous and infinitely varied data of experience.
These images are never, of course, exact reproductions of the
physical and social environment. They cannot motivate and
direct action unless they are drastic simplifications, yet if the
impulse toward clarity of form is not controlled by some
process of verification, symbols and myths can become

dangerous by inciting behavior grossly inappropriate to the given historical situation. The special status accorded agriculture in federal legislation shows that Congress is still markedly influenced by the now archaic myth of the Garden.

In addition to the acknowledgments in the original Preface, I wish to record here my special indebtedness to Barry Marks, Roy H. Pearce, and Alan Trachtenberg for perceptive criticism of *Virgin Land;* to Albert Johannsen for detailed comment on the labyrinthine bibliography of Beadle publications;[3] and to Robert Hirst for expert editorial assistance.

H. N. S.

BERKELEY, CALIFORNIA
OCTOBER 1969

---

[1] "The Concept of Myth in *Virgin Land*," *American Quarterly*, V, 71–76 (Spring 1953).

[2] In an unpublished paper entitled "Myth, History and Literature in *Virgin Land*" which was read at a meeting of the American Studies Association of Northern California, Stanford University, 30 August 1967.

[3] Even before the publication of his imposing two-volume work, *The House of Beadle and Adams and Its Dime and Nickel Novels. The Story of a Vanished Literature* (Norman, Oklahoma, 1950), Dr. Johannsen was kind enough to send me a letter clarifying some problems of dating that I had been unable to solve on the basis of the notable collection of dime novels in the Henry E. Huntington Library.

PREFACE TO THE FIRST PRINTING

The terms "myth" and "symbol" occur so often in the following pages that the reader deserves some warning about them. I use the words to designate larger or smaller units of the same kind of thing, namely an intellectual construction that fuses concept and emotion into an image. The myths and symbols with which I deal have the further characteristic of being collective representations rather than the work of a single mind. I do not mean to raise the question whether such products of the imagination accurately reflect empirical fact. They exist on a different plane. But as I have tried to show, they sometimes exert a decided influence on practical affairs.

In the course of a long preoccupation with this subject I have contracted intellectual debts that I shall never be able to repay, and can not even fully acknowledge. John H. McGinnis and J. Frank Dobie first opened my eyes to the significance of the West within American society. Howard M. Jones and Frederick Merk directed the studies from which the present book has grown. Bernard DeVoto has more than once pointed me toward materials I should otherwise have missed. My former students Leo Marx and J. C. Levenson have tried hard to save me from antiquarianism. Kenneth McLean and A. Whitney Griswold showed the true scholar's disinterestedness by offering expert advice to a stranger whose only claim on their attention was a common interest in ideas. Louis B. Wright, Robert G. Cleland, Bernard De-Voto, and Theodore Hornberger have read the entire manuscript and have given me the benefit of their learning and wisdom, although of course they are not accountable for my vagaries. I have received much help from the staffs of libraries, especially the Harvard College Library, the Mirabeau B. Lamar Library of the University of Texas, the Library of the University of Minnesota, and the Henry E. Huntington Library and Art Gallery. The Huntington Library and the Rockefeller Foundation subsidized a year's leave of absence from teaching which enabled me to write the book, and I have also been given generous financial aid from the Research Fund of the Graduate School of the University of Minnesota.

Portions of this work, sometimes slightly revised, have appeared in the *Huntington Library Quarterly*, the *Mississippi Valley Historical Review*, the *Pacific Spectator*, and the *Southwest Review*. I wish to thank the editors of these journals for permission to reprint material from their pages.

H. N. S.

MINNEAPOLIS
CHRISTMAS 1949

CONTENTS

BOOK THREE: THE GARDEN OF THE WORLD

ILLUSTRATIONS

(following page 98)

CERES IN THE GARDEN OF THE WORLD

Frontispiece of Charles Mead's *Mississippian Scenery* (Philadelphia, 1819). An allegorical grouping of the major symbols of the dream of an agricultural utopia in the Mississippi Valley. The goddess of fertility leans upon the sacred plow. In the background one pioneer fells a tree with the other great Western implement, the axe, while his companion sets about breaking the newly cleared earth. A primitive steamboat in the middle distance suggests future commercial development.

SERIES ONE

VERSIONS OF THE PERSONA OF LEATHERSTOCKING

THE EARLIEST GRAPHIC REPRESENTATION OF LEATHERSTOCK-ING

From a drawing by Henry Inman (1801–1846) for the original edition of Cooper's *The Pioneers* (Philadelphia, 1823). Judge Temple, patron of the new community on the upstate New York frontier, has accidentally wounded Oliver Effingham, the hero. Leatherstocking is depicted in the background, where he technically belongs in a novel built about upper-class characters. He wears a fur cap and a hunting shirt of deerskin, and carries a long rifle, but the artist does not insist on these details.

SETH JONES, PRINCIPAL DESCENDANT OF LEATHERSTOCKING IN THE EARLY DIME NOVELS

Frontispiece for Edward S. Ellis's *Seth Jones; or, The Captives of the Frontier* (originally Beadle's Dime Novels No. 8, New York, copyright 1860; this edition was published in London in 1861. Beadle's editor, Orville Victor called *Seth Jones* "the perfect Dime Novel." It eventually sold 400,000 copies in the United States and England. The character of the aged hunter illustrated here is literally a *persona*, a disguise adopted by the elegant young hero. The cap is almost pedantically shown to be made of coonskin, the hunting shirt, leggings, and moccasins are drawn with minute fidelity, and the rifle, powderhorn, and hunting knife conform to regulations. The beard has been added in accordance with changing styles in the nation at large.

LEW DERNOR CONDUCTING EDITH SUDBURY TO SAFETY

Cover illustration for Edward S. Ellis's *The Riflemen of the Miami* (Beadle's Dime Novels No. 36, New York, copyright 1862). This hunter wears the standard costume, with a beard like Seth Jones's, but a transformation has begun. The frontiersman now has genteel sensibility. He feels the pangs of love as his horny palm grasps the heroine's almost fairy hand, and he will eventually be allowed to marry her.

DEADWOOD DICK BUYS SALAMANDER SAM'S DAUGHTER AT AUCTION

Cover illustration for Edward L. Wheeler's *Blonde Bill; or, Deadwood Dick's Home Base. A Romance of the "Silent Tongues"* (Beadle's Half Dime Library No. 138, New York, copyright 1880). Salamander Sam sells his daughter Dashing Dol at auction. The man at the extreme right is the villainous Congressman Ray Vernon of Ohio who wishes to buy the girl for base purposes. The figure at the extreme left is Deadwood Dick disguised as Blonde Bill, who pays ten thousand dollars for the girl and gives her her liberty.

BUFFALO BILL, THE KING OF BORDER MEN

From *New York Weekly*, December 23, 1869. An illustration for the opening instalment of Ned Buntline's first serial about Buffalo Bill, which ran in Street & Smith's *New York Weekly* from December 1869 to March 1870. It will be noted that, except for his felt hat, the hero wears an authentic Leatherstocking costume, with deerskin leggings and moccasins. He carries a muzzle-loading rifle, and is on foot. His beard resembles that of Lew Dernor. In 1872, when Buntline's second serial about Buffalo Bill began in the *Weekly*, the hero was depicted with a moustache but no beard. The familiar goatee first appeared with the second instalment of this story.

BUFFALO BILL IN THE GRAND CANYON

Cover illustration for *Buffalo Bill's Spy-Shadower; or, The Masked Men of Grand Canyon,* by Prentiss Ingraham (Beadle's New York Dime Library No. 777, New York, copyright 1893). Wild Western costume has undergone a decided evolution. The deerksin leggings have been replaced by expensive top-boots; the hunting shirt has been shortened for a horseman's use and touched up with embroidery. Buffalo Bill's weapon is now a repeating rifle. Because of his strong ties with the past, he is slow to adopt the revolver that other Wild Western heroes are coming to prefer.

THE EMIGRANT'S DREAM OF KANSAS

From page 217 of John H. Beadle's *The Undeveloped West,* copyright 1873. This fantasy gently satirizes the "Kansas fever" of the years immediately following the Civil War, an epidemic resembling the Kentucky fever that raged after the Revolution and the Oregon and Texas fevers of the 1840's.

SERIES TWO
DIME-NOVEL HEROINES

CORA RICHTER, WIFE OF A YOUNG MISSIONARY, ABDUCTED BY AN INDIAN

Cover illustration for Edward S. Ellis's *The Lost Trail: A Legend of the Far West* (Beadle's Dime Novels No. 71, New York, copyright 1864). As this illustration shows, the early Dime Novels take over Cooper's distressed female without change. She is a passive victim of Indian warfare. The side that retains possession of the heroine wins the match, but she herself has no real function in the plot. According to the rules of Wild Western fiction, the lady herself is in no danger of indignity from her captor.

WILD EDNA, THE GIRL BRIGAND

Cover illustration for Edward L. Wheeler's *Old Avalanche, The Great Annihilator; or, Wild Edna, the Girl Brigand* (Beadle's Half Dime Library No. 45; "Thirteenth Edition," New York, copyright 1878). In the late 1870's Dime-Novel writers begin to use heroines thirsting for revenge upon evil men who have injured them or their parents. Such Amazons adopt a feminine version of the Leatherstocking costume, carry a rifle and pistols, and possess the skills of the frontier. But for a time they preserve their maidenly dignity.

DENVER DOLL, THE DETECTIVE QUEEN

Cover illustration for Edward L. Wheeler's *Denver Doll, the Detective Queen; or, Yankee Eisler's Big Surround* (Beadle's Half Dime Library No. 277, New York, copyright 1882). Dime-Novel heroines soon grow bolder and less refined. Denver Doll has adopted the Western gambler's boiled shirt and diamond stick-pin, Buffalo Bill's top-boots, and a bright sash with Mexican connotations.

CALAMITY JANE, FEMALE COUNTERPART OF DEADWOOD DICK

Cover illustration for Edward L. Wheeler's *Deadwood Dick in Leadville; or, A Strange Stroke for Liberty* (Beadle's Pocket Library No. 88, New York, copyright 1885). The heroine is now as tough as anybody. She smokes, drinks, swears, and is handy with the pistols that are at last becoming the standard weapons of Wild Western fiction. This story had appeared in Beadle's Half-Dime Library in 1879, but possibly with a different cover illustration.

ACKNOWLEDGMENTS

"CERES IN THE GARDEN OF THE WORLD" IS REPRODUCED THROUGH THE COURTESY OF THE HARVARD UNIVERSITY LIBRARY; "BUFFALO BILL, THE KING OF BORDER MEN" IS REPRODUCED THROUGH THE COURTESY OF THE LIBRARY OF CONGRESS; AND ALL THE OTHER ILLUSTRATIONS ARE REPRODUCED THROUGH THE COURTESY OF THE HENRY E. HUNTINGTON LIBRARY.

PROLOGUE ☆ ☆ ☆

EIGHTEENTH-CENTURY ORIGINS

I discern . . . a new power, the People
occupied in the wilderness . . . .

> — WILLIAM GILPIN, *The Central Gold
> Region* (1860)

Eighteenth-Century Origins

What is an American? asked St. John de Crèvecœur before the Revolution, and the question has been repeated by every generation from his time to ours. Poets and novelists, historians and statesmen have undertaken to answer it, but the varying national self-consciousness they have tried to capture always escapes final statement. Men of Thomas Jefferson's day emphasized freedom and republicanism as the defining characteristics of American society; the definitions of later thinkers stressed the cosmopolitan blending of a hundred peoples into one, or mechanical ingenuity, or devotion to business enterprise. But one of the most persistent generalizations concerning American life and character is the notion that our society has been shaped by the pull of a vacant continent drawing population westward through the passes of the Alleghenies, across the Mississippi Valley, over the high plains and mountains of the Far West to the Pacific Coast.

This axiom, which was grasped at least in part by Crèvecœur, before him by Benjamin Franklin, and subsequently by Emerson, by Lincoln, by Whitman, by a hundred others, comes to us bearing the personal imprint of a Wisconsin historian, Frederick Jackson Turner, who gave it its classic statement in a paper on "The Significance of the Frontier in American History" read before the American Historical Association at the Chicago World's Columbian Exposition in 1893. Although Turner asserted that the westward movement was about to come to an end with what he believed to be the closing of the frontier of free land in the West, a whole generation of historians took over his hypothesis and rewrote American history in terms of it. Despite a growing tendency of scholars to react against the Turner doctrine, it is still by far the most familiar interpretation of the American past.

Brilliant and persuasive as Turner was, his contention that the frontier and the West had dominated American development could hardly have attained such universal acceptance if it had not found an echo in ideas and attitudes already current. Since the enormous currency of the theory proves that it voices a massive and deeply-held conviction, the recent debate over what Turner actually meant and over the truth or falsity of his hypothesis is much more than a mere academic quibble. It concerns the image of themselves which many — perhaps most — Americans of the present day cherish, an image that defines what Americans think of their past, and therefore what they propose to make of themselves in the future.

The present study traces the impact of the West, the vacant continent beyond the frontier, on the consciousness of Americans and follows the principal consequences of this impact in literature and social thought down to Turner's formulation of it. Whatever the merits of the Turner thesis, the doctrine that the United States is a continental nation rather than a member with Europe of an Atlantic community has had a formative influence on the American mind and deserves historical treatment in its own right.

At the opening of the eighteenth century the image of the West beyond the Appalachian Mountains was very dim in the minds of those subjects of the British crown who inhabited the fringe of colonies along the Atlantic coast. The unsettled forest no longer seemed, as it had to Michael Wigglesworth in 1662, a "Devils den,"

> A waste and howling wilderness,
>   Where none inhabited
> But hellish fiends, and brutish men
>   That devils worshiped.[1]

Yet few English-speaking colonists had reliable knowledge of the interior of the continent. In so far as the West had come under European control at all, it was French. The English colonists had been engaged in war against this enemy as early as the 1690's, but not even the boldest prophet could imagine a day when the

English power would extend over the unmeasured expanse of the Mississippi Valley. The imperial development of Britain was moving in another direction, toward dominion over the seven seas rather than toward the blank and remote hinterland of North America.

The earliest analyses of British policy in the Mississippi Valley proceed from these assumptions. Settlement in the interior might be expedient as a means of defense against the French or as an incident of the fur trade, but it had no meaning in itself. There was no reason for the government to encourage inland colonization because agricultural commodities were far too bulky to be transported from the interior to the seacoast and such colonies could have no part in the sea-borne commerce upon which the British Empire was based. The Council of Trade and Plantations declared in a memorial submitted to George I in 1721 that "all the settlemts. that may at any time hereafter be made beyond the mountains, or on ye lakes, must necessarily build their hopes of support much more upon ye advantage to be made by the Indian trade, than upon any profits to arise from planting at so great a distance from the sea." [2]

Even as late as 1763, when the French had been defeated and it was clear that British sovereignty would be extended over the Mississippi Valley, Lord Egremont, Secretary of State, proposed with perfect logic that Americans with an itch for emigration should be forbidden to move out into the interior. They should be directed instead to Nova Scotia or Georgia, near the sea, "where they would be useful to their Mother Country instead of planting themselves in the Heart of America out of reach of Government where from the great difficulty of procuring European commodities, they would be compelled to commerce and manufactures to the infinite prejudice of Britain. . . ." [3]

This was a rational analysis of the problem of the Empire. Colonies were sources of raw materials for which British merchants could find a market either in the United Kingdom or on the continent of Europe. Europe was still largely self-sufficient in the production of foodstuffs except for specifically subtropical items like sugar. There was a British or a European market for furs, for tobacco, and for "naval stores" — turpentine, pitch, timber suitable for shipbuilding, and so on. But it seemed unlikely that farmers in the Ohio Valley would be able to produce any commodities worth transporting to a transatlantic market. Hard-headed economic thinking supported the faction in Parliament which opposed taking over the Mississippi Valley from France. And the economic argument was reinforced by the obvious ad-ministrative difficulties which would be created by expansion of population beyond easy reach of the seacoast.

But the American West was nevertheless there, a physical fact of great if unknown magnitude. It strongly influenced the debate over the nature of the Empire which preceded the Revolution. The interior of North America was an almost infinite expanse of arable land capable of supporting a large population. It was potential wealth on an unprecedented scale. The magnetic attrac-tion of this untouched natural resource interfered with the con-ception of an empire based on maritime commerce by suggesting the quite different vision of a populous agricultural society, largely self-contained, in the Mississippi Valley. The West there-fore posed a major question: Could the fabric of the Empire be made flexible enough to allow agricultural expansion in North America without breaking the economic and political integration centered in London?

It was possible for a sincere "imperial patriot" to maintain that such a creative development of the British system was both inevitable and desirable. The decision of William Pitt, for ex-ample, to take over the French possessions in America at the Peace of Paris in 1763 indicated his acceptance of this general view.[4] And the American colonies had already produced in Benjamin Franklin a far-seeing theorist who understood what a portentous role North America might play in the future develop-ment of British power. Franklin's pamphlets on western settle-ment were occasioned by his interest in various land companies that were seeking grants in the Ohio Valley from the Crown, but his conclusions were a remarkably accurate prevision of what this new force would mean in the development of American society.

First of all, he grasped an elementary principle distilled from more than a century of English colonial experience in the New

World: he saw that agriculture would long continue to be the
dominant economic enterprise of continental America. Orthodox
theory, which presupposed trade as the basis of British power,
had been developed from the point of view of the merchant, and
in this broad sense may b   for convenience, called mercantilist.
Franklin, on the other ha   s an agrarian. He starts out
from the "political arithr   Sir William Petty,
and their followers in   ury, a method
which showed the first   study of trends
in population. But he   birth rate, under
the influence of an ab   d waiting always
just beyond the fron   birth rate of "full-
settled old Countri   in the New World
doubles every twer   al progression leads
to staggering con   years, he asserts, the
population of th   s in America will be
"more than the   e greatest Number of
Englishmen wil   r." [5]

Here was a r   ish statesmen must deal.
They might striv   slation forbidding settlement in the inte   blandly avoided saying
until his patience wore t..   eated failures to secure the
land grants he wanted — such law   ere not likely to have much
effect. Besides, a brilliant and constructive alternative lay open
to the makers of British policy. The merchants of England must
realize that colonies like those in North America were vastly
more important as potential markets than simply as sources of
raw materials. Franklin undertakes to demonstrate that agricultural settlement of the interior, far from being meaningless to
imperial trade, will provide the greatest of all outlets for British
manufactures. Developing almost as an aside the theory that was
to have currency down to our own day as the "safety-valve"
doctrine, he points out that free land will constantly attract
laborers from the cities and thus keep wages high. Manufacturing
will continue to be unprofitable for Americans on this account
in any foreseeable future, and the British merchant will enjoy a
natural monopoly of a constantly expanding market for exports.
The argument is set forth with admirable clarity in a pamphlet

prepared in collaboration by Franklin and Richard Jackson, London agent for the colony of Pennsylvania:

The new settlements will so continually draw off the spare hands from the old, that our present colonies will not . . . find themselves in a condition to manufacture even for their own inhabitants, to any considerable degree, much less for those who are settling behind them.

Thus our *trade* must, till that country becomes as fully peopled as *England*, that is for centuries to come, be continually increasing, and with it our naval power; because the ocean is between us and them, and our ships and seamen must increase as that trade increases.[6]

The vision roused Franklin to one of his rare moments of enthusiasm. "What an Accession of Power to the *British* Empire by Sea as well as Land!" he exclaimed with an emotion that we need not judge insincere. "What Increase of Trade and Navigation! What Numbers of Ships and Seamen!" [7]

Nevertheless, Franklin's blueprint for a new Empire could hardly fail to arouse misgivings in English minds. He exhibits an unaccustomed naïveté in a letter to Lord Kames in 1760: "I have long been of opinion, that the *foundations of the future grandeur and stability of the British empire lie in America* . . . ." [8] It was asking too much of Englishmen to look forward with pleasure to the time when London might become a provincial capital taking orders from an imperial metropolis somewhere in the interior of North America. Yet the idea had found expression long before Franklin seized upon it. Bishop Berkeley had written with gentle melancholy in the 1720's that "Westward the course of empire takes its way," [9] and Englishmen were familiar with his notion of a fated succession of world states. The empire of Greece had given way to that of Rome, Rome had yielded preëminence to northern Europe, the empires of France and Spain had waned as Britain had waxed in power. Was America fated to be the next inheritor of universal sway? By 1774 a contributor to the *Middlesex Journal* noted with disapproval that the idea of America as the future seat of empire was widely current in England, and a humorous skit in *Lloyd's Evening Post*, to which the mid-twentieth century has lent a grim dramatic irony, pictured two Americans visiting London in 1974 and finding it in ruins like Balbec or Rome.[10]

Americans naturally took such ideas more seriously than did Englishmen. The theme, for example, is developed at length in a poem on "The Rising Glory of America" written by Philip Freneau and Hugh Henry Brackenridge for the Princeton commencement of 1771. "Say," exclaim the class laureates,

> shall we ask what empires yet must rise,
> What kingdoms, pow'rs and states where now are seen
> But dreary wastes and awful solitude,
> Where melancholy sits with eye forlorn
> And hopes the day when Britain's sons shall spread
> Dominion to the north and south and west
> Far from th' Atlantic to Pacific shores? [11]

In 1771 the vision was ambiguous: the question of whether Britain's sons on the Pacific shore would still be loyal subjects of the crown was left tactfully vague. But with the achievement of American independence, the belief in a continental destiny quickly became a principal ingredient in the developing American nationalism. In 1784 Thomas Hutchins, a protégé of George Croghan who was interested in western land speculations and had been named "Geographer to the United States," published in his *Historical Narrative and Topographical Description of Louisiana, and West-Florida* a prophecy concerning the future development of the new nation that left little to be added by the philosophers of Manifest Destiny in the 1840's. Using the traditional notion of a series of world empires, he finds in the natural resources of the North American continent promise of a power greater than any in the past. He estimates the habitable area of the continent — including Spanish possessions — at three and a half million square miles, and announces: "If we want it, I warrant it will soon be ours." The inhabitants of the potent empire which had already begun to develop in the New World,

so far from being in the least danger from the attacks of any other quarter of the globe, will have it in their power to engross the whole commerce of it, and to reign, not only lords of America, but to possess, in the utmost security, the dominion of the sea throughout the world, which their ancestors enjoyed before them.

In a word, "North-America . . . as surely as the land is now in being, will hereafter be trod by the first people the world ever knew." [12]

Even conservative New England responded to the soaring theme when Timothy Dwight included in his *Greenfield Hill* a rhapsody on westward expansion:

> All hail, thou western world! by heaven design'd
> Th' example bright, to renovate mankind.
> Soon shall thy sons across the mainland roam;
> And claim, on far Pacific shores, their home;
> Their rule, religion, manners, arts, convey,
> And spread their freedom to the Asian sea.
> Where erst six thousand suns have roll'd the year
> O'er plains of slaughter, and o'er wilds of fear,
> Towns, cities, fanes, shall lift their towery pride;
> The village bloom, on every streamlet's side;
> Proud Commerce' mole the western surges lave;
> The long, white spire lie imag'd on the wave;
> O'er morn's pellucid main expand their sails,
> And the starr'd ensign court Korean gales.

There is even a hint of the vision of world brotherhood to be set forth later in Whitman's "Passage to India":

> Then to new climes the bliss shall trace its way,
> And Tartar desarts hail the rising day;
> From the long torpor startled China wake;
> Her chains of misery rous'd Peruvia break;
> Man link to man; with bosom bosom twine;
> And one great bond the house of Adam join:
> The sacred promise full completion know,
> And peace, and piety, the world o'erflow.[13]

Thomas Jefferson had already made a more concrete analysis of the process by which he believed the entire continent was to be peopled from the "original nest" of the Atlantic settlements. The inhabited parts of the United States, he noted in 1786, had already attained a density of ten persons to the square mile, and "wherever we reach that the inhabitants become uneasy, as too much compressed, and go off in great numbers to search for vacant country." The lesson of Daniel Boone's venture beyond the mountains had become clear:

We have lately seen a single person go & decide on a settlement in Kentucky, many hundred miles from any white inhabitant, remove thither with his family and a few neighbors, & though perpetually harassed by the Indians, that settlement in the course of 10 years has acquired 30.000 inhabitants, it's numbers are increasing while we are writing, and the state of which it formerly made a part has offered it independence.[14]

At this rate, he estimated all the territory east of the Mississippi would be occupied within forty years. Then the people would begin settling beyond the river, and eventually, no doubt, pour into South America as well.

Even before the treaty of peace that officially marked the end of the Revolution, Philip Freneau had elaborated his vision of future glory in the West. The North American empire of the future, he wrote in 1782, would bring agriculture to the summit of perfection and make the nations brothers by disseminating the riches of the New World throughout the earth. The world's great age would begin anew, "those days of felicity . . . which are so beautifully described by the prophetic sages of ancient times." As in a hundred yet unwritten rhapsodies on the West, the physical fact of the continent dominates the scene. The American interior is presented as a new and enchanting region of inexpressible beauty and fertility. Through stately forests and rich meadows roam vast herds of animals which own no master, nor expect their sustenance from the hands of man. A thousand rivers flow into the mighty Mississippi,

who from a source unknown collecting his remotest waters, rolls forward through the frozen regions of the north, and stretching his extended arms to the east and west, embraces those savage groves, as yet uninvestigated by the traveller, unsung by the poet, or unmeasured by the chain of the geometrician; till uniting with the Ohio, and turning due south, receiving afterwards the Missori [sic] and a hundred others, this prince of rivers, in comparison of whom the Nile is but a Rivulet and the Danube a mere ditch, hurries with his immense flood of waters to the Mexican sea, laving the shores of many fertile countries in his passage, inhabited by savage nations as yet almost unknown, and without a name.[15]

The emotions that have gone into this passage are even more remarkable than its overt content. The stately trees, the buffalo (somehow transformed into mild sweet-breathed dairy herds, perhaps through the connotations of "meadows"), the bland climate, are bathed in a golden mist of utopian fantasy. The charming hint of frontier-boasting in the comparison between the Mississippi and rivers known to fame in the Old World serves as comic seasoning for the solemn and elevated prose; and the whole is pulled together at the end on a note of remoteness, strangeness, yet haunting potential accessibility. What traveler should penetrate the groves and solitudes, what explorer name the nameless savage tribes, what poet sing the westward-flowing rivers?

The early visions of an American Empire embody two different if often mingled conceptions. There is on the one hand the notion of empire as command of the sea, and on the other hand the notion of empire as a populous future society occupying the interior of the American continent. If these two kinds of empire are not mutually exclusive — for we can readily concede that patriots would want to claim every separate glory for their country — they nevertheless rest on different economic bases and imply different policies. Engrossing the trade of the world is an ambition evidently taken over from the British mercantilist ideal. On the other hand, creating new states in the dreary solitudes of the West is an enterprise that depends upon the increase of population resulting from agricultural expansion into an empty, fertile continent. This second version of the American Empire, based on agrarian assumptions, more nearly corresponds to the actual course of events during the nineteenth century.

Both these conceptions predict the outcome of the westward movement. Empire conceived as maritime dominion presupposes American expansion westward to the Pacific. The idea draws upon the long history and rich overtones of the search for a northwest passage to Asia, or, in Whitman's phrase, a "passage to India." It will occupy our attention in Book One. The hunter and trapper who served as the pathfinder of overland expansion and became one of the fixtures of American mythology forms the subject of Book Two. The very different idea of a continental empire dependent upon agriculture, and associated with various images of the Good Society to be realized in the West, may be called the theme of the Garden of the World. Its development will be traced in Book Three.

BOOK ONE ✰ ✰ ✰

*Start now on that farthest western way,
which does not pause at the Mississippi
or the Pacific, nor conduct toward a
worn-out China or Japan, but leads on
direct a tangent to this sphere, summer
and winter, day and night, sun down,
moon down, and at last earth down too.*

— HENRY DAVID THOREAU, *Walden* (1854)

CHAPTER I

A Highway to the Pacific:
Thomas Jefferson and the Far West

Although Jefferson, as we have seen, believed that all North America would eventually be peopled by descendants of the original English colonists, this prospect belonged to a remote and rather dim future. His immediate attitude toward the Far West was in some respects like that of the British authorities toward the Ohio Valley before the Revolution: he thought of it as an area to be occupied by fur traders rather than farmers. He does not seem to have felt that his devout agrarianism was applicable to the area beyond the Mississippi. A certain instinct for order, and perhaps also the attacks of his Federalist opponents, led him to suggest at the time of the Louisiana Purchase that the right bank of the river should be turned into an Indian reservation for at least fifty years. Emigrants should be forbidden to cross the river "until we shall have filled up all the vacant country on this side." [1]

Nevertheless, Jefferson was clearly the intellectual father of the American advance to the Pacific. Early in his career he began collecting materials relating to the vast hinterland which he believed to be included within the original grant to the colony of Virginia. During his five years of diplomatic service in Paris, from 1784 to 1789, as he wrote later, he formed "a pretty full collection of the English, French and Spanish authors, on the subject of Louisiana." [2] Not content with buying books and compiling notes, he began a long series of efforts to bring about actual exploration of the trans-Mississippi area. In Paris he

worked out a plan whereby the Connecticut traveler John Ledyard was to go eastward through Siberia to the Pacific Northwest
and thence overland across North America to Virginia, but the
venture was frustrated by the Empress Catherine. Back in
America as Secretary of State in Washington's cabinet, Jefferson
arranged for the French scientist André Michaux to explore the
Pacific Northwest under the auspices of the American Philosophical Society. This plan likewise failed when Michaux became
involved in the filibustering intrigues of the French ambassador
Genêt.[3]

After Jefferson's inauguration as President in 1801 he was at
last in a position to carry out the projected exploration of the
Far West by sending Meriwether Lewis and William Clark up
the Missouri and over the Rocky Mountains to the mouth of the
Columbia. The ostensible purpose of the expedition was the
one mentioned by Jefferson when he sought permission from
Madrid for Lewis and Clark to enter Spanish territory: it was a
scientific enterprise. But a responsible statesman was not likely
to forget that geographical knowledge was a necessary preliminary to economic penetration and eventual political domination.
Scientific knowledge was to be sought for the sake of the fur
trade. The North West Company of Montreal was expanding
westward across Canada; Alexander Mackenzie had reached the
Pacific in 1793. British fur traders were already established far
down into present Minnesota and the Dakotas. Indeed, as Lewis
and Clark found when they wintered from 1804 to 1805 at the
Mandan Villages near present Bismarck, North Dakota, the
British were in undisturbed control of the fur trade of the upper
Missouri.

American trappers had to be encouraged to move into this
area as an offset to the British, whose strong economic position
might easily lead to the extension of their sovereignty over most
of the trans-Mississippi.[4] The best means of inducing American
fur companies to enter the area was to make it profitable for
them, and this in turn meant finding a better trade route than
the British could command. Jefferson pointed out to Congress
that the Canadian route along the line of lakes and rivers from
Montreal to the Rocky Mountains "could bear no competition

with that of the Missouri," which was shorter, offered a continuous water route without portages, and might possibly lead to the Pacific with only a short land carriage over the mountains.[5]

The concrete plans outlined in this famous message to Congress proved unworkable when brought to the test of practice. The prospect of an advance up the Missouri to the area where American fur traders might come to grips with the British faded when the hostility of the Blackfoot Indians effectively closed the waterway. And the effort to find a commercial route over the Continental Divide and down the Columbia to the Pacific failed because of difficulties of terrain. Even Meriwether Lewis was forced to admit that 340 miles of land carriage, 140 miles of it "over tremendious [sic] mountains which for 60 miles are covered with eternal snows," would be necessary along the most practicable communication across the continent by way of the Missouri and the Columbia.[6]

But these practical difficulties were of minor consequence beside Jefferson's continental breadth of vision. The importance of the Lewis and Clark expedition lay on the level of imagination: it was drama, it was the enactment of a myth that embodied the future. It gave tangible substance to what had been merely an idea, and established the image of a highway across the continent so firmly in the minds of Americans that repeated failures could not shake it. John Jacob Astor's ambitious plan of establishing trade between the Columbia Valley and the Orient from a base at Astoria was upset by the British navy, which captured the fort during the War of 1812 and supervised a virtually forced sale of the property to the North West Company. But the American fur traders were determined to penetrate the northern Rockies and in the 1820's William Ashley and Jedediah Smith developed an overland route through the Platte Valley and over South Pass.[7] For the next two decades British and American trappers struggled for economic domination of the Northwest. In this contest the Americans were worsted once again. After all, they were fighting the greatest mercantile empire in the world. In the Hudson's Bay Company, which had absorbed the North West Company in 1821, they had an adversary enjoying the advantage of vigorous governmental support as well as the practical experience of more than two centuries of British chartered trading companies. As long as the contest for Oregon remained in the stage of imperial rivalry based on the fur trade, the British proved impregnable.

On the other hand, the discovery of the overland route that became the Oregon Trail had an ultimate consequence of far greater moment than the fur trade. In the late 1830's and early 1840's widespread economic distress in the Mississippi Valley led Westerners to look longingly at the free land and the supposedly better markets of Oregon. When the frontier farmer learned that he could take his family all the way to the Pacific with no more equipment than his rifle, his wagon, and his livestock, his new energies were thrown into the contest against Britain in the Northwest.[8] Within five years after the first significant migration of American settlers to the Willamette Valley the mercantilist colossus of the Hudson's Bay Company gave up and quit. The Treaty of 1846, establishing the boundary where it now is, at the forty-ninth parallel, merely records officially the fact that the American agricultural frontier had been pushed out to Oregon.

CHAPTER II

Passage to India:
Thomas Hart Benton and Asa Whitney

When Lewis and Clark reached the shore of the Pacific in 1804 they reactivated the oldest of all ideas associated with America — that of a passage to India. Columbus had been seeking the fabled wealth of the Orient when he discovered that a New World lay between Europe and Asia. Since his day, explorers of many nationalities had engaged in an almost continuous search for a route through or around this obstacle without traversing the Spanish possessions in America. Several expeditions were organized in Virginia during the seventeenth century "to find out the East India Sea," as Governor William Berkeley wrote in 1669 concerning his own plans.[1] The distance was at that time not believed to be very great — perhaps ten days' journey beyond the Alleghenies. But as men gradually realized the enormous bulk of North America, they had given up this project in favor of an equally unavailing search for a northwest passage around the continent by sea.

Until the very end of the eighteenth century the West beyond the Mississippi was so shadowy and remote that it could be pictured in almost any guise that might occur to a writer's imagination. Nevertheless, some of these fantasies bear faint marks of purposiveness and a continuing tradition. The Freneau-Brackenridge commencement poem of 1771, for instance, in elaborating the idea of a westward course of empire, predicts that analogues of various imperial capitals of the Old World will spring up in the America of the future: a St. Petersburg amid the

snows of the far north, a Babylon in Mexico, a Nineveh on the
Orinoco in South America. In the Far West the future reveals

> A new Palmyra or an Ecbatan
> And sees the slow pac'd caravan return
> O'er many a realm from the Pacific shore,
> Where fleets shall then convey rich Persia's silks,
> Arabia's perfumes, and spices rare
> Of Philippine, Cœlebe and Marian isles,
> Or from the Acapulco coast our India then,
> Laden with pearl and burning gems of gold.[2]

If this is hardly more than a pretty conceit, one can find in as
sober a writer as Thomas Hutchins the notion that North America
would eventually dominate the trade of the Orient.[3]

That Jefferson fully grasped the relation of the Pacific Northwest to Asia is evident in his plan for John Ledyard to approach
the American coast by way of Siberia, and in the emphasis he
gave to finding a trade route "between the higher parts of the
Missouri and the Pacific ocean" in the instructions he prepared
for Michaux.[4] This document was composed in January, 1793.
By that time enterprising American ship captains sailing out of
Atlantic ports around Cape Horn had developed a lucrative trade
between the Pacific Northwest and China by way of the Sandwich
Islands, so that Jefferson could hardly have discussed the possibility of a transcontinental route without having the China
trade in mind. The idea was current in the American press: in
February, 1795 the *Kentucky Gazette* picked up from a New
York paper a notice that Alexander Mackenzie had reached the
Pacific overland. "This circumstance," the dispatch noted, "will,
in the course of time, be of the utmost consequence to this country, as it opens a direct communication with China, and may
doubtless lead to further discoveries." [5]

It is true that Jefferson himself nowhere dwells on the value
of the Asiatic trade. Perhaps his desire for maintaining a simple
agricultural society in the United States prevented him from
growing enthusiastic over this commercial possibility. But his
private instructions to Meriwether Lewis probably took for
granted the importance of trade with the Orient:

The object of your mission is to explore the Missouri river, & such principal stream of it as, by it's course & communication with the waters of the Pacific Ocean, may offer the most direct & practicable communication across this continent, for the purposes of commerce.[6]

Furthermore, Lewis's confidential letter to Jefferson from St. Louis immediately after his return from the expedition seems to refer to a previous discussion of access to the Far East:

We vew this passage across the continent as affording immence advantages to the fir trade but fear that advantages wich it offers as a communication for the productions of the East Indias to the United States and thence to Europe will never be found equal on an extensive scale to that by the way of the Cape of good hope. still we beleive that many articles not bulky brittle nor of a perishable nature may be conveyed to the U'. States by this rout with more facility and less expence than by that at present practiced.[7]

This plan, however, could hardly be taken seriously in view of Lewis's rather lame suggestion that freight could be carried from the head of navigation on the Missouri to the head of navigation on the Columbia by means of horses, which could be procured "in immence numbers and for the most trivial considerations from the natives." [8]

It is not clear what means of transport John Jacob Astor intended to use along the overland route to Astoria, the trading post he built in 1811 near the mouth of the Columbia. He meant to supply his fort mainly by sea, but he sent Wilson P. Hunt westward from the Missouri in the hope of finding a better route than Lewis's proposed combination of river boating and a packhorse portage. Hunt's men had an even worse time getting over the Rockies than Lewis and Clark, but a party of returning Astorians led by Robert Stuart discovered South Pass in 1813.[9] Ten years later William Ashley's demonstration that wagons could be driven through the Pass suggested an overland wagon road to Oregon and revived the old dream of Asiatic trade. Caleb Atwater of Ohio declared in 1829 with stout Western confidence: "That this will be the route to China within fifty years from this time, scarcely admits of a doubt." He foresaw a dense population all along the way, with corresponding wealth, grandeur, and glory for the American people.[10] It was nevertheless a long haul for wagons from Independence, Missouri, to the Columbia. The

hardy frontiersman might learn how to plow it through with his
family and household goods in four or five months, if he had luck,
but Asa Whitney, an early propagandist for a Pacific railway, was
justified in pouring scorn on the notion that the Oregon Trail was
any better than the Lewis and Clark route as a highway for
Oriental imports. "I presume no man," he exclaimed, "will think
of an overland communication with teams through a wilderness
and desert of more than two thousand miles in extent!" [11] Only in
the 1840's, when a transcontinental railroad began to be seriously
discussed, did the notion of bringing Asiatic goods eastward
across the continent come to deserve practical consideration.

Yet the idea of a passage to India, with its associated images
of fabulous wealth, of ivory and apes and peacocks, led a vigorous
existence on the level of imagination entirely apart from its
practicability. So rich and compelling was the notion that it remained for decades one of the ruling conceptions of American
thought about the West. It was almost an obsession with Thomas
Hart Benton of Missouri, who during the thirty years following
the death of Jefferson was the most conspicuous and best-informed
champion of westward expansion in Congress. Benton's public
career extended from the beginnings of the Santa Fé Trail and
the heyday of the Rocky Mountain fur trade to the eve of the
Civil War. During all this time he was indefatigable in analyzing
the problems of the West and urging the cause of expansion.
Defeated for the Senate in 1850 because of his free-soil views, he
returned to the House of Representatives in 1854 and threw his
energies into the cause of a Pacific railway. Almost to the day of
his death in 1858 he was making speeches in behalf of the railway
and the general development of the West.

Benton was a devoted follower of Thomas Jefferson. He believed, according to his daughter Jessie Benton Frémont, that a
visit he paid to the aged statesman at Monticello late in 1824
was the occasion of a laying on of hands, a ceremony at which
Benton received the mantle of the first prophet of American
expansionism.[12] So strong was Benton's piety, in fact, that he
read into Jefferson ideas of his own which were not there, or
at most were present in an embryonic state. The point is not of
great significance, but it is suggestive enough to warrant passing

notice. In his *Thirty Years' View* Benton wrote that Jefferson sent
Lewis and Clark out to open commercial communication with
Asia. "And thus Mr. Jefferson," he added, "was the first to propose the North American road to India, and the introduction of
Asiatic trade on that road; and all that I myself have either said
or written on that subject . . . is nothing but the fruit of the
seed planted in my mind by the philosophic hand of Mr. Jefferson." [13] Jessie Benton is even more explicit concerning Jefferson's
conception of the Lewis and Clark expedition. Paraphrasing this
passage from her father's memoirs, she says that Jefferson told
Congress the Lewis and Clark expedition

would '*open overland commercial relations with Asia*; and enlarge the
boundaries of geographical science' — putting as the first motive a
North-American road to India, and the introduction of Asiatic trade
over that road.[14]

The words enclosed in quotation marks do not occur in Jefferson's message to Congress proposing the expedition, or indeed
in any other statement of Jefferson known to me. The notion of
trade with Asia was so strong in the Benton tradition eighty years
after the message was delivered that it actually colored Jessie
Benton's memory.

Benton's interest in the passage to India grew out of an elaborate philosophy of westward expansion. After a childhood and
youth in North Carolina and Tennessee, he served under Jackson
with the Tennessee militia in 1812. His daughter says that this
experience determined him to identify himself with the West, the
vast basin of the Mississippi, and to repudiate "the exclusively
English and seaboard influences to which he had been born and
in which he had been trained." The Atlantic coast, for father
and daughter alike, is identified with European tradition: it is
"the English seaboard," and is viewed as an influence stifling the
development of the American personality by imposing deference
to precedent and safe usage. By contrast, access to Asia becomes
a symbol of freedom and of national greatness for America.
Benton adopts the role of a Moses leading his people out of
bondage. Jessie Benton cites the inscription on her father's statue
in St. Louis: "There is the East; there lies the road to India," a

quotation from a speech he made in the Senate in 1825 favoring military occupation of Oregon.[15]

The image of Asia became for Benton the key to all modern history, which he saw as a series of conflicts between Britain and her successive rivals for world dominance. Jessie Benton asserts that when her father moved to St. Louis after the War of 1812,

he found himself confronting English aggression in another form. The little French town so far in the centre of our continent found itself direct heir to the duel of a century between England and France for the New World and the Asiatic trade, and, France having withdrawn, was meeting the added resentment of English feeling against her late subjects, who now replaced France in that contest.[16]

Defeated in the struggle for the Mississippi Valley, the English still hoped by controlling San Francisco to dominate the Asiatic trade across the Pacific. American seizure of California would thus be an act of defiance to England rather than to Mexico, and would mean a great deal more than a mere occupation of territory.[17]

Benton's thought concerning the passage to India and the related theme of Anglo-American rivalry can be traced through almost four decades of public discussion: (1) in a series of editorials written for the St. Louis *Enquirer* in 1818–1819, before the admission of Missouri as a state; (2) in his famous speech on the Oregon question, delivered in the Senate in 1825; (3) in his fostering of the exploring expeditions of his son-in-law, Lieutenant John Charles Frémont, during the 1840's; and (4) in his concern with the proposed railway to the Pacific during the 1850's.

The editorials in the *Enquirer* were occasioned by the Treaty of 1818 with Britain providing for joint occupation of Oregon, and the Spanish Treaty of 1819 establishing the Sabine and the Red River as the boundary between Spanish and American possessions in the Southwest. Benton's position is that John Quincy Adams, who negotiated the Spanish treaty, and Albert Gallatin, who negotiated the treaty with Britain, had made outrageous concessions to foreign powers at the expense of westward expansion. He insists upon the value of the western half of the

Mississippi Valley and the inevitability of American commercial expansion toward the Pacific. Elaborating the theory of the course of empire, he declares that westward advance has been throughout recorded time "the course of the heavenly bodies, of the human race, and of science, civilization, and national power following in their train." This vast perspective suggests grandiose reflections. Soon the American pioneers will complete "the circumambulation of the globe" when they reach the Pacific and look out toward that Asia in which their first parents were originally planted.[18] The Arkansas, the Platte, and the Yellowstone rivers, their sources interlocking with those of streams emptying into the western ocean, will become for the people of the United States "what the Euphrates, the Oxus, the Phasis, and the Cyrus were to the ancient Romans, lines of communication with eastern Asia, and channels for that rich commerce which, for forty centuries, has created so much wealth and power wherever it has flowed." [19]

For thousands of years merchants loaded with gold and silver have traversed the deserts on camels or the trackless sea in ships, in quest of the rich productions of the East. From the ancient Phoenicians to the English, the nation which has commanded the trade of Asia in each successive era has been the leader of the world in civilization, power, and wealth. It is her monopoly of this trade that has enabled England to triumph single-handed over the combined powers of Europe and to impress her policy upon every quarter of the globe. American mariners have already made inroads upon the English monopoly; and this enterprise, embryonic though it may be, forms the richest vein of American commerce. What then would be the consequences if Americans could perfect their own route to Asia, shorter than that open to the English? [20]

Lewis and Clark have demonstrated that such a route exists, by way of the Columbia River. Nothing is wanted but a second Daniel Boone to lead the way through the wilderness. Benton translates maritime commerce, which had always been carried on by wealthy merchants, into Jacksonian terms. The shortness of the American road to India will make it easy for men of moderate means to embark in the trade, which, by being made more accessible to all classes of the community, will be more valuable to the nation. Most important of all is the prospect that trade with the Orient will emancipate the United States from its dependence on Europe. No longer will Americans be "servile copyists and imitators," branded with Buffon's stigma of biological inferiority. They have built their own system of government; let them go on to nationalize their character by establishing a system of commerce adapted to their geographical position and free from European interference.[21]

Five years later Benton returned to the theme of contact with Asia in his speech on the occupation of Oregon. He had now become more fully aware of the agricultural resources of the Pacific coast, and predicted that within one hundred years a population greater than that of the present United States would exist beyond the Rocky Mountains. American pioneers would bring science, liberal principles in government, and the true religion to the peoples of Asia, and the oldest and the newest, the most despotic and the freest of nations might become friends united in opposition to a Europe which was determined to dominate and exploit them both.[22]

Yet despite Benton's exuberant expansionism his fidelity to Jeffersonian tradition exerted a markedly conservative influence on his thinking. Still cherishing the old fear, stemming from Montesquieu, that a republican government could not survive too great an extension of its boundaries, he considered it inevitable and desirable that the descendants of Americans who would settle the Pacific Coast should form an independent nation. The Rocky Mountains were a convenient, natural, and everlasting western boundary for the United States. There "the statue of the fabled god, Terminus, should be raised . . . , never to be thrown down." Such a delimitation of territory would in no way hamper American commercial expansion into the Orient because the new Pacific republic would stand beside the United States against the combined powers of the Old World.[23]

The next phase of Benton's interest in Far Western expansion was the most significant of his career. By 1841 emigrants from the Missouri frontier, encouraged by the passage of a Senate bill donating 640 acres of land in Oregon to every settler (even though the bill failed to pass the House), were beating a broad path up the valley of the Platte River and through South Pass to Fort Hall and Oregon. The following year Benton was able to secure passage of a bill authorizing his son-in-law, John Charles Frémont of the Topographical Corps, to map the trail as far as South Pass. Publication of Frémont's report of the expedition, in a form owing much to the literary flair of Jessie Benton, fostered an increased migration out the Oregon Trail in succeeding summers. The further expeditions of Frémont, leading him eventually into California at the outbreak of the Mexican War, were a conspicuous and carefully publicized phase of the burst of expansionism that extended the boundaries of the United States to the Pacific by 1848.

Out of the war grew yet another development of Benton's program for the West, again in the spirit of his emphasis on westward movement, on the passage to India. On February 7, 1849, he introduced a bill to appropriate a part of the proceeds from the sales of public lands for building a Central National Road from the Pacific Ocean to the Mississippi River. As a forerunner of the eventual federal subsidy for a Pacific railway, Benton's plan has an air of archaism. He favored construction of a railway as far as practicable, but was prepared for reliance upon sleighs through the snowy passes. The railway was to be built by the federal government and then leased to contractors who would operate trains over it. And throughout the entire length of the highway was to be built "a plain old English road, such as we have been accustomed to all our lives — a road in which the farmer in his wagon or carriage, on horse or on foot, may travel without fear, and without tax — with none to run over him, or make him jump out of the way." [24]

This homespun conception, with its imaginative fusion of the Cumberland Road across the Alleghenies, the actual Oregon Trail with its covered wagons, and the Union Pacific Railway of the future, was balanced in Benton's speech by one of the majestic historical parallels with which he habitually dignified his remarks on westward expansion. He quotes Gibbon on the Roman roads that connected the remotest provinces of the Empire. Like these ancient highways, the road to the Pacific would

facilitate sending troops to protect the frontiers. It would foster
political unity by connecting the Atlantic and the Pacific states.
(Benton has dropped the idea of the god Terminus at the Continental Divide.) But commercial considerations were most important of all, for here was Benton's ancient and preferred theme,
the passage to India. Each time he returned to this notion he
added fresh ornaments to it. As he said, it was always for him
"a boundless field, dazzling and bewildering the imagination
from its vastness and importance." A pageant of universal history
opened before him portraying the events which would follow
completion of a transcontinental highway:

The trade of the Pacific Ocean, of the western coast of North America,
and of Eastern Asia, will all take its track; and not only for ourselves,
but for posterity. That trade of India which has been shifting its
channels from the time of the Phoenicians to the present, is destined
to shift once more, and to realize the grand idea of Columbus. The
American road to India will also become the European track to that
region. The European merchant, as well as the American, will fly
across our continent on a straight line to China. The rich commerce
of Asia will flow through our centre. And where has that commerce
ever flowed without carrying wealth and dominion with it? Look at its
ancient channels, and the cities which it raised into kingdoms, and
the populations which upon its treasures became resplendent in science, learning, and the arts. Tyre, Sidon, Balbec, Palmyra, Alexandria,
among its ancient emporiums, attest the power of this commerce to
enrich, to aggrandize, and to enlighten nations. Constantinople, in the
middle ages, and in the time of the crusades, was the wonder of
Western Europe; and all, because she was then a thoroughfare of
Asiatic commerce. Genoa and Venice, mere cities, in later time, became the match of kingdoms, and the envy of kings, from the mere
divided streams of this trade of which they became the thoroughfare.
Lisbon had her great day, and Portugal her preëminence during the
little while that the discovery of the Cape of Good Hope put her in
communication with the East. Amsterdam, the city of a little territory
rescued from the sea, and the Seven United Provinces, not equal in
extent to one of our lesser States, became great in arms, in letters, in
wealth, and in power; and all upon the East India trade. And London,
what makes her the commercial mistress of the world — what makes an
island no larger than one of our first class States — the mistress of
possessions in the four quarters of the globe — a match for half of
Europe — and dominant in Asia? What makes all this, or contributes
most to make it, but this same Asiatic trade? In no instance has it
failed to carry the nation, or the people which possessed it, to the

highest pinnacle of wealth and power, and with it the highest attain-
ments of letters, arts, and sciences.[25]

This imperial destiny, like the eighteenth-century dream of
an American Empire, had two different aspects which seldom
received equal emphasis at a given moment. There was on the
one hand the world-historical mission of dominion over the seven
seas, like that of Venice, or Amsterdam, or London, which could
carry a nation to greatness without regard to its internal resources
and population. The theme of the passage to India, as Benton
developed it during most of his career, belongs to this aspect of
the notion of empire. The economic basis which it emphasizes is
that of ocean-borne commerce. But the highway to the Pacific
was potentially more than a means of connecting the wharves of
the seaport with the warehouses of merchants in the interior. It
was not only an instrument of distribution: it could also become
an instrument of production, or at least of creating facilities for
production, in the area through which it passed. In the conclusion of his speech of 1849 Benton for the first time took cogni-
zance of the internal development of the West which the highway would bring about. "An American road to India through the
heart of our country," he declared, "will revive upon its line all
the wonders of which we have read — and eclipse them. The
western wilderness, from the Pacific to the Mississippi, will start
into life under its touch." [26]

This puts the problem in an entirely new light. It is no longer
a question merely of extending the maritime commerce of the
United States, but also of developing the trans-Mississippi region:
the transition has begun from an outward-looking to an introspective conception of empire. The idea of gaining access to the
trade of Asia had served as a rationale of American expansion
to the Pacific, but with the formal acquisition of Oregon in 1846
and California in 1848, expansionism had reached the natural
boundary of the ocean. Its goal had been achieved and the impulse itself was ceasing to be a major concern of American society. The debate was now to become one over federal policy
concerning the development of the vast new area which had been
added to the national domain.

Beyond the Missouri there was no natural equivalent for the

network of navigable rivers that had so magnificently furthered the agricultural occupation of the eastern half of the Mississippi Valley. The Far Western farmer would evidently have to depend on railroads to get his crops to market. But how should the railroads be built?

In this phase of the discussion Benton was joined by a man who for a five-year period, without holding office or commanding any established organ for reaching the public, made himself a national figure through the sole agency of his thinking on the subject of a Pacific railway. This crusader was Asa Whitney, a New York merchant of New England origins who, after failing in business in the Panic of 1837, went out to the Orient as a mercantile agent and returned in 1844 with a fortune which gave him a comfortable income for the rest of his life. In January, 1845 Whitney laid before Congress a request for a gigantic land grant to finance the construction of a railway from Lake Michigan to the Pacific. The audacity of the proposal — he asked for a tract of land sixty miles wide throughout the distance to be traversed by his road — together with the spectacular publicity campaign he conducted, aroused an interest which temporarily obscured the impractical nature of his scheme.

When Whitney first entered the discussion, Benton, after twenty-five years' fervent devotion to the memory of Thomas Jefferson, was finding it difficult to understand the importance of the railroad. In a speech on the Oregon question delivered in May, 1846, which Whitney quoted with justifiable delight in a later altercation, Benton declared with all the emphasis of his momentous rhetoric: "Lewis and Clarke were sent out to discover a commercial route to the Pacific Ocean; and so judiciously was their enterprise conducted that their return route must become, and forever remain, the route of commerce. . . ." The implication was that once Jefferson had made up his mind, the geography had jolly well better get into line. Benton was willing to concede something to the wagon road of his friends the St. Louis fur traders — "the route further south, through the South Pass . . . will be the travelling road" — but nothing could be conceded to New Yorkers and technological innovation: "commerce will take the water line . . . crossing the Rocky Mountains in latitude 47, through the North Pass." [27] The reason why Benton showed such a monumental inability to understand the revolution in transport that was under way was that he thought in terms of a tradition, a century of preoccupation with the network of natural waterways overspreading the Mississippi Valley. St. Louis, his home, was the metropolis of the trans-Mississippi trade because it dominated the Missouri, having the same relation to that river that New Orleans had to the Mississippi. The imaginary American East India merchant of the future (a significantly old-fashioned figure who dominates Benton's thinking until near the end of his career), having come by boat up the Columbia and then by an overland portage which may just conceivably depend upon the "steam car" for a short distance in the mountains, stands at last beside the Great Falls of the Missouri, head of steamboat navigation upstream from St. Louis. Here his troubles are over. Before him he sees a thousand markets inviting his approach, each readily accessible along the rivers.[28] What place had the railroad in such a panorama?

Yet Whitney was right in insisting that the railroad must be the technological basis both for the Asiatic trade and for large-scale settlement in the trans-Mississippi. The rivers of the Far West could not compare with those of the eastern Mississippi Valley as commercial routes. The country could not be developed by any other means than the railroad. Benton himself finally conceded the point. As we have seen, for four or five years between 1848 and 1853 he advocated a railway to the Pacific constructed by the federal government.[29] But he opposed Whitney's scheme on the very sensible ground that no individual could safely be trusted with the power conveyed by so vast a land grant.[30] Convinced at last that sectional rivalries made federal action to build the road impossible, Benton turned to the private capitalists he had once so strongly criticized and threw his weight into promoting a Pacific railroad corporation headed by Abbott Lawrence of Massachusetts.

A discourse which Benton delivered before the Boston Mercantile Library Association in December, 1854 (and repeated in substance before a Baltimore audience and on the floor of the House of Representatives) sets forth the final state of his thinking about westward expansion. Its most remarkable feature is its attention to the internal development of the trans-Mississippi as

contrasted with the theme of the passage to India: Benton was
at last renouncing his lifelong devotion to an archaic mercantilist
point of view and was beginning to confront the theme of the
"garden of the world" which was destined to supplant it in the
main stream of American thought about the West. He brings to
this new conception as contagious an enthusiasm as he had
brought to the older one. Benton was not the man to do this
sort of thing by halves; and the cause was one for which he was,
as he said, perfectly capable of becoming a Peter the Hermit to
wander about preaching a crusade. Proclaiming that a line of
states will be created between the Missouri frontier and California as great as the line stretching from the Atlantic to the
Mississippi, he demonstrates how each proposed far-western
commonwealth abounds in natural resources. Kansas has a soil
"rich like Egypt and tempting as Egypt would be if raised above
the slimy flood, waved into gentle undulations, variegated with
groves and meadows, sprinkled with springs, coursed by
streams. . . ." [31] In similar fashion he deals with Colorado, the
lyrically beautiful parks of the Rocky Mountains, and the Interior
Basin beyond, emphasizing iron and coal when he can not manage
to praise the fertility of the soil, and citing the ease of irrigation
by artesian wells when he concedes an inadequate rainfall.

The same procedure enables him to say of a route through
the Rockies of southern Colorado still considered impracticable
for a railroad, that there was "Not a tunnel to be made — a mountain to be climbed — a hill to be crossed — a swamp to be seen —
or desert, or movable sand to be encountered, in the whole distance." [32] One feels a kind of awe in the presence of a faith so
triumphantly able to remove mountains; but a more appropriate
attitude would be that which greets the ecstatic lover praising
his mistress. For Benton was in love with the Far West. He had
never seen it, except vicariously, through the delegated eyes of
Frémont; but perhaps his love was only the more intense for
being ideal and Platonic. We may leave him as he bedecks his
mistress with jewels, fabulous cities-to-be strung upon the thread
of the railway from St. Louis to San Francisco —

the channel of Asiatic commerce which has been shifting its bed from
the time of Solomon, and raising up cities and kingdoms wherever it

went — (to perish when it left them) — changing its channel for the last time — to become fixed upon its shortest, safest, best, and quickest route, through the heart of our America — and to revive along its course the Tyres and Sidons, the Balbecs, Palmyras, and Alexandrias, once the seat of commerce and empire; and the ruins of which still attest their former magnificence, and excite the wonder of the oriental traveller.[33]

Coming into the field more than twenty years after Benton had begun proclaiming the value of Oriental trade, Whitney took over Benton's main positions and added to them the fruits of two years' residence in China. Like Benton he declared that the commerce of Asia had been the foundation of all commerce since the earliest ages, controlling the rise and fall of nations, and furnishing the basis of Britain's greatness. He touched the familiar theme of how the Asiatic trade would in turn bring the United States to a peak of unexampled and permanent grandeur. "Here we stand forever," he exclaimed; "we reach out one hand to all Asia, and the other to all Europe, willing for all to enjoy the great blessings we possess, claiming free intercourse and exchange of commodities with all, seeking not to subjugate any, but *all* . . . tributary, and at our will subject to us." [34]

A controversy between Whitney and Stephen A. Douglas, embodied in a public exchange of letters in 1845, brought out an interesting and basic disagreement between the Easterner Whitney and this emerging western leader concerning the development of the trans-Mississippi. Speaking in behalf of the frontier farmer with his half-anarchic individualism, Douglas refused to endorse Whitney's plan because it was too contrived, too consciously planned from above, too little adapted to what Douglas conceived to be the way all American frontiers must advance. A Pacific railway, he agreed, was necessary and would eventually be built. But not all at once, and not according to any rational blueprint. A Pacific railway constructed according to the principle of "squatter sovereignty," as Douglas's doctrine came to be called later when he applied it to the problem of slavery in the territories, would be the work of years. It would have to

progress gradually, from east to west, keeping up a connected chain of communication, and following the tide of emigration, and the settlement of the country. In addition to the India and China trade, and the vast commerce of the Pacific ocean, which would pass over this route, you must create a further necessity for the road, by subduing the wilderness, and peopling it with a hardy and industrious population, who would soon have a surplus produce, without the means of getting it to market, and require, for their own consumption, immense quantities of goods and merchandize [*sic*], which they could not obtain at reasonable rates, for want of proper facilities of transportation.[35]

Douglas, spokesman for the West, considered the individual farmer with his primitive agriculture to be the ultimate source of social values and energies — an assumption derived, however remotely, from the agrarian tradition of Franklin and Jefferson. On the other hand, the New York merchant, Whitney, set out from the assumption that the prime source of social values and achievements is commerce. The notion seems at first glance hardly applicable to an agricultural frontier. But Whitney was as consistent as Douglas. If Douglas insisted that the individual farmer would create the Pacific railway, Whitney was as certain that only the railway could create the far-western farmer, in the sense of making him a useful member of society. The settler in the trans-Mississippi, Whitney pointed out, had no way of getting produce to market. In the wilderness, remote from civilization, destitute of comforts, he was but a "demi-savage." It was true that his labor produced food from the earth: in this limited sense the ideal of subsistence farming was valid. But since he could not "exchange with the different branches of industry," that is, had no place in the commercial system, he was not a source of wealth or power to the nation, and from the mercantilist point of view could hardly be said to exist.[36] It was in this fashion that Whitney conceived what his friend and supporter Senator John M. Niles of Connecticut called "the *creative* power of a railroad." [37] The railroad was the only means by which the wilderness from the Great Lakes to the Pacific could ever be developed. Without it, this immense area must remain forever useless to mankind, "being the greater part without timber, and without navigable streams to communicate with civilization or markets." Whitney was in fact so little disposed to count upon Douglas's squatters that he planned to import European laborers to construct his railway.[38]

CHAPTER III

The Untransacted Destiny: William Gilpin

The Mexican War with its territorial acquisitions realized Ben-ton's twenty-year-old dream of westward expansion but ironically put an end to his career in the Senate by bringing the slavery issue to a head. The same years of decision matured the thinking of a young associate of Benton's who was to become the principal heir of his geopolitical thought, as he had been of Jefferson's. This man, William Gilpin, born in 1813 and therefore thirty years younger than his mentor, had grown up in a distinguished Philadelphia household of which Andrew Jackson was an intimate. One brother was a Democratic appointee in the consular service, and another, Henry D. Gilpin, a lawyer of literary and artistic interests, was prominent in the fight against Biddle's Bank of the United States and became Attorney General in Van Buren's cabinet.

William Gilpin himself was a personal friend of Jackson, who appointed him to West Point. Although he was not graduated from the Academy, he served for a time as a volunteer officer in the Seminole War. In 1838 Gilpin went to St. Louis as editor of the *Missouri Argus* for the express purpose of securing the reëlection of Benton and James Linn to the Senate. Yet a further step toward identification with the Benton tradition was Gilpin's accidental meeting with Frémont on the trail to Oregon in 1843. He went out to Walla Walla with Frémont; pushed on westward by himself to spend two months as a not over-welcome guest of the Hudson's Bay Company at Fort Vancouver; participated in the convention for establishing a government in

Oregon, March, 1844; took back to Washington the petition drawn up at this meeting asking for American occupation of the territory; and became an expert adviser to Benton, Buchanan, Polk, and other statesmen in those crowded months of Manifest Destiny.[1]

But this was only the beginning, for within a year Gilpin emerged as a major in Doniphan's famous First Missouri Volunteers. After the victory over Mexico he commanded expeditions against the Pawnees and Comanches. A decade later, having cast the only vote for Lincoln in Jackson County, Missouri, he was one of thirteen men who accompanied the president-elect from Springfield to Washington. He served in the volunteer bodyguard of one hundred who slept in the White House during the first tense weeks of the new administration, and was appointed by Lincoln as the first governor of Colorado Territory.[2]

The appointment was appropriate on several grounds. Not only had Gilpin earned it according to the canons of party politics; his military abilities were essential because of the danger of a Confederate effort to seize the territory. Besides, Gilpin had been a prominent writer and speaker about the West for fifteen years. His utterances on this theme include two letters on Western matters published in government documents in 1846; several articles in magazines during the 1850's; and a collection of public addresses published in 1860 under the title *The Central Gold Region. The Grain, Pastoral and Gold Regions of North America.* In 1873 he brought out a revised edition of this work entitled *The Mission of the North American People*; and in 1890, at the age of seventy-seven, he published an even more elaborate treatise called *The Cosmopolitan Railway.* This impressive body of writing, extending over more than forty years, gives Gilpin a claim to be considered the most ambitious student of the Far West during the second half of the nineteenth century.

Despite the grandeur of many of Gilpin's ideas, his writings bear directly on practical politics, in the style of open-air stump speaking. His prose has many traits in common with Benton's — the headlong rhythms, the hyperboles, the devices of ornamentation — but there is one important difference. Where Benton's oratory is in the polemic mode of Congressional debates and reaches its full development only when it can take the form of an attack on an adversary (the East, the Past, the British Empire, anti-expansionists, and so on), Gilpin is too much a bardic seer to argue with anyone. He is a mystic, burning with certainty, striving to convey to his audience the contagion of his own ecstatic vision. He seems to himself to be uttering self-evident axioms rather than pleading a lawyer's brief.

Gilpin takes over from Benton the theory of a succession of empires arising along a "hereditary line of progress" culminating in the Republican Empire of North America.[3] Just as each successive empire of the past has been superior to its predecessors, according to a general law of progress, so has each successive phase of American development emerged upon a higher level with its westward thrust. This theory, so flattering to the West, becomes a guiding command to the American people in moments of decision. Only by a heroic response to the challenge of universal history can the nation fulfill its mission, which Gilpin describes in apocalyptic language:

The *untransacted* destiny of the American people is to subdue the continent — to rush over this vast field to the Pacific Ocean — to animate the many hundred millions of its people, and to cheer them upward . . . — to agitate these herculean masses — to establish a new order in human affairs . . . — to regenerate superannuated nations — . . . to stir up the sleep of a hundred centuries — to teach old nations a new civilization — to confirm the destiny of the human race — to carry the career of mankind to its culminating point — to cause a stagnant people to be reborn — to perfect science — to emblazon history with the conquest of peace — to shed a new and resplendent glory upon mankind — to unite the world in one social family — to dissolve the spell of tyranny and exalt charity — to absolve the curse that weighs down humanity, and to shed blessings round the world![4]

The material means for bringing about this millennial consummation was a Pacific railway. In contrast with Whitney's plan for a northern transcontinental route, and various other schemes for a railway from Memphis or New Orleans via El Paso, Gilpin was certain that the line must be built along a central route, passing through his adopted home town of Independence, Missouri, and traversing the Rocky Mountains by way of South Pass. Such a railway, bridging the American continent and

destined to serve as the line of communication between Europe
and Asia, would inaugurate a new era in human affairs by bringing to maturity the North American Empire.

The force which pushes America irresistibly onward toward
her historical destiny is the westward movement of the frontier,
and the standard-bearers in this movement toward the Pacific
are the farmers of the West.

Let us not forget [wrote Gilpin in 1846] to estimate magnanimously
the unparalleled enterprise now being accomplished, under our eyes,
by the pioneers of America, upon the shores of the Pacific. Armies
have plunged into deserts, or scaled prodigious mountains — some to
conquer, and some to perish. . . . Upon the western edge of our
Union, at the confluence of the Kansas and Missouri rivers, there
assembled during May, 1843, American citizens with their families to
the number of one thousand, each one on himself alone dependant
[*sic*], and animated by impulses driving him irresistibly towards the
west. Surrounded by his wife and children, equipped with wagon,
ox-team, and provisions, such as the chase does not furnish, accompanied by his rifle and slender outfit of worldly goods, did these hardy
men embark upon the unmeasured waste before them. Plunged into
the immense plains which slope up to the Rocky Mountains, contending with great rivers, and surrounded by the uncertain dangers of an
Indian foe, a government and a discipline, at once republican and
military, was created for the common safety, and implicitly obeyed by
this moving people. . . . Arriving after an immense journey upon
the unpeopled shores of the Pacific at the season of the closing in of
winter, exhausted and destitute, neither despondency nor hesitation
palsied for a moment the undertaken work; but with energies over-
powering all obstacles, the opening spring beheld farms, houses, mills,
and towns, growing apace, as with the pith and sinews of many years.
Suffice it to say, that this hardy band, accompanied by 122 wagons,
in the short space of five months penetrated to the Pacific, opening
and traveling along a road of 1,000 miles of plains and 1,500 of vast
mountains, on whose summits the eternal snows are perpetually visible,
without other guide than an indomitable perseverance, or other protection than their invincible rifles, and the wives and progeny clustered
around them.[5]

It was the pioneer farmers whom Gilpin represented as demanding "a National Railway to the ocean which they seek." [6]
This is in some respects nearer to Douglas's view than to Whitney's, for it makes of the individual settler the prime force in the
development of the West. But Gilpin's main ideas are Benton's.

He shares Benton's allegiance to Jefferson and Jackson; his hatred for Britain, the Hartford Convention, and the Southern secessionists; his certainty that the Asiatic trade will bring incalculable wealth to the United States; and his vision of magnificent cities springing up along the line of the Pacific railway. To this intellectual patrimony Gilpin adds important new ideas derived from the developing science of physical geography. In particular, he affirms his debt to the "oracular inspiration" and "divine eloquence" of the German geographer Alexander von Humboldt, who was almost as great a scientist as Gilpin said he was.[7]

The most important idea Gilpin derived from Humboldt was that of the isothermal zodiac, "a serpentine zone of the north hemisphere of the globe" approximately thirty-five degrees in width, whose axis "alternates above and below the 40th degree of latitude, as the neighborhood or remoteness of the oceans modifies the climates of the continents." Gilpin believed that this geographical theory provided a scientific basis for the old idea of the westward course of empire. Along the isothermal zodiac, he pointed out, had arisen one by one the empires that had determined the history of the world — from China and India to Persia, Greece, Rome, Spain, and Britain. The advance of the pioneer army across the trans-Mississippi region was inaugurating the greatest of them all, the Republican Empire of North America, which consummated the westward tendency of the ages and would become permanent mistress of the world.[8] "This mission of civic empire," Gilpin proclaims, "has for its oracular principle the physical characteristics and configuration of our continent, wherein the *Basin of the Mississippi* predominates as supremely as the sun among the planets." [9] On the east and on the west the Mississippi Valley is bounded by a mountain rim so that the continent has a generally concave structure. All parts of the vast interior are drawn into integration by a network of rivers. Asia and Europe, dissected by central mountain chains and plateaus, have produced disunited civilizations constantly at war with one another. But the topography of North America is such that the dominant character of the society developed there will be integration, harmony, union. This conception, which Gilpin had developed in the 1840's, acquired a peculiar urgency as the Civil

War drew near. In 1860 he returned to it with almost desperate insistence: ". . . the holy question of our *Union*," he wrote, "lies in the bosom of *nature* . . . it lies not in the trivial temporalities of political taxation, African slavery, local power, or the nostrums of orators however eminent." [10]

When Gilpin reaches this point in his reasoning the conception of nature, the physical conformation of the earth, has all but supplanted the theories of expansionism based on the course of empire or the primacy of Asiatic trade in determining the fate of nations. It even overshadows the notion of the frontier farmer as the instrumental force that makes history happen. Physical nature, conceived according to Humboldt's great principle as an organic whole, governs the development of human communities. From the perspective of the physical geographer the continents and oceans, the mountain ranges and river systems group themselves into a system having a supreme and unbreakable order which is at the same time absolutely good. This order will ultimately determine the condition of the civilizations of the earth, elevating the United States above all other nations.

Gilpin derived his faith in the benevolence of nature from Humboldt, whose mind had been formed in the optimistic intellectual climate of the eighteenth century. But the tendency to identify nature with the specific geographical setting of the North American continent gave to the term a much narrower reference than it had had for eighteenth-century thinkers. Where in that earlier day nature had usually been conceived as a force permeating the physical universe, a vast system of relationships, even, in Pope's phrase, a "clear, *unchang'd*, and *Universal Light*," [11] the nineteenth century had tended to fix attention on this or that specific aspect of the great whole and had seen nature more and more concretely. Thus a science of physical geography which in one direction invited the observer to contemplate all the continents and the seas of the earth as parts of a single harmonious pattern, could in another direction focus attention upon the relation of organic life to its environment in a very limited area. The first of these tendencies was broad and cosmopolitan; the second restrictive and even provincial. The first was appropriate to a citizen of the world like Humboldt; the second to a nationalist and sectionalist like Gilpin. But the two tendencies, so different in their consequences, were aspects of a single ruling idea.

The cosmopolitan Humboldt's doctrine could be made to nourish American nationalism and Western sectionalism in yet another way. If the earth is the final arbiter of human destinies, then the student of society should direct his gaze toward nature rather than to history. The important thing about man is not his past, not a cultural tradition, but his biological adjustment to his milieu, which is a matter of the present and of the future. This inference from the science of physical geography coincided neatly with that hostility to the East and to Europe which formed so important a part of Benton's and Gilpin's sectional chauvinism. Yet if Humboldt's thought yielded conclusions like these it was because Gilpin was merely using geography to rationalize a well-established Western prejudice. The same science could be made to support an exactly contrary, if equally prejudiced, view of the relation between East and West. At the moment when Gilpin was invoking geography to prove that the West was certain to dominate the East, a European geographer whose affiliations were with the Atlantic seaboard was using the new ideas to prove that the East would always dominate the West.

Arnold Guyot, a Swiss scientist who came to this country at the invitation of Louis Agassiz in 1848 and subsequently had a long and distinguished career on the faculty of Princeton, delivered a series of lectures in French at the Lowell Institute of Boston in January and February, 1849.[12] Translated by Cornelius C. Felton of Harvard under the title *The Earth and Man,* the lectures had an enormous vogue both in the newspaper press and in repeated reissues of the book. Guyot sees North America as a continent just emerging into world history, toward which the old nations of Europe, "exhausted by the difficulties of every kind which oppose their march, turn with hope their wearied eyes . . . ." He agrees with Gilpin that

the simplicity and the grandeur of its forms, the extent of the spaces over which it rules, seem to have prepared it to become the abode of the most vast and powerful association of men that has ever existed on the surface of the globe.

And Guyot's itemized list of the geopolitical advantages of North
America likewise recalls the philosophers of manifest destiny:

The fertility of the soil; its position, in the midst of the oceans, between the two extremes of Europe and Asia, facilitating commerce
with these two worlds; the proximity of the rich tropical countries of
Central and South America, towards which, as by a natural descent,
it is borne by the waters of the majestic Mississippi, and of its thousand
tributary streams; all these advantages seem to promise its labor and
activity a prosperity without example. It belongs not to man to read
in the future the decrees of Providence. But science may attempt to
comprehend the purposes of God, as to the destinies of nations, by
examining with care the theatre, seemingly arranged by Him for the
realization of the new social order, towards which humanity is tending
with hope. For the order of nature is a foreshadowing of that which
is to be.[13]

Yet Guyot is far from agreeing with Benton and Gilpin that
the United States should abandon its ties to Europe and accept its
relation to Asia as defining its future. What, he asks,

would . . . become of the present destinies, the entire future of this
continent, were it necessary to cross the desert table lands of California,
and their high mountain ranges, in order to reach the Mississippi from
the Atlantic coast? What would become of its important relations with
the Old World, if America, averted from the civilized nations, looked
only towards the Pacific Ocean and China?[14]

The civilization of the United States is derived from that of Europe: Europe thinks, America acts; and only in a true marriage of
these complementary principles can America achieve her highest
development.[15] Thus the Atlantic seaboard, fronting toward Europe, will always be the dominant region in the New World. A
Boston audience could hardly have been displeased to hear that
". . . both in point of nature and of history, the maritime zone of
every continent enjoys a superiority over all others not to be
questioned or disputed." "It is in this region," Guyot declared,
". . . that life is unfolded in its most intense and diversified
forms. . . ." All civilized nations have lived on the margins of
oceans.

And in this new world of North America, now entering on its great
career among the nations under so many happy auspices, is it not on
the shores of the Atlantic that life is developed to its most active, most

intense, and most exalted form? Is this merely a chance consequence of the accidental debarkation at that point of the colonists of the Ancient World? No, gentlemen, brilliant as may be the prospects the West may aspire to from the exuberance of its soil, life and action will always point toward the coast, which can only derive fresh accessions of prosperity from the prosperity of the interior.[16]

Guyot's shrewd perception that the East would long be able to maintain its economic control over the West contained a hard core of truth upon which Western regionalisms other than Gilpin's were to wreck themselves.

CHAPTER IV

Walt Whitman and Manifest Destiny

Walt Whitman, the poet who gave final imaginative expression to
the theme of manifest destiny, was a native and lifelong resident
of the Atlantic seaboard.[1] He was drawn into contact with the
Western intellectual tradition not through firsthand experience —
for he had not even traveled beyond the Mississippi when he
wrote his principal poems — but through his burning conviction
that the society and the literature of the United States must be
adapted to the North American continent. This obsession led him
to declare with Benton (and of course also with Emerson) that
America must turn away from the feudal past of Europe to build
a new order founded upon nature:

I swear there is no greatness or power that does not emulate those of
    the earth!
I swear there can be no theory of any account, unless it corroborate
    the theory of the earth![2]

He wrote in the preface to the first edition of *Leaves of Grass* in
1855 that the poet of America "incarnates its geography and natural life and rivers and lakes":

Mississippi with annual freshets and changing chutes, Missouri and
Columbia and Ohio and Saint Lawrence with the falls and beautiful
masculine Hudson, do not embouchure where they spend themselves
more than they embouchure into him. . . . When the long Atlantic
coast stretches longer and the Pacific coast stretches longer he easily
stretches with them north or south. He spans between them also from
east to west and reflects what is between them.[3]

As this statement implies, Whitman originally set out to sing
the whole continent, East and West, North and South; and inter-

mittently throughout his life he returned to the impartial celebration of all the regions. But the Atlantic seaboard after all represented the past, the shadow of Europe, cities, sophistication, a
derivative and conventional life and literature. Beyond, occupying
the overwhelming geographical mass of the continent, lay the
West, a realm where nature loomed larger than civilization and
where feudalism had never been established. There, evidently,
would grow up the truly American society of the future. By 1860
Whitman had become aware that his original assumptions logi-
cally implied the Western orientation inherent in the cult of manifest destiny. "These States tend inland, and toward the Western
sea," he wrote, "and I will also." [4] He made up his mind that his
future audience would be found in the West: "I depend on being
realized, long hence, where the broad fat prairies spread, and
thence to Oregon and California inclusive." [5] It was in inland
America that he discovered the insouciance, the self-possession,
the physical health which he loved.[6] He declared that his *Leaves*
were made for the trans-Mississippi region, for the Great Plains
and the Rocky Mountains and the Pacific slope, and dwelt with
ecstasy upon "a free original life there . . . simple diet, and clean
and sweet blood, . . . litheness, majestic faces, clear eyes, and
perfect physique there . . . ." Above all, he foresaw "immense
spiritual results, future years, inland, spread there each side of the
Anahuacs." [7]

At the same time, Whitman had become interested in the conception of a fated course of empire leading Americans to the
shores of the Pacific and bringing them into contact with Asia. In
"Enfans d'Adam" he gives the ancient idea a vivid restatement:

Inquiring, tireless, seeking that yet unfound,
I, a child, very old, over waves, toward the house of maternity, the
    land of migrations, look afar,
Look off over the shores of my Western sea — having arrived at last
    where I am — the circle almost circled;
For coming westward from Hindustan, from the vales of Kashmere,
From Asia — from the north — from the God, the sage, and the hero;
From the south — from the flowery peninsulas, and the spice islands,
Now I face the old home again — looking over to it, joyous, as after
    long travel, growth, and sleep;
But where is what I started for, so long ago?
And why is it yet unfound? [8]

The plaintive question at the end of this passage does not belong to the jubilant Western tradition and indeed represents but a passing moment of melancholy in Whitman himself. Three poems in the collection *Drum-Taps*, published in 1865, return to the course of empire with an optimism more appropriate to Whitman's philosophy as a whole and to the intimations of manifest destiny. "Pioneers! O Pioneers," his most celebrated although not his best poem about the westward movement, depicts the march of the pioneer army in phrases that often suggest Gilpin's description of the Great Migration to Oregon. The peoples of the Old World are weakening; the youthful and sinewy pioneers take up the cosmic burden. Having conquered the wilderness and scaled the mighty mountains, they come out upon the Pacific coast. Their advent inaugurates a new era in the history of mankind: "We debouch upon a newer, mightier world . . ." [9]

"Years of the Unperform'd" (the title may echo Gilpin's phrase, "the *untransacted* destiny of the American people") [10] launches the westward-moving pioneer out upon the waters of the Pacific and equips him with the weapons of a developing technology:

Never was average man, his soul, more energetic, more like a God;
Lo, how he urges and urges, leaving the masses no rest;
His daring foot is on land and sea everywhere — he colonizes the
    Pacific, the archipelagoes;
With the steam-ship, the electric telegraph, the newspaper, the whole-
    sale engines of war,
With these, and the world-spreading factories, he interlinks all
    geography, all lands. . . . [11]

And the idea of an American empire in the Pacific is carried even farther in "A Broadway Pageant," celebrating the arrival of the first Japanese embassy in New York in 1860:

I chant the world on my Western Sea; . . .
I chant the new empire, grander than any before — As in a vision it
    comes to me;
I chant America, the Mistress — I chant a greater supremacy;
I chant, projected, a thousand blooming cities yet, in time, on those
    groups of sea-islands; . . .
I chant commerce opening, the sleep of ages having done its work —
    races, reborn, refresh'd. . . .

For the long circuit of the globe is drawing to its close: the children of Adam have strayed westward through the centuries, but with the arrival of the American pioneers in the Pacific a glorious millennium begins.[12]

Elaborate as these ideas are, Whitman was not yet done with the theme of the course of empire. He returned to it in 1871 in "Passage to India," which he said was an expression of "what, from the first, . . . more or less lurks in my writings, underneath every page, every line, every where."[13] Again he depicts the myriad progeny of Adam and Eve moving westward around the globe, "wandering, yearning, curious . . . with questionings, baffled, formless, feverish — with never-happy hearts . . . ."[14] God's purpose, hidden from men through countless ages, is revealed at last when the Suez Canal, the Atlantic submarine cable, and especially the Pacific railway connect the nations of the earth with a single network:

> The people [are] to become brothers and sisters,
> The races, neighbors, to marry and be given in marriage,
> The oceans to be cross'd, the distant brought near,
> The lands to be welded together.[15]

But the new era begun with the closing of the cycle of history meant even more than the mingling of peoples: it was to restore man's lost harmony with nature. The secret of impassive earth was to be uttered at last. The "strong, light works of engineers" encircling the globe were to lead man into a full understanding of nature and a permanently satisfying communion with her:

All these hearts, as of fretted children, shall be sooth'd,
All affection shall be fully responded to — the secret shall be told;
All these separations and gaps shall be taken up, and hook'd and link'd together;
The whole earth — this cold, impassive, voiceless Earth, shall be completely justified; . . .
Nature and Man shall be disjoin'd and diffused no more,
The true Son of God shall absolutely fuse them.[16]

This is a mysticism difficult for the twentieth century to follow, but it moves in a straight line from Benton's first intimation that the course of empire would lead the American people westward to fabulous Asia. In view of the less attractive inferences that other thinkers have drawn from the notion of an American empire in the Pacific, one is grateful for the intrepid idealism that so triumphantly enabled Whitman to see in the march of the pioneer army a prelude to peace and the brotherhood of nations.

BOOK TWO ✩ ✩ ✩

THE SONS OF LEATHERSTOCKING

The friendly and flowing savage, who is he?
Is he waiting for civilization, or past it and mastering it?

Is he some Southwesterner rais'd out-doors? is he
*   Kanadian?*
Is he from the Mississippi country? Iowa, Oregon,
*   California?*
The mountains? prairie-life, bush-life? or sailor from the
*   sea?*
Wherever he goes men and women accept and desire
*   him,*
They desire he should like them, touch them, speak to
*   them, stay with them.*

Behavior lawless as snow-flakes, words simple as grass,
*   uncomb'd head, laughter, and naivetè,*
Slow-stepping feet, common features, common modes
*   and emanations,*
They descend in new forms from the tips of his fingers,
They are wafted with the odor of his body or breath,
*   they fly out of the glance of his eyes.*

— Walt Whitman, *Song of Myself*

CHAPTER V

Daniel Boone: Empire Builder
or Philosopher of Primitivism?

During the summer of 1842, following his sophomore year at
Harvard, Francis Parkman made a trip through northern New
York and New England. After spending several days admiring the
scenery along the shores of Lake George, he noted in his journal:
"There would be no finer place of gentlemen's seats than this, but
now, for the most part, it is occupied by a race of boors about as
uncouth, mean, and stupid as the hogs they seem chiefly to delight
in." [1] The tone is even blunter than that of Timothy Dwight's
famous description of backwoodsmen in this area a generation
earlier, but it embodies a comparable aristocratic disdain. Observers from Eastern cities made similar comments about uncultivated farmers along every American frontier. The class bias
underlying the judgment was one of the dominant forces shaping
nineteenth-century attitudes toward the West.

When Parkman got away from farms and hogs, out into the
forest, his tone changed completely. He wrote, for example, that a
woodsman named James Abbot, although coarse and self-willed,
was "a remarkably intelligent fellow; has astonishing information
for one of his condition; is resolute and independent as the
wind." [2] The young Brahmin's delight in men of the wilderness
comes out even more forcibly in the journal of his Far Western trip
four years later. *The Oregon Trail* presents the guide Henry Cha-
tillon, a French-Canadian squaw man, as a hero of romance —
handsome, brave, true, skilled in the ways of the plains and mountains, and even possessed of "a natural refinement and delicacy
of mind, such as is rare even in women." [3]

Parkman's antithetical attitudes toward backwoods farmers and the hunters and trappers of the wilderness illustrate the fact that for Americans of that period there were two quite distinct Wests: the commonplace domesticated area within the agricultural frontier, and the Wild West beyond it. The agricultural West was tedious; its inhabitants belonged to a despised social class. The Wild West was by contrast an exhilarating region of adventure and comradeship in the open air. Its heroes bore none of the marks of degraded status. They were in reality not members of society at all, but noble anarchs owning no master, free denizens of a limitless wilderness.

Parkman's love of the Wild West implied a paradoxical rejection of organized society. He himself was the product of a complex social order formed by two centuries of history, and his way of life was made possible by the fortune which his grandfather had built up as one of the great merchants of Boston. But a young gentleman of leisure could afford better than anyone else to indulge himself in the slightly decadent cult of wildness and savagery which the early nineteenth century took over from Byron. Historians call the mood "primitivism." Parkman had a severe case. In later life he said that from his early youth "His thoughts were always in the forest, whose features possessed his waking and sleeping dreams, filling him with vague cravings impossible to satisfy." [4] And in a preface to *The Oregon Trail* written more than twenty years after the first publication of the book he bewailed the advance of humdrum civilization over the wide empty plains of Colorado since the stirring days of 1846.[5]

Such a mood of refined hostility to progress affected a surprising number of Parkman's contemporaries. Nevertheless, it could hardly strike very deep in a society committed to an expansive manifest destiny. A romantic love of the vanishing Wild West could be no more than a self-indulgent affectation beside the triumphant official cult of progress, which meant the conquest of the wilderness by farms and towns and cities. If there was a delicious melancholy for sophisticated and literary people in regretting the destruction of the primitive freedom of an untouched continent, the westward movement seemed to less imaginative observers a glorious victory of civilization over savagery and barbarism. For such people — and they were the vast majority — the Western hunter and guide was praiseworthy not because of his intrinsic wildness or half-savage glamor, but because he blazed trails that hard-working farmers could follow.

One of the most striking evidences of the currency of these two conflicting attitudes toward the westward movement is the popular image of Daniel Boone. The official view was set forth in a greatly admired piece of allegorical sculpture by Horatio Greenough in the National Capitol, which depicted the contest between civilization and barbarism as a fierce hand-to-hand struggle between Boone and an Indian warrior.[6] George C. Bingham's painting "The Emigration of Daniel Boone" (1851) showed the celebrated Kentuckian leading a party of settlers with their wives and children and livestock out into a dreamily beautiful wilderness which they obviously meant to bring under the plow.[7]

These empire-building functions were amply documented by the facts of history. Boone had supervised the Treaty of Sycamore Shoals which extinguished the Indian claim to much of Kentucky, he had blazed the Wilderness Trail through the forest, and after leading the first settlers to Boonesborough in 1775, he had stoutly defended this outpost of civilization against the Indians during the troubled period of the Revolution.[8] His functions as founder of the commonwealth of Kentucky had been celebrated as early as 1784 by John Filson, first architect of the Boone legend, in *The Discovery, Settlement and Present State of Kentucke.* Filson represents Boone as delighting in the thought that Kentucky will soon be one of the most opulent and powerful states on the continent, and finding in the love and gratitude of his countrymen a sufficient reward for all his toil and sufferings.[9] The grandiose epic entitled *The Adventures of Daniel Boone*, published in 1813 by Daniel Bryan, nephew of the hero, is even more emphatic concerning his devotion to social progress. Complete with Miltonic councils in Heaven and Hell, the epic relates how Boone was chosen by the angelic Spirit of Enterprise to bring Civilization to the trans-Allegheny wilderness.[10] When he is informed of his divine election for this task, Boone's kindling fancy beholds Refinement's golden file smoothing the heathen encrustations from the savage mind, while Commerce, Wealth, and all the brilliant Arts spread over the land.[11] He informs his wife in a Homeric leave-taking that the sovereign law of Heaven requires him to tread the adventurous stage of grand emprise, scattering knowledge through the heathen wilds, and mending the state of Universal Man.[12] Faithful to his mission even in captivity among the Indians, he lectures the chief Montour on the history of the human race, concluding with reflections on

> How Philanthropy
> And social Love, in sweet profusion pour
> Along Refinement's pleasure-blooming Vales,
> Their streams of richest, life-ennobling joy.[13]

By the side of Boone the empire builder and philanthropist, the anonymous popular mind had meanwhile created an entirely different hero, a fugitive from civilization who could not endure the encroachment of settlements upon his beloved wilderness. A dispatch from Fort Osage in the Indian territory, reprinted in *Niles' Register* in 1816, described an interview with Boone and added: "This singular man could not live in Kentucky when it became settled. . . . he might have accumulated riches as readily as any man in Kentucky, but he *prefers the woods*, where you see him in the dress of the roughest, poorest hunter." [14]

Boone's flight westward before the advance of the agricultural frontier — actually dictated by a series of failures in his efforts to get and hold land — became a theme of newspaper jokes. The impulse that produced Western tall tales transformed him into the type of all frontiersmen who required unlimited elbow room. "As civilization advanced," wrote a reporter in the New York *American* in 1823, "so he, from time to time, retreated" — from Kentucky to Tennessee, from Tennessee to Missouri. But Missouri itself was filling up: Boone was said to have complained, "I had not been two years at the licks before a d—d Yankee came, and settled down *within an hundred miles of me*!!" He would soon be driven on out to the Rocky Mountains and would be crowded there in eight or ten years.[15] Edwin James, chronicler of the Stephen H. Long expedition, visiting Fort Osage in 1819, heard that Boone felt it was time to move again when he could no longer fell a tree for fuel so that its top would lie within a few yards of the door of his cabin. This remark set James, a native of Vermont, to thinking about the irrational behavior of frontiersmen. He had observed that most inhabitants of new states and territories had "a manifest propensity, particularly in the males, to remove westward, for which it is not easy to account." There was an apparently irresistible charm for the true Westerner in a mode of life "wherein the artificial wants and the uneasy restraints inseparable from a crowded population are not known, wherein we feel ourselves dependent immediately and solely on the bounty of nature, and the strength of our own arm. . . ." [16] The Long party came upon a man more than sixty years old living near the farthest settlement up the Missouri who questioned them minutely about the still unoccupied Platte Valley. "We discovered," noted James with astonishment, "that he had the most serious intention of removing with his family to that river." [17]

Seizing upon hints of Boone's flight before the advance of civilization, Byron paused in his description of the siege of Ismail in the eighth canto of *Don Juan* to insert an extended tribute to him. Although Byron's Boone shrank from men of his own nation when they built up unto his darling trees, he was happy, innocent, and benevolent; simple, not savage; and even in old age still a child of nature, whose virtues shamed the corruptions of civilization. Americans quoted these stanzas eagerly.[18]

Which was the real Boone — the standard-bearer of civilization and refinement, or the child of nature who fled into the wilderness before the advance of settlement? An anonymous kinsman of Boone wrestled with the problem in a biographical sketch published a few years after the famous hunter's death in 1820. It would be natural to suppose, he wrote, that the Colonel took great pleasure in the magnificent growth of the commonwealth he had founded in the wilderness. But such was not the case. Passionately fond of hunting, "like the unrefined Savage," Boone saw only that incoming settlers frightened away all the game and spoiled the sport. He would "certainly prefer a state of nature to a state of Civilization, if he were obliged to be confined to one or the other." [19]

Timothy Flint's biography, perhaps the most widely read book about a Western character published during the first half of the nineteenth century, embodies the prevalent confusion of attitudes.

Flint says that Boone delighted in the thought that "the rich and boundless valleys of the great west — the garden of the earth — and the paradise of hunters, had been won from the dominion of the savage tribes, and opened as an asylum for the oppressed, the enterprising, and the free of every land." The explorer of Kentucky

had caught some glimmerings of the future, and saw with the prophetic eye of a patriot, that this great valley must soon become the abode of millions of freemen; and his heart swelled with joy, and warmed with a transport which was natural to a mind so unsophisticated and disinterested as his.[20]

Yet we learn only a few pages later that he was driven out of Kentucky by "the restless spirit of immigration, and of civil and physical improvement." [21] Even in Missouri, "the tide of emigration once more swept by the dwelling of Daniel Boone, driving off the game and monopolizing the rich hunting grounds." In despair,

he saw that it was in vain to contend with fate; that go where he would, American enterprize seemed doomed to follow him, and to thwart all his schemes of backwoods retirement. He found himself once more surrounded by the rapid march of improvement, and he accommodated himself, as well as he might, to a state of things which he could not prevent.[22]

On yet other occasions Flint credits Boone with a sophisticated cult of pastoral simplicity greatly resembling his own, which he had imitated from Chateaubriand. When the frontiersman seeks to induce settlers to go with him into the new land, he is represented as promising them that the original pioneers, in their old age, will be surrounded by

consideration, and care, and tenderness from children, whose breasts were not steeled by ambition, nor hardened by avarice; in whom the beautiful influences of the indulgence of none but natural desires and pure affections would not be deadened by the selfishness, vanity, and fear of ridicule, that are the harvest of what is called *civilized and cultivated life.*[23]

The debate over Boone's character and motives lasted into the next decade. The noted Western Baptist minister and gazetteer, John M. Peck, prepared a life of Boone for Jared Sparks's Library of American Biography in 1847 which repeatedly attacked the current conception of the hero as a fugitive from civilization. Peck says that Boone left North Carolina for the Kentucky wilderness because of the effeminacy and profligacy of wealthy slaveowners who scorned the industrious husbandman working his own fields. But by the time the biographer interviewed the aged hero in Missouri in 1818, Boone had become aware of an imposing historical mission. Although he had not consciously aimed to lay the foundations of a state or nation, he believed that he had been "a creature of Providence, ordained by Heaven as a pioneer in the wilderness, to advance the civilization and the extension of his country." [24]

James H. Perkins of Cincinnati, writing in 1846 in the *North American Review*, was equally interested in the problem of Boone's motives, but inclined to a more modest interpretation. Boone, he said, was a white Indian. Although he and his companions were not at all like the boasting, swearing, drinking, gouging Mike Finks of the later West, they were led into the wilderness not by the hope of gain, nor by a desire to escape the evils of older communities, nor yet by dreams of founding a new commonwealth, but simply by "a love of nature, of perfect freedom, and of the adventurous life in the woods." Boone "would have pined and died as a nabob in the midst of civilization. He wanted a frontier, and the perils and pleasures of a frontier life, not wealth; and he was happier in his log-cabin, with a loin of venison and his ramrod for a spit, than he would have been amid the greatest profusion of modern luxuries." [25]

If one detects a patronizing note in this account, it goes along with a greater respect for the simple, hearty virtues that are left to the frontiersman. Such a view seems to have become general in the 1840's. William H. Emory of the Army of the West which invaded New Mexico in 1846 invoked the figure of the Kentuckian to convey his impression of an American settler in the Mora Valley northeast of Santa Fé: "He is a perfect specimen of a generous open-hearted adventurer, and in appearance what, I have pictured to myself, Daniel Boone, of Kentucky, must have been in his day." [26]

Yet the issue long remained unsettled. As a character in fiction Boone could still be made the spokesman of a stilted primitivism. Glenn, the young Eastern hero of John B. Jones's shoddy *Wild*

Western Scenes, published in 1849, is traveling in the vicinity of
Boone's last home in Missouri, and there encounters the venerable
pioneer. The highly implausible conversation between the two
men indicates to what unhistorical uses the symbol of Boone could
be put. The Westerner asks Glenn whether he has become disgusted with the society of men. Glenn, who happens to be just
such a rhetorical misanthrope as the question implies, welcomes
the opportunity to set forth his views:

I had heard [he declares] that you were happy in the solitude of the
mountain-shaded valley, or on the interminable prairies that greet the
horizon in the distance, where neither the derision of the proud, the
malice of the envious, nor the deceptions of pretended love and friend-
ship, could disturb your peaceful meditation; and from amid the
wreck of certain hopes, which I once thought no circumstances could
destroy [it is a matter of disappointment in love], I rose with a determined vow to seek such a wilderness, where I would pass a certain
number of my days engaging in the pursuits that might be most congenial to my disposition. Already I imagine I experience the happy
effects of my resolution. Here the whispers of vituperating foes cannot
injure, nor the smiles of those fondly cherished, deceive.

Boone clasps the young coxcomb's hand in enthusiastic agreement.[27] If Daniel Bryan's epic represents the limit of possible absurdity in making Boone the harbinger of civilization and refinement, this may stand as the opposite limit of absurdity in making
him a cultural primitivist. The image of the Wild Western hero
could serve either purpose.

CHAPTER VI

Leatherstocking
and the Problem of Social Order

Although Boone was not exactly the prototype of Cooper's Leatherstocking, there is a haunting similarity between the two figures. Cooper based a part of chapters X and XII of *The Last of the Mohicans* on a well-known exploit of Boone in conducting the rescue of Betsey and Fanny Callaway and Jemima Boone, his daughter, from the Cherokees.[1] Betsey Callaway, like Cora Munro in Cooper's novel, tried to aid her rescuers by breaking twigs to mark the trail, and was detected by her Indian guards.[2] The rescue also furnished Cooper with several other details for his story.[3]

Near the opening of *The Prairie* Cooper sets his stage by describing the migration of Americans from Ohio and Kentucky across the Mississippi immediately after the Louisiana Purchase. Although Boone actually settled in Missouri in 1799, Cooper names him among the emigrants of 1804:

This adventurous and venerable patriarch was now seen making his last remove; placing the "endless river" between him and the multitude, his own success had drawn around him, and seeking for the renewal of enjoyments which were rendered worthless in his eyes, when trammelled by the forms of human institutions.[4]

In a footnote added to the revised edition, Cooper elaborates this passage with the remark that Boone emigrated beyond the Mississippi "because he found a population of ten to the square mile, inconvenient."[5] The aged Leatherstocking has likewise "been driven by the increasing and unparalleled advance of population, to seek a final refuge against society in the broad and tenantless plains of the west . . . ."[6]

The similarities between Boone and Leatherstocking were analyzed at length by a perceptive writer in *Niles' Register* in 1825, when Leatherstocking had appeared in only one novel, *The Pioneers*. The critic points out that both these heroes love the freedom of the forest, both take a passionate delight in hunting, and both dislike the ordinary pursuits of civilized men. As testimony to the fidelity of Cooper's characterization, the writer quotes a letter from a traveler through the Pennsylvania mountains who came upon herdsmen and hunters reminiscent both of Boone and of Leatherstocking. One of their number, celebrated throughout the West as having once been a companion of Boone, had set out for Arkansas when he was almost a hundred years old, and was reported to be still alive, a solitary hunter in the forest. A nephew of the emigrant who remained in Pennsylvania, himself athletic and vigorous at the age of seventy, shared Leatherstocking's love of hunting and his antipathy for "clearings" to such a marked degree that the traveler felt he must have sat as a model for Cooper.[7] A similar point was made by the poet Albert Pike, who after graduating from Harvard went out the Santa Fé Trail and later settled in a very primitive Arkansas. "I cannot wonder that many men have chosen to pass their life in the woods," wrote Pike in 1834, "and I see nothing overdrawn or exaggerated in the character of Hawkeye and Bushfield." He listed as the prime attractions of the lonely hunter's life its independence, its freedom from law and restraint, its lack of ceremony.[8]

For at least one section of the reading public, then, Leatherstocking, like Boone, was a symbol of anarchic freedom, an enemy of law and order. Did this interpretation conform to Cooper's intention in drawing the character?

The original hunter of *The Pioneers* (1823) clearly expresses subversive impulses. The character was conceived in terms of the antithesis between nature and civilization, between freedom and law, that has governed most American interpretations of the westward movement. Cooper was able to speak for his people on this theme because the forces at work within him closely reproduced the patterns of thought and feeling that prevailed in the society at large. But he felt the problem more deeply than his contemporaries: he was at once more strongly devoted to the principle of social order and more vividly responsive to the ideas of nature and freedom in the Western forest than they were. His conflict of allegiances was truly ironic, and if he had been able — as he was not — to explore to the end the contradictions in his ideas and emotions, the Leatherstocking series might have become a major work of art. Despite Cooper's failures, the character of Leatherstocking is by far the most important symbol of the national experience of adventure across the continent.[9] The similarities that link Leatherstocking to both the actual Boone and the various Boones of popular legend are not merely fortuitous.

The Pioneers illustrates these aspects of Cooper's work with almost naïve directness. After a negligible first novel, *Precaution*, he had turned to the matter of the American Revolution in *The Spy*, which had had a sensational success. The Preface to *The Pioneers*, his next book, has a jaunty air bespeaking the apprentice novelist's growing confidence. Cooper announces that he is now writing to please himself alone.[10] We may well believe him, for the scene is the Cooperstown of his childhood, and the character of Judge Marmaduke Temple, patron of the infant community, landed proprietor, justice of the peace, and virtual lord of the manor, has much in common with that of the novelist's father William Cooper. Not only did both William Cooper and Judge Temple buy land on the New York frontier and oversee the planting of a town on the shores of Lake Otsego; they resemble one another even in the minor detail of springing from Quaker forebears but having given up formal membership in the sect.[11] When an author turns to autobiographical material of this sort and introduces a central character resembling his father, one does not have to be very much of a Freudian to conclude that the imagination is working on a deeper level than usual. This is certainly the case in *The Pioneers*.

Still very much an amateur in the externals of his craft, Cooper contrived for his story of Cooperstown a flimsy plot that hinges upon a childish misunderstanding about Judge Temple's administration of the property of his old friend Major Effingham, but the plot is merely a framework to hold together a narrative focussed about an entirely different problem. The emotional and literary center of the story is a conflict between Judge Temple and the old hunter Leatherstocking which symbolizes the issues raised by the advance of agricultural settlement into the wilderness. In the management of this theme Cooper is at his best. From the opening scene, when Judge Temple claims as his own a deer that Leatherstocking's young companion has shot, until the moment when the Judge sentences the old hunter to a fine and imprisonment because of his resistance to legal procedures he cannot understand, the narrative turns about the issue of the old forest freedom versus the new needs of a community that must establish the power of law over the individual.[12] One aspect of the conflict is of course the question of a primitive free access to the bounty of nature — whether in the form of game or of land — versus individual appropriation and the whole notion of inviolable property rights. Not far in the background are the further issues of the rough equality of all men in a state of nature as against social stratification based on unequal distribution of property; and of formal institutional religion versus the natural, intuitive theology of Leatherstocking, who has little regard for theological niceties or the minutiæ of ritual.

The profundity of the symbol of Leatherstocking springs from the fact that Cooper displays a genuine ambivalence toward all these issues, although in every case his strongest commitment is to the forces of order. The social compact, with all its consequences, is vividly and freshly realized, as it had to be realized with every new community planted in the wilderness. And all the aspects of authority — institutional stability, organized religion, class stratification, property — are exhibited as radiating from the symbol of the father. But if the father rules, and rules justly, it is still true that in this remembered world of his childhood Cooper figures as the son. Thus he is able to impart real energy to the statement of the case for defiance and revolt.

But we are not concerned with Cooper's personal relation to his materials so much as with his treatment of the themes arising from the advance of the agricultural frontier. The broader setting for the story is indicated in an exclamation of Elizabeth Temple:

"The enterprise of Judge Temple is taming the very forests! How rapidly is civilization treading on the footsteps of nature!" [13] When Elizabeth, with a burst of womanly sympathy for the imprisoned Leatherstocking, declares he must be innocent because of his inherent goodness, her father makes a crucial distinction: "Thou hast reason Bess, and much of it too, but thy heart lies too near thy head." The Judge himself means to pay Leatherstocking's fine, but he cannot brush aside the sentence of imprisonment which he imposed as the spokesman of necessary justice. He sends Elizabeth with a purse to visit the hunter and comfort him: ". . . say what thou wilt to the poor old man; give scope to the feelings of thy warm heart; but try to remember, Elizabeth, that the laws alone remove us from the condition of the savages; that he has been criminal, and that his judge was thy father." [14]

Another interesting scene occurs when the sonless Judge Temple invites Oliver Effingham to enter his household as a secretary. Oliver hesitates. Richard, the Judge's pompous factotum, says in an aside to Elizabeth, "This, you see, cousin Bess, is the natural reluctance of a half-breed to leave the savage state. Their attachment to a wandering life is, I verily believe, unconquerable." The Judge remarks that the unsettled life of a hunter "is of vast disadvantage for temporal purposes, and it totally removes one from within the influences of more sacred things." But this rouses Leatherstocking, who bursts out:

No, no, Judge . . . take him into your shanty in welcome, but tell him the raal thing. I have lived in the woods for forty long years, and have spent five years at a time without seeing the light of a clearing, bigger than a wind-row in the trees; and I should like to know where you'll find a man, in his sixty-eighth year, who can get an easier living, for all your betterments, and your deer-laws; and, as for honesty, or doing what's right between man and man, I'll not turn my back to the longest winded deacon on your Patent.

This states the issue as succinctly as possible. Cooper is unable to solve it, and resorts to a compromise statement that represents exactly his unwillingness or inability to accept the full implications of the conflict he has stated. The Judge answers, "nodding good-naturedly at the hunter": "Thou art an exception, Leatherstocking; for thou hast a temperance unusual in thy class, and a hardihood exceeding thy years. But this youth is made of materials too precious to be wasted in the forest." [15]

The Judge's reply expresses the unfailing regard for status which qualified Cooper's attitude toward the idea of nature as a norm. Leatherstocking, noble child of the forest, is nevertheless of inferior social status; whereas even in disguise, Oliver's gentle birth is palpable to the Judge's Falstaffian instinct. Leather-stocking began life as a servant of Major Effingham, and he is wholly illiterate. The fact that he speaks in dialect is a constant reminder of his lowly origin. It is true that the social status of the old hunter was not to prove significant during the long passages of adventure in *The Last of the Mohicans* and *The Prairie*, which deal with Indian warfare and the rescue of Cooper's distressed heroines from their captors. Here Leatherstocking's prowess with the rifle, his talents as a strategist, and his skill in following trails could be exploited with little regard for gradations in rank. But the problem of the hunter's status could not be permanently ignored. The response of readers to this symbol of forest freedom and virtue created a predicament for the novelist by revealing to him that his most vital character occupied a technically inferior position both in the social system and in the form of the sentimental novel as he was using it. The store of emotion associated with the vast wilderness in the minds of both Cooper and his audience was strikingly inharmonious with the literary framework he had adopted.

A more self-conscious or experimentally inclined writer might have found in this situation a challenge to devise a new form proceeding functionally from the materials. But Cooper was not the man to undertake a revolution, either in life or in literature. He chose a different course of action; he set about modifying the traditional form of the novel as far as he could without actually shattering it, and at the same time altering his materials as much as possible to make them fit.

Cooper's efforts to solve his problem can be traced in the last two novels of the Leatherstocking series, *The Pathfinder* and *The Deerslayer*, which appeared in 1840 and 1841. In *The Prairie*, published thirteen years before, he had described the death of

Leatherstocking, and had at that time meant to abandon the character forever. This decision seems to have been due in part to the technical difficulty mentioned above, for in later years Cooper told his daughter he wished he had left out of *The Prairie* the genteel hero and heroine, Inez de Certavallos and Captain Middleton, retaining only those characters who properly belonged to the locale.[16] But if the upper-class hero and heroine were to be omitted, and Leatherstocking was to be promoted to the post of official hero, how was the plot to be managed? It is at this point that Cooper's reluctance to break with the conventions of the sentimental novel becomes most glaringly apparent. A novel, according to canons which he considered binding, was a love story. The hero of the novel was the man who played the male lead in the courtship. If Leatherstocking was to be promoted to this rank, he must be made to fall in love with a heroine. In *The Pathfinder*, Cooper accordingly sets to work with great good will to exhibit Leatherstocking in love. The problem was to construct a female character, sufficiently refined and genteel to pass muster as a heroine, but sufficiently low in social status to receive the addresses of the hunter and scout without a shocking and indecent violation of the proprieties.

The object of Leatherstocking's affection, Mabel Dunham, is the daughter of a sergeant — not an officer — in the British army. When she is first introduced in the company of Cap, her seafaring uncle, who occupies "a station little, if any, above that of a common mariner," Cooper is careful to point out that Mabel is "a maiden of a class in no great degree superior to his own." [17] She is, therefore, technically accessible to the lower-class Leatherstocking. But before she can qualify as a heroine Mabel has to be given some of the attributes of gentility. Cooper explains elaborately that upon the death of her mother Mabel had been taken in charge by the widow of a field-officer of her father's regiment. Under the care of this lady Mabel had acquired "some tastes, and many ideas, which otherwise might always have remained strangers to her." The results of this association

were quite apparent in her attire, her language, her sentiments, and even in her feelings, though neither, perhaps, rose to the level of those which would properly characterize a lady. She had lost the coarser and less refined habits and manners of one in her original position, without having quite reached a point that disqualified her for the situation in life that the accidents of birth and fortune would probably compel her to fill.[18]

In particular, Mabel had acquired a degree of sensibility that caused her to respond in approved fashion to the beauty of landscape — an index in Cooper almost as infallible as that of language for distinguishing the upper classes from the lower.

Ironically enough, the novelist's care in refining Mabel creates a fresh problem for him. The modifications of her character that qualify her for the role of heroine raise her somewhat above the actual range of Leatherstocking's manners and tastes. When Mabel's father proposes the marriage Leatherstocking is timid about it. He fears that a "poor ignorant woodsman" cannot hope to win the girl's affection. The sergeant compels the scout to admit that he is a man of experience in the wilderness, well able to provide for a wife; a veteran of proved courage in the wars; a loyal subject of the King. But Leatherstocking still demurs: "I'm afeard I'm too rude, and too old, and too wild like, to suit the fancy of such a young and delicate girl, as Mabel, who has been unused to our wilderness ways, and may think the settlements better suited to her gifts and inclinations." Pressed still further, Leatherstocking makes an avowal that throws a flood of light on Cooper's conception of the social relationships prevailing within his standard tableau of a captured heroine in the process of being rescued by Leatherstocking and a genteel hero:

I have travelled with some as fair, and have guided them through the forest, and seen them in their perils and in their gladness; but they were always too much above me, to make me think of them as more than so many feeble ones I was bound to protect and defend. The case is now different. Mabel and I are so nearly alike, that I feel weighed down with a load that is hard to bear, at finding us so unlike. I do wish, serjeant, that I was ten years younger [the scout was then presumably in his early thirties], more comely to look at, and better suited to please a handsome young woman's fancy!

In short, "I am but a poor hunter, and Mabel, I see, is fit to be an officer's lady." [19] She is indeed, as appears in the course of the story when the regimental quartermaster wants to marry her: or is she?

Cooper subsequently causes this officer to prove a traitor, perhaps because of an unconscious impulse to punish him for his subversive disregard of class lines. In any event, when the actual moment of Leatherstocking's proposal arrives, Mabel's superior refinement is so unmistakable that it decides the issue. One of Cooper's very few valid comic inventions causes her, in her confusion, to use a more and more involved rhetoric that Leatherstocking cannot follow at all. He has to resort to his characteristic query, "Anan?" [20] The match is quite unsuitable and in the end Leatherstocking has the exquisite masochistic pleasure of giving his blessing to her union with Jasper Western, the young, handsome, and worthy Great Lakes sailor.[21]

If Leatherstocking could hardly be imagined as married, however, a feeling for symmetry would suggest that he at least might be shown as himself hopelessly beloved. This is the formula of the last novel of the series, *The Deerslayer*, which removes the obstacle of the hero's age by going back to the period of his early youth and thus represents the utmost possible development of Leatherstocking into a hero of romance. In this story he is loved by Judith Hutter, beautiful daughter of a somewhat coarse backwoodsman. But Judith's reputation is stained by past coquetries: she is obviously not an appropriate mate for the chaste Leatherstocking, and at the end of the novel is reported to be living in England as the mistress of a British officer.

Despite these late experiments in depicting Leatherstocking in his youth, the persistent image of the hunter was that of his first appearance, as a man of venerable age. This trait of Leatherstocking was strengthened by whatever parallels were felt to exist between him and Daniel Boone. When John Filson's biography of Boone appeared in 1784, the Kentuckian, at fifty, already seemed a patriarchal figure, his active days of fighting in the past. The folk cult of Boone that developed after 1815 emphasized the picturesque conception of an octogenarian huntsman. Cooper himself gives testimony to the popular tendency to exaggerate Boone's age when he remarks in a note to the revised edition of *The Prairie* that the famous hunter emigrated to Missouri "in his ninety-second year." [22] Boone was actually sixty-five when that event occurred. The many Western hunters created in the image of Leatherstocking who people Western fiction through most of the nineteenth century are characteristically of advanced age.

If Leatherstocking was, so to speak, intrinsically aged, this fact hindered his transformation into a hero of romance as seriously as did his low social status. Cooper was thus led to experiment with younger heroes who had Leatherstocking's vital relation to the forest, but were more easily converted into lovers. The character of Oliver Effingham in *The Pioneers* had early suggested the idea of a young hunter, wearing the garb and following the vocation of Leatherstocking. In *The Prairie* the impulse to double the role of the hunter in this fashion yields the character of Paul Hover, who, like Oliver, appears as an associate of Leatherstocking but is a real instead of merely a pretended child of the backwoods. Paul is a native of Kentucky and has a dialect that is the unmistakable badge of lowly status. It is true that he is merely a bee hunter rather than a hunter of deer and bear, but his sentiments concerning the rifle and his skill at marksmanship arouse Leatherstocking's enthusiastic approval. The most interesting thing about Paul is that, despite the presence in this novel of the official genteel hero and heroine, he is treated as an embryonic hero himself. He is young and handsome and virtuous, and in the end is allowed to marry Ellen Wade, who has carefully been given appearance, manners, speech, and sensibility superior to those of her crude companions — a distinct foreshadowing of Mabel Dunham's status and character in *The Pathfinder*. The Paul–Ellen love affair in *The Prairie*, in fact, seems to have furnished Cooper with the germ of his experiments in the two later novels.

Near the end of his life the novelist made a final effort to construct a story with a Western hero in *The Oak Openings* (1848). Like Paul Hover twenty years earlier, Ben Boden is a bee hunter of admirable character. In the absence of a genteel hero, however, he has to be refined somewhat beyond Paul Hover's level. This process is indicated in terms of the significant criterion of language. We are told twice in the first chapter that he used surprisingly pure English for one in his social class, and he has the further genteel trait of highly moral views concerning whiskey.[23] Margaret Waring, the heroine, like Ellen Wade, is related to a coarse frontiersman, but is made as refined as possible within the iron limits of her status. Although *The Oak Openings* is one of Cooper's weakest novels, the fault lies in his uncontrollable tendency to preach on any current topic that happens to come into his mind. The basic conception is very promising.

The novel begins as if Cooper were determined to see what might have been made of *The Prairie* if he had carried out his project of omitting the genteel hero and heroine. If this conjecture is valid, then Ben Boden represents Cooper's ultimate achievement in trying to use a man of the wilderness as a technical hero. After the dangers of Indian warfare in early Michigan have been endured by the young lovers, the novelist feels compelled to add an epilogue that exhibits Ben Boden in his old age as a substantial farmer, a man of influence in the community, and a state senator. This career "shows the power of man when left free to make his own exertions." [24] But if Boden's Jacksonian rise in the world gives retroactive sanction to Cooper's choice of him as a hero, it dissolves whatever imaginative connection he may have had with the mysterious and brooding wilderness.

Cooper's twenty-five years' struggle to devise a Wild Western hero capable of taking the leading role in a novel yielded the following results: (1) Since the basic image of Leatherstocking was too old for the purposes of romance, the novelist doubled the character to produce a young hunter sharing the old man's habits, tastes, skills, and, to some extent, his virtues. (2) The earliest of the young hunter companions of Leatherstocking, Oliver Effingham, could be a hero because he was revealed as a gentleman temporarily disguised as a hunter. That is, the hero retained all his genteel prerogatives by hereditary right, and at the same time claimed the imaginative values clustering about Leatherstocking by wearing a mask, a *persona* fashioned in the image of the old hunter. But this was so flagrant a begging of the question that Cooper could not be satisfied with it. He therefore undertook further development of the young hunter produced by doubling the character of Leatherstocking, and this process yielded (3) the Paul Hover–Ben Boden type of hero, a young and handsome denizen of the wilderness, following the gentler calling of a bee hunter and thus free from even the justifiable taint of bloodshed involved in Leatherstocking's vocation. This young Western hero is given a dialect less pronounced than that of Leatherstocking except in Leatherstocking's most exalted moments. His actual origin is left vague. He is not a member of the upper class, but he is nowhere specifically described as having once been a servant. Finally, the young hero has none of the theoretical hostility to civilization that is so conspicuous in Leatherstocking. These changes make it technically possible for a Wild Westerner to be a hero of romance, but they destroy the subversive overtones that had given Leatherstocking so much of his emotional depth.

CHAPTER VII

The Innocence and Wildness of Nature:
Charles W. Webber and Others

The Wild Western hunter and scout descended from Leather‹ stocking could reach full status as a literary hero only at the cost of losing contact with nature. Before we follow this interesting character in his later adventures we may profitably glance for a moment at what he was giving up.

Leatherstocking's own debt to nature was of course very great. "I have been a solitary man much of my time," he exclaimed in his old age, "if he can be called solitary, who has lived for seventy years in the very bosom of natur', and where he could at any instant open his heart to God without having to strip it of the cares and wickednesses of the settlements . . . ." [1] The two principal ideas implicit in this statement — the negative doctrine that civilization is wicked and the positive doctrine that untouched nature is a source of strength, truth, and virtue — occur sporadically in writing about the Wild West far into the nineteenth century. Thomas J. Farnham, for example, on his way out to Oregon in 1839, records an interview with a remarkable and perhaps largely fictitious Indian whom he says he met on the Arkansas River west of Fort Bent. The Indian is not presented as an untutored noble savage (he was educated at Dartmouth) but as a philosopher whose views Farnham finds impressive.

As soon as you thrust the plowshare under the earth [declares the articulate Red Man], it teems with worms and useless weeds. It increases population to an unnatural extent — creates the necessity of penal enactments — spreads over the human face a mask of deception and selfishness — and substitutes villainy, love of wealth and power,

and the slaughter of millions for the gratification of some royal cut-
throat, in place of the single-minded honesty, the hospitality, honour
and the purity of the natural state.[2]

Civilization is pernicious also because it interposes a veil of arti-
ficiality between the individual and the natural objects of experience. The sophisticated art of the cities substitutes a copy for the
realities of things "as they live in their own native magnificence
on the eternal mountains, and in the secret untrodden vale." That
other boasted triumph of civilization, science, may point to its
shallow successes in the realm of mere physical manipulation of
natural forces; but the true savage scorns the aid of such trivial
tools, and "looks through Nature, without the aid of science, up to
its cause." [3]

Something resembling this set of ideas was almost certain to
be used sooner or later in imaginative interpretation of the Wild
West. The man who went farthest in such a direction was one
Charles W. Webber, a forgotten writer who nevertheless in his
day created quite a stir. Webber was appropriately enough a native of Kentucky. He spent some time in Texas in the late 1830's
and subsequently entered the Princeton Divinity School. Finding
himself troubled by theological doubts, he went to New York and
embarked on a prolific career as a writer for the magazines. Between 1844, when his story "Jack Long; or, The Shot in the Eye"
had a sensational success, and 1856, when he met his death while
filibustering with Walker in Nicaragua, he wrote several books
and some two dozen articles, essays, and stories, many of them
related to his experiences in Texas.

Webber started with the simple exploitation of violence on the
frontier that was to furnish the substance of so many hundreds of
subliterary tales in the Beadle period and after. Encouraged by
the popularity of "Jack Long" to think of himself as an interpreter
of the West, he began to affect the manner of a philosopher and
wrote two ambitious novels. Of these, *Old Hicks, the Guide* (1848)
is the more interesting because it shows so clearly how the author
tried and failed to construct an interpretation of the Western
wilderness within the framework of primitivism.

Chapters V to VIII of *Old Hicks* contain, according to Webber,
extracts from the journal of an actual trip which he made from the

headwaters of the Trinity River in north central Texas to the upper Canadian River, near the present boundary between Texas and New Mexico.[4] At the end of Chapter VIII Webber inserts the words "End of the Journal," and immediately introduces his characters to a fabulous "Peaceful Valley" where are discovered a heroine, Emilie, and a villain, Count Albert, both of them Parisians. The narrator functions as hero. Webber seems to have intended a contrapuntal arrangement of related themes of primitivism — the decadent impulse to go back to nature peculiar to the overcivilized, and the original harmony with nature enjoyed by virtuous savages. But he faces the same problem of plot construction that confronted Cooper: for incident he can contrive only a love story and an Indian fight. It is true that he handles these familiar materials in an unprecedented fashion. Since Emilie is French she would be felt by the author and his readers as possibly immoral, or at least less rigidly proper than Cooper's females. Besides, she is married to the wicked Count. This contretemps interposes an obstacle to the hero's love for her which gives Webber the opportunity to contrast the intuitive ethics of the wilderness with the bigotry of urban society.[5] As for the Indians, Comanches whom Count Albert has made into a disciplined cavalry enslaved to his will, they are presented as children of the ancient mother nature. They are, for instance, skilled in the art of healing by the purely natural means of cold water or sweat baths. This Indian accomplishment launches Webber on an extended passage of moralizing called "The Philosophy of Savage Life." He declares that

the highest truths in many departments of human investigation, which it has taken our complex civilization many centuries to arrive at or approach, are recognized and acted upon intuitively in the savage or elementary forms of the social state. . . . The great geniuses are, and have been, essentially savages in all but the breech-clout. They arrive at truth by much the same processes; they equally scorn all shackles but those of the God-imposed senses, whether corporeal or spiritual, and, with like self-reliance, rule all precedents by the Gospel as revealed within themselves! [6]

Although there is more of this sort of thing in Webber's discussion of his implausible Comanches, the crux of his literary

problem is of course what he is going to do with his love story on
the basis of the philosophical apparatus he has so elaborately constructed. His solution is not very impressive. He introduces a
brother of Emilie who kills Albert when he discovers that the
Count has deceived his sister by the familiar device of a spurious
marriage ceremony. The situation would seem to depend entirely
upon civilized and even genteel conceptions of propriety. But
Webber justifies the brother's action on the score that frontiersmen, having withdrawn from civilization "to get rid of what, to
their free instinct, seemed merely conventional and unnatural
requisitions," have based their stern moral code upon the light of
nature — that is, upon "those conscious instincts of honor, justice,
and right, which are common to all mankind." [7]

Another supposed aspect of frontier morality leads Webber
in a different direction. If the rangers' intuitive sense of honor and
justice demands the death of the villain for his seduction of the
heroine, the same instinct leads them to approve their leader's
love for her even when they think she is the lawful wife of the
Count. The author's point, reached after rather devious reasoning, is that the Texan rangers' freedom from all shackles upon
the physical life has released them at the same time from moral
bigotry.

With them [he declares] the primitive virtues of a heroic manhood
are all-sufficient, and they care nothing for reverences, forms, duties,
&c., as civilization has them, but respect each other's rights, and recognize the awful presence of a benignant God in the still grandeur of
mountain, forest, valley, plain, and river, through, among, and over
which they pass.
    With them, loyalty to the God of truth and nature is first, and
loyalty to race and comrade next.
    This is their creed in short.
    Such men do not look back to society except with disgust, and
look into the face of God as revealed in his natural world, and into
the instincts of their own souls and hearts for what is just and true.
To them all that is true, fitting, and natural in a passion, is proper
and legitimate. [8]

The rangers are thus prepared to accept their leader's love for
Emilie. But surely this is a long preamble to a simple tale. Since
the narrator performs no action more remarkable than winning

the love of the heroine, he hardly represents a significant advance in the development of a characteristic Western hero.

Webber's determination to develop his primitivistic theory leads him into an elaborate description of the Peaceful Valley as "a new Eden of unsophisticated life" where the antelope are so tame they walk up to sniff the saddles the Texans have thrown upon the grass.

> These graceful creatures [he explains] had been shut out, by their steep hills in this enchanting recess, from any knowledge of the gloomy and bloody strife which man has been waging with himself and all God's creatures since sin and death came into the world.[9]

No one in the party was cruel enough to fire at such an unsuspecting prey, "to be, willingly, the first messenger of terror to announce to these innocent creatures that the curse was upon the world, smiting with a red right hand its sunny heart." The theme of conflict seems to have had a peculiar importance for Webber; his tributes to a natural as contrasted with a civilized life return again and again to the notion that the essence of civilization is struggle. His symbols are loosely managed, but a genuine, if somewhat formless, emotion comes through the tinsel rhetoric:

> I felt the better instincts of my nature uplift themselves in a revolt against the harsh and fierce conditions of that endless struggle with all being and all peace, in which my life had been so long involved. Was this stern antagonism natural? Did it include the higher purposes of our lives — touch our nobler capacities of bliss? I felt weary at these thoughts, and as if I could sink forever upon the placid bosom of our mother earth and sleep a sweet sleep of dreamlessness; for that would, at least, be peace.[10]

Upon a first encounter with this farrago one might well conclude that Webber's adventure in primitivism was a mere idiosyncrasy. But to his contemporaries he was a far from negligible figure. Shortly before his death in 1856 the Duyckincks gave him an impressive amount of space in their *Cyclopaedia of American Literature*, speaking with approval of his "healthy sense of animal life," his "inner poetical reflection," and his "mental enthusiasm"[11] — phrases which show an accurate if uncritical perception of the writer's intentions and manner. In reviewing *The Gold Mines of the Gila*, Webber's second novel, *Graham's* stated that "if the author would concentrate his energies, he might produce a novel which would give him a place in the front rank of our original minds." [12] This comment, together with certain other contemporary remarks to be considered presently, suggests that Webber's readers correctly evaluated his careless, headlong, improvisatory method. At the same time, they believed that he was moving in an interesting direction and that his central ideas, with greater discipline and rigor, might well support an important work. The primitivism that now seems merely pompous and absurd did not seem so to professional critics of the mid-century.

The impression Webber made on his contemporaries is best shown by the fact that two leading journals compared him with Melville, in both instances to Webber's advantage. *Graham's* declared flatly that *Old Hicks* showed "more genius than Typee or Omoo" [13] and the *Democratic Review* said that *Old Hicks* resembled *Omoo* in its "remarkable *vraisemblance*" but had "more of earnestness and poetry . . . ." In fact, the anonymous critic for the *Democratic Review* seemed on the point of becoming a convert to Webber's faith. He remarked that "We have evidently much to learn yet of these Camanches," and described the chapter on "The Philosophy of Savage Life" as "a manly exposition of truths, which have for a long time puzzled the heads of our wiseacres . . . ." [14]

As for *vraisemblance*, a modern reader finds *Old Hicks* so signally deficient in this regard after the opening chapters that he can hardly believe the reviewer was saying what he meant. But the comparisons with *Typee* and *Omoo* are more illuminating. Both Melville and Webber wrote of adventures among primitive peoples in remote parts of the world. Both novelists drew heavily upon their own experiences and cast their narratives in the first person. Both perceived in the simple life of savages values strikingly in contrast with the official doctrines of American society, and drew inferences not flattering to refinement, gentility, and civilization. Webber, of course, was vastly inferior to Melville either as thinker or as artist, and his subsequent development demonstrates what now seems evident on every page of *Old Hicks*, namely that he was far too careless and irresponsible to mature and integrate his art. Melville went on to *Moby Dick* while Webber was trifling with miscellaneous sketches of animals, outdoor life, and hunting. Both men had, so to speak, lived among cannibals, but Webber was never able to get beyond this experience.

The comparison with Melville nevertheless has the advantage of suggesting why no one besides Webber made a serious effort to develop a literature of the Wild West in terms of primitivism, and why Webber's effort failed. The strain of exoticism which colored Webber's Peaceful Valley on the Upper Canadian as well as Melville's idyllic valley in the South Seas gave to both these symbols an essentially static, dreamlike quality. They derived their vitality from an attenuated form of the idea of communion with nature. This idea, as Melville was later to proclaim with unmatched force, was no longer tenable; but Webber was unable to confront the fact. He could do no more than exemplify the bankruptcy of primitivism. He did not have the intellectual or imaginative force of a Melville, to build a new art from the ruins of his earlier doctrine of nature. And his career strongly suggests that a valid literary interpretation of the West could not be based upon a conception of nature that was losing force with every passing year.

Yet if the Wild West considered as untouched nature proved to be unsuitable material for major literature, it had a considerable attraction for American writers at the middle of the century. Emerson noted in 1844 that "The imagination delights in the woodcraft of Indians, trappers and bee-hunters." "We fancy that we are strangers," he continued, "and not so intimately domesticated in the planet as the wild man and wild beast and bird." Men who felt themselves divorced from nature seemed to hope that by dwelling upon these symbols they might regain a lost imaginative contact with some secret source of virtue and power in the universe. Emerson considered the quest vain: primitive man, and even animals, had no more root in the deep world than civilized man; "the world is all outside; it has no inside." [15] But among Emerson's younger contemporaries, Thoreau and Melville were still able to find some meaning in the virgin West.

Even though the Western wilderness no longer seemed benevolent in the old fashion, its very wildness could nourish Thoreau's rejection of the organized society he surveyed with such superb detachment. He conceded, grudgingly, that for the wise man civilization offered advantages superior to those of the savage state. But he felt that these advantages had been secured only at a grievous cost in individual freedom and spontaneity.[16] In an often-quoted passage from his posthumous essay on "Walking" he declares that the West draws him by an indescribable magnetic attraction. "The future lies that way to me, and the earth seems more unexhausted and richer on that side." To the East lay the city, to the West the wilderness, "and ever I am leaving the city more and more, and withdrawing into the wilderness."[17] This westward impulse led Thoreau momentarily to envision a Whitmanesque future society composed of men whose hearts should correspond in breadth and depth and grandeur to the topography of the West.[18] But more often, and more deeply, the West was for him "but another name for the Wild." And he believed that "in Wildness is the preservation of the World. . . . From the forest and wilderness come the tonics and barks which brace mankind."[19] At the very moment when he was celebrating transcendental "higher laws" in *Walden* he noted that he felt an equal impulse toward a primitive rank and savage life. "I love the wild not less than the good."[20] "I would have every man," he declared in the essay on "Walking," "so much like a wild antelope, so much a part and parcel of Nature, that his very person should . . . sweetly advertise our senses of his presence, and remind us of those parts of Nature which he most haunts."[21]

Thoreau opposes the vital wildness of the West to the dead tameness of civilization. To the extent that he affirms a supreme good in the trackless wilderness he falls into the pattern of all cultural primitivisms. But to Melville the Wild West, like nature in general, came to seem in the highest degree ambiguous. It was not more certainly good than bad, yet in either case it was terrible and magnificent. The point is worth making because metaphorical material derived from the Wild West plays such an important part in *Moby Dick*. Toward the agricultural West of the Ohio Valley Melville had an attitude not unlike that of most conservative Easterners in the 1840's. *Mardi* makes a conventional attack on Western politicians with their cult of manifest destiny, and paints an unsympathetic picture of the Gold Rush.[22] But the West beyond the frontier had a different value for him. The two images developed at greatest length in the pivotal Chapter XLII of *Moby Dick*, "The Whiteness of the Whale," are those of the White Steed of the Prairies and the Vermont colt maddened by the scent of a buffalo robe. These Wild Western images are used to establish the incantation of whiteness, the sinister blend of majesty and terror which Ishmael perceives in the White Whale and of course by implication in the suprasensible reaches of the universe. Yet at the same time Melville adopts the theme of the paradisiacal innocence of the Wild West which had attracted Webber. The White Steed, in this celebrated passage, is

a magnificent milk-white charger, large-eyed, small-headed, bluff-chested, and with the dignity of a thousand monarchs in his lofty, overscorning carriage. He was the elected Xerxes of vast herds of wild horses, whose pastures in those days were only fenced by the Rocky Mountains and the Alleghanies. At their flaming head he westward trooped it like that chosen star which every evening leads on the hosts of light. The flashing cascade of his mane, the curving comet of his tail, invested him with housings more resplendent than gold and silver-beaters could have furnished him. A most imperial and archangelical apparition of that unfallen, western world, which to the eyes of the old trappers and hunters revived the glories of those primeval times when Adam walked majestic as a god, bluff-browed and fearless as this mighty steed. Whether marching amid his aides and marshals in the van of countless cohorts that endlessly streamed it over the plains, like an Ohio; or whether with his circumambient subjects browsing all around at the horizon, the White Steed gallopingly reviewed them with warm nostrils reddening through his cool milkiness; in whatever aspect he presented himself, always to the bravest Indians he was the object of trembling reverence and awe. Nor can it be questioned from what stands on legendary record of this noble horse, that it was his spiritual whiteness chiefly, which so clothed him with divineness; and that this divineness had that in it which, though commanding worship, at the same time enforced a certain nameless terror.[23]

The frenzy aroused in the colt in his peaceful Vermont valley by the savage musk of the pelt from distant Oregon testifies to the demonism in the world: it calls up associations of the gorings of wild creatures trampling some deserted wild foal of the prairies. For Ishmael, as for the sheltered Vermont colt, such nameless evil things must exist. And at this point comes the sentence that conveys more than any other passage of similar length what Melville meant by his novel: "Though in many of its aspects this visible world seems formed in love, the invisible spheres were formed in fright." [24] The native wildness of the West served him as a means of expressing one of his major intuitions.

CHAPTER VIII

The Mountain Man
as Western Hero: Kit Carson

The first generation of fictional Wild Western heroes after Cooper — the sons of Leatherstocking — were primarily symbols of anarchic freedom. The notion that men who ranged the wilderness had fled from the restraints of civilization — for better or for worse, according to the social philosophy of the observer — had been greatly strengthened during the 1830's by the spectacular development of the Rocky Mountain fur trade. The fur trapper, or Mountain Man, was much more clearly uncivilized than Daniel Boone had been. The prime theater of his activities lay hundreds of miles distant from the frontier beyond the Great American Desert, and was not a region that invited agricultural settlement. He had adopted many more Indian ways than had the typical pioneers of the area east of the Mississippi. His costume, his speech, his outlook on life, often enough his Indian squaw, gave him a decidedly savage aspect. Yet the trappers dominated the exploration of the trans-Mississippi region, and the successor of Boone and Leatherstocking in the role of typical Wild Western hero was certain to be a mountain man. Cooper had acknowledged this fact in *The Prairie* by transporting Leatherstocking beyond the Mississippi and trying halfheartedly to make him over into a trapper. But Leatherstocking did not really belong in the Far West — a region about which his creator knew next to nothing. Besides, the old hunter considered the vocation of a trapper somewhat beneath his dignity.

This low opinion of the fur trade was shared by Timothy

Flint, whose *The Shoshonee Valley*, published in 1830, is the first novel in which mountain men figure as characters. It is true that Flint divides his trappers into two classes. A few, potentially virtuous, experience in the presence of mountain landscapes "a certain half chill sensation of the awful and sublime" which will be recognized as evidence of at least rudimentary ethical nobility. But by far the greater number of the trappers are as insensitive as deer to the charms of the scenery, and therefore by implication vulgar or wicked.[1] These "strange, fearless, and adamantine men," Flint says,

renouncing society, casting off fear, and all the common impulses and affections of our nature . . . finding in their own ingenuity, their knife, gun and traps, all the Divinity, of which their stern nature and condition taught them the necessity . . . became almost as inaccessible to passions and wants, and as sufficient to themselves, as the trees, or the rocks with which they were conversant.[2]

Such an existence satisfies man's baser impulses. Few who have tasted its dangerous joys can return with pleasure to the tedious routine of the settlements. Life in the mountains is especially attractive because of its unrestricted love and licensed polygamy. All the trappers have

an instinctive fondness for the reckless savage life, alternately indolent and laborious, full and fasting, occupied in hunting, fighting, feasting, intriguing, and amours, interdicted by no laws, or difficult morals, or any restraints, but the invisible ones of Indian habit and opinion.[3]

Charles Sealsfield, although he was not committed to the essentially theocratic social theory of the New Englander Flint, was equally certain that the Western trapper was a monster, peculiar to America, produced by the absolute freedom of wilderness life. He asserts that the fur trade is carried on by men to whose intractable minds even the rational liberty of the settled portions of the United States seemed an intolerable constraint.[4] Having fled to the wilderness to escape the control of law, the trappers come to regard a wild freedom as the one absolute necessity of existence. In this situation, every man must rely upon his own physical prowess. Warlike skills, practical cunning, and sheer ferocity are developed to the highest degree. The true trapper hates mankind and kills any rival with "a real fiendish joy." [5]

The picture of the mountain man presented in David H. Coyner's fictionalized narrative *The Lost Trappers* (1847) is in substantial agreement with Sealsfield's, although it has less of his overstraining and love of hyperbole. Coyner asserts that the mountain man rejects civilized life deliberately because he despises its

dull uniformity and monotony . . . when compared in his mind with the stirring scenes of wild western adventure. The security and protection of the laws have no attraction for him; for he wants no other means of defence than his rifle, which is his daily companion. He is impatient of the formalities and the galling restrictions of well organized society, and prefers the latitude and liberty of a life in the woods.[6]

Emerson Bennett, whose novel *The Prairie Flower* may have been based upon a narrative composed by an actual traveler on the Oregon Trail, introduces a few passages of remarkably accurate dialogue in the scenes dealing with the four trappers who figure in the story; one of them tells tall tales which belong to the authentic tradition of Davy Crockett.[7] But Bennett has nothing to contribute to the interpretation of the mountain man's character. He merely reshuffles the standard themes — the trapper's love of freedom, his indifference to hardship and danger, his hatred of the dull life of settled communities.[8] The novelist is noncommittal concerning the ethical character of the trapper, mingling hints of primitivistic approval with contradictory suggestions of moral condemnation, and concludes tamely that the mountain man is "a strange compound of odds and ends — of inexplicable incongruities — of good and evil." [9] As a straw in the wind pointing to the future development of the Wild Western hero we may note that Bennett's trappers, to the horror of the genteel hero Frank Leighton, delight in scalping Indians.[10] Leatherstocking, who always insisted that the white man and the Indian had different "gifts," had never condoned scalping by whites. As the literary Western hero moves beyond the Mississippi he is becoming more and more fully assimilated to the mores of the Indian.

At the same time, he is conceived as more and more completely autonomous, isolated, and self-contained. This is in accord with factual reporting by firsthand observers in the mountains. Lewis H. Garrard's autobiographical narrative *Wah-To-Yah*, for example, places great emphasis upon the mountain men's anarchic freedom and self-sufficiency. In the trappers' camps Garrard experienced "a grand sensation of liberty and a total absence of fear." There was no one to say what he should do; no "conventional rules of society constrained him to any particular form of dress, manner, or speech." It is true that Garrard was a youngster on his first vacation away from home, but he reports other attitudes than his own. He quotes the kindly advice of an old mountaineer:

If you see a man's mule running off, do n't stop it — let it go to the devil; it is n't yourn. If his possible sack falls off, do n't tell him of it; he'll find it out. At camp, help cook — get wood an' water — make yourself active — get your pipe, an' smoke it — do n't ask too many questions, an' you'll pass! [11]

The dissolution of the bonds that tie man to man in society could hardly be carried farther than this.

The best known mountain man was Kit Carson, who owed his fame to Jessie Benton Frémont's skillful editing of her husband's reports on his exploring expeditions in the early 1840's.[12] Although these narratives had been widely read before 1846, the Mexican War created an even greater audience for them by bringing to bear on everything related to the winning of the West the yeasty nationalism aroused by the conflict. The momentary effect was to make of the fur trapper and mountain man just such a pioneer of empire as the glorifiers of Kentucky had tried to make of Boone in earlier decades. This in turn implied that Carson must be depicted according to canons of progress and civilization and even gentility that had not previously been invoked in discussion of the mountain man. Carson, like Boone, had now to be transformed into

one of the best of those noble and original characters that have from time to time sprung up on and beyond our frontier, retreating with it to the west, and drawing from association with uncultivated nature, not the rudeness and sensualism of the savage, but genuine simplicity and truthfulness of disposition, and generosity, bravery, and single heartedness to a degree rarely found in society.

Barbaric life in the wilderness held grave dangers for the ethical purity considered obligatory in national heroes. But if the typical Wild Westerner was, as the contemporary journalist just quoted was forced to admit, "uncurbed," a prey to his own base passions, still an unassailable formula could be found for Carson: "In the school of men thus formed by hardships, exposure, peril, and temptation, our hero acquired all their virtues, and escaped their vices." [13] This almost exactly reproduces Timothy Flint's characterization of Boone and Cooper's characterization of Leatherstocking.

The pure and noble Carson was developed in later years by a series of biographers. The first of these, DeWitt C. Peters, was an army surgeon who had been stationed near the famous scout's home in New Mexico during the 1850's, and who made use of an autobiographical narrative dictated by the hero. The Peters biography appeared in 1858 before Kit's death and established the genteel interpretation of his character. Kit himself complained that Peters "laid it on a leetle too thick." [14] One instance will illustrate the doctor's method. Commenting upon the return of a trapping expedition under command of Ewing Young to Santa Fé in 1831, Peters confronts the fact that according to Carson's own account the mountain men went on a long spree. But this will never do. The biographer therefore commits the following extravaganza:

Young Kit, at this period of his life, imitated the example set by his elders, for he wished to be considered by them as an equal and a friend. He, however, passed through this terrible ordeal, which most frequently ruins its votary, and eventually came out brighter, clearer and more noble for the conscience-polish which he received. He contracted no bad habits, but learned the usefulness and happiness of resisting temptation, and became so well schooled that he was able, by the caution and advice of wisdom, founded on experience, to prevent many a promising and skillful hand from grasping ruin in the same vortex.[15]

Two subsequent biographies of Carson, one by an obscure novelist named Charles Burdett in 1862, and one by the famous

popularizer of history, John S. C. Abbott, in 1873, are based on
Peters and the Frémont reports, with various flourishes on the
theme of the mountain man's spectacular refinement. Burdett
implies that Carson never touched liquor, and emphasizes his
extreme frugality amid men who loved to spend a year's earnings
in a single splurge.[16] Abbott, accepting these positions as established, goes to the further extreme of maintaining that no oath
ever passed Carson's lips. As Abbott remarks, "Even the rude and
profane trappers around him could appreciate the superior dignity of such a character." [17] The historian also invoked the outworn theme of communion with nature (in this instance, in the
Yellowstone country) as the source of his hero's virtue:

> Men of little book culture, and with but slight acquaintance with
> the elegancies of polished life, have often a high appreciation of the
> beauties and the sublimities of nature. Think of such a man as Kit
> Carson, with his native delicacy of mind; a delicacy which never
> allowed him to use a profane word, to indulge in intoxicating drinks,
> to be guilty of an impure action; a man who enjoyed, above all things
> else, the communings of his own spirit with the silence, the solitude,
> the grandeur, with which God has invested the illimitable wilderness;
> think of such a man in the midst of such scenes as we are now de-
> scribing.[18]

This sort of thing could lead only to more and more acute
distress in the reader. The future belonged to a different Kit
Carson who had been developed entirely apart from the genteel
conception — the Indian fighter, the daredevil horseman, the
slayer of grizzly bears, the ancestor of the hundreds of two-gun
men who came in later decades to people the Beadle dime novels.
The rip-roaring Kit Carson made a brief appearance in Emerson
Bennett's *The Prairie Flower* in 1849,[19] and came fully into his
own in a thriller called *Kit Carson, The Prince of the Gold
Hunters*, by one Charles Averill. This is probably the book dealing with his exploits that Kit found in October of that year amid
the plunder taken by Apaches from a wagon train they had
stampeded. He was decently embarrassed by it.[20]

Averill's novel was one of the consequences of a literary trend
that had almost as much to do with Kit's rise to fame as did his
association with Frémont. The subliterary story of adventure

deliberately contrived for a mass audience, called "steam literature" because it was printed on the newly introduced rotary steam presses, was developed by editors of the weekly story papers established in imitation of the penny daily newspaper in the late 1830's and early 1840's. The earliest of these weeklies were the Boston *Notion* and *New World,* and *Brother Jonathan* of New York. At first the story papers relied heavily on pirated British fiction. Thus in 1842 both the *New World* and *Brother Jonathan* brought out Bulwer-Lytton's *Zanoni* at a "shilling," that is 12½¢.[21] In 1844 Maturin M. Ballou, then twenty-five years old, Boston-born son of the noted Universalist minister Hosea Ballou, joined forces with another young writer named Frederick Gleason in publishing three sea stories that Ballou had written under the pseudonym "Lieutenant Murray." The tales were highly successful — the first, *Fanny Campbell,* sold 80,000 copies within a few months — and the two young partners immediately expanded their publishing venture by hiring writers to grind out novelettes for them, including a few, such as Mrs. Ann S. Stephens, who later found steady employment on Beadle's staff. The Ballou-Gleason series of tales, selling at a shilling, was the ancestor of the many comparable series published during the second half of the century by Beadle and his competitors. Gleason and Ballou also pioneered the development of a national system of distribution by maintaining agents in nine cities, including Samuel French of New York.[22]

In 1846 Gleason and Ballou established a weekly story paper, *The Flag of Our Union,* which soon outstripped the *Boston Notion* and its other competitors to dominate the field. After holding the lead for five years it yielded in turn to the *New York Ledger,* which Robert Bonner bought in 1851 and publicized by the most sensational methods.[23] But Ballou had plenty of energy left. In 1854 he forced Gleason to sell out to him, and after various experiments, in 1857 inaugurated a series called *The Weekly Novelette,* selling for four cents. Each issue carried one-fifth of a story, so that the whole story cost twenty cents.[24] In that year Ballou's publications included *The Flag of Our Union,* a story weekly with a circulation of 80,000; *The Dollar Magazine,* a monthly with a circulation of 100,000; and *Ballou's Pictorial,* an illustrated weekly with a circulation of 140,000. To provide fiction for these various periodicals Ballou had enlarged his staff. Several of the newly added writers also went over to Beadle later, including Dr. John Hovey Robinson, A. J. H. Duganne, and the veteran E. Z. C. Judson ("Ned Buntline"). Ballou himself was the author of at least two stories published later by Beadle. Under Ballou's guidance these writers, by the late 1850's, had developed the standard procedures of the popular adventure story.[25] They could turn with ease from pseudo-Gothic tales of knights in armor to yarns about pirates in the Caribbean; but popular demand brought most of them back in the end to the standard subjects of the American past: the Revolution, Kentucky, and, with increasing frequency, the Far West. Bennett's and Averill's stories belong to this class.[26]

The cast of characters in Averill's *Kit Carson* is substantially that standardized by Cooper — a genteel hero, a heroine, assorted villains, and the faithful guide — but the pattern has undergone a significant evolution. The logic of the Far Western materials has begun to make itself felt. Although the upper-class Eastern hero is still present, he has sunk into insignificance, and is hardly more than a vestigial remnant beside the gigantic figure of Carson. Furthermore, Kit is presented without any mystical or genteel mummery; he is notable for his prowess and his courage alone. He is introduced to both the official hero and the reader by the device of a miniature, described with a quaint hagiological charm which is only increased by the contrast between subject and medium. The painting depicts

a man on horseback, in the dress of a western hunter, equipped like a trapper of the prairies; his tall and strongly knit frame drawn up, erect and lithe as the pine tree of his own forests; his broad, sun-burnt face developing a countenance, on which a life of danger and hardship had set its weather-beaten seal, and placed in boldest relief the unerring signs of a nature which for reckless daring and most indomitable hardihood, could know scarce a human superior.

Far in the background of the painting, rolled the waving grass of a boundless prairie; amid the silent wilderness of which, towered the noble figure of the hunter-horseman, half Indian, half whiteman in appearance, with rifle, horse and dog for his sole companions, in all that dreary waste; though to the right a yelling pack of wolves were seen upon his track, and on his left the thick, black smoke, in curling wreaths, proclaimed the prairie fire, while in the clear, gray eye that looked from the thrilling picture forth, there seemed to glance a look of proud indifference to all, and the conscious confidence of ennobling self-reliance! [27]

This figure, which the reader will recognize has little physical resemblance to the actual Kit Carson, is the Leatherstocking of *The Prairie*, made younger, mounted on a horse, and given an appreciably greater degree of self-assurance. Gone is the humility of the former servant, but gone also is the power to commune with nature. The Wild Western hero has been secularized — if the term may be employed in this connection — and magnified. He no longer looks to God through nature, for nature is no longer benign: its symbols are the wolves and the prairie fire. The scene has been shifted from the deep fertile forests east of the Mississippi to the barren plains. The landscape within which the Western hero operates has become, in Averill's words, a "dreary waste." It throws the hero back in upon himself and accentuates his terrible and sublime isolation. He is an anarchic and self-contained atom — hardly even a monad — alone in a hostile, or at best a neutral, universe.

This portrait of Kit Carson establishes the lines along which the Wild Western story was to develop for the next half century, until it should reach the seemingly indestructible state of petrifaction which it exhibits in our own day and is apparently destined to maintain through successive geological epochs while subtler and more ambitious literary forms come and go. In Averill's tale the stage is already set for the entrance of Erastus Beadle.[28]

CHAPTER IX

The Western Hero in the Dime Novel

I. FROM SETH JONES TO DEADWOOD DICK

In 1858 Erastus Beadle, a native of Cooper's country near Lake Otsego who had become a successful publisher in Buffalo, moved to New York in order to launch an ambitious project of cheap publishing for a mass audience. When a number of his song books and handbooks priced at ten cents made an immediate hit, he was encouraged to begin a weekly series of orange-backed "Dime Novels." The first of these appeared in June, 1860. It was followed by more than three hundred tales in the original series, and in due course by thousands of similar titles in more than thirty distinct series issued over a period of forty-five years.

The Beadle stories — they were hardly novels, for they seldom ran to more than thirty thousand words — were patterned after the thrillers that Gleason and Ballou had been publishing in Boston since the 1840's, although there was probably a greater emphasis on Western adventure. What Beadle contributed was persistence, a more systematic devotion to the basic principles of big business, and the perception that Boston was yielding first place as a publishing center to New York.[1] Beadle's editor was Orville J. Victor, a former newspaperman from Sandusky, Ohio, who supervised the production of dime novels and other series for thirty years. The distribution of the tales was handled at first through jobbers, but after 1864 by the American News Company, which was closely affiliated with the firm of Beadle & Adams.[2] The usual print order for a dime novel was sixty thousand, but many titles were reprinted again and again. Edward S. Ellis's *Seth Jones*, which appeared as No. 8 of the original series, eventually sold more than four hundred thousand copies. Beadle's total sales between 1860 and 1865 approached five millions.[3] These figures are not sensational by modern standards but they mark a revolution in nineteenth-century American publishing. An audience for fiction had been discovered that had not previously been known to exist. Beadle has some claim to rank among the industrial giants of his day. In his field, as an organizer and promoter of a basic discovery made by his predecessors, he was a figure comparable to Rockefeller or Carnegie.

Large-scale production implies regularity of output. The customer must be able to recognize the manufacturer's product by its uniform packaging — hence the various series with their characteristic formats. But a standard label is not enough; the product itself must be uniform and dependable. Victor's contribution to Beadle's success was the perfection of formulas which could be used by any number of writers, and the inspired alteration of these formulas according to the changing demands of the market. Victor was what would now be called a born "mass" editor; that is, he had an almost seismographic intuition of the nature, degree, and direction of changes in popular tastes.[4]

Writers on Victor's staff composed at great speed and in unbelievable quantity; many of them could turn out a thousand words an hour for twelve hours at a stretch. Prentiss Ingraham, son of the author of *The Prince of the House of David*, produced more than six hundred novels, besides plays and short stories.[5] He is said to have written a thirty-five-thousand-word tale on one occasion in a day and a night.[6] Fiction produced in these circumstances virtually takes on the character of automatic writing. The unabashed and systematic use of formulas strips from the writing every vestige of the interest usually sought in works of the imagination; it is entirely subliterary. On the other hand, such work tends to become an objectified mass dream, like the moving pictures, the soap operas, or the comic books that are the present-day equivalents of the Beadle stories. The individual writer abandons his own personality and identifies himself with the reveries of his readers. It is the presumably close fidelity of the Beadle stories to the dream life of a vast inarticulate public that renders them valuable to the social historian and the historian of ideas.

Eventually, however, the industrial revolution in publishing leads to more and more frenzied competition among producers, and destroys even this value in the dime novel. Orville Victor said that when rival publishers entered the field the Beadle writers merely had to kill a few more Indians.[7] But it went farther than that. The outworn formulas had to be given zest by a constant search after novel sensations. Circus tricks of horsemanship, incredible feats of shooting, more and more elaborate costumes, masks, and passwords were introduced, and even such ludicrous ornaments as worshippers of a Sun God devoted to human sacrifice in a vast underground cavern in the region of Yellowstone Park.[8] Killing a few more Indians meant, in practice, exaggerating violence and bloodshed for their own sakes, to the point of an overt sadism. By the 1890's the Western dime novel had come to hinge almost entirely upon conflicts between detectives and bands of robbers that had little to do with the ostensibly Western locales.

The thirty-year development preceding this final period of stasis reveals the working out of internal necessities already perceptible long before in the work of Cooper. The derivation of the Beadle Westerns from the Leatherstocking series, evident enough on the basis of internal evidence, is certified by Orville Victor's explicit testimony. In 1884 he told a reporter for the *Boston Evening Transcript* that the Beadle stories "followed right after 'Cooper's Tales,' which suggested them." [9] What does this mean in terms of themes, characters, and plots?

The strongest link connecting the Beadle Westerns with Cooper is the representation of a benevolent hunter without a fixed place of abode, advanced in age, celibate, and of unequalled prowess in trailing, marksmanship, and Indian fighting. That this group of characteristics, within certain limits of variation, had come to exist as a *persona*, a mask, is already evident in Paulding's Kentucky hunter Bushfield in *Westward Ho!* (1832). The nineteenth-century fondness for disguises on the stage and in fiction, a taste which encouraged actors to exploit mimicry and make-up as a form of sensationalism, would immediately suggest using the

Leatherstocking *persona* as a disguise. This is done in the most famous of all Beadle Westerns, Edward S. Ellis's *Seth Jones; or, The Captives of the Frontier*, which Orville Victor called "the perfect Dime Novel." [10] Not until the end of the tale does the reader learn that the aged and eccentric hunter who has dominated the action is the gently bred young Eugene Morton in disguise. The pretext for Morton's odd persistence in concealing his identity is so flimsy (he had heard that his sweetheart had ceased to care for him while he was away fighting in the Revolution) that one feels Ellis must be employing the *persona* for its own sake. It is the hero's assumed role that gives the title to the book, is illustrated on the cover, and engrosses the author's attention. The reader who has followed the earlier analysis of Cooper's procedures will recognize the device as a neat maneuver for combining the picturesque appeal of the "low" hunter with the official status of the "straight" upper-class hero.

Ellis long continued to be a prolific contributor to the various Beadle series, and his handling of traditional formulas and stereotypes retained its appeal for decades. As late as 1877, for example, the firm reprinted for the third time a tale by Ellis (*Kent, the Ranger; or, The Fugitives of the Border*,[11] first published in 1860) which is almost pure Cooper. The action takes place in southern Ohio in the early nineteenth century. The heroine, Rosalind, daughter of Sir William Leland, is captured by the Indians; the pursuit is undertaken by Rosalind's brother George and her lover Roland Leslie, the traditional straight hero, with the indispensable aid of the wandering hunter and ranger Kent Whiteman, who has the requisite dialect and other traits of the Leatherstocking type.[12] After Rosalind is rescued and united in marriage to Leslie, the old hunter is often a welcome guest in their household.[13]

The number of such more or less exact replicas of Leatherstocking is quite large. Mrs. Ann S. Stephens, for example, the majestic woman of letters who wrote *Malaeska*, the first of the Beadle Dime Novels, in 1862 turned her gaze from the classic ground of the Hudson Valley to write *Esther: A Story of the Oregon Trail*.[14] This story introduces a "Nature's Nobleman," Kirk Waltermyer, who combines the characteristics of Leatherstocking with the historic mission that had been ascribed to Daniel Boone. Mrs. Stephens is fully conscious that the *persona* exists, both for her and for her readers. Waltermyer, she says, strong dialect, deerskin costume, and all, was "the very *beau ideal* of that pioneer race who, scorning the ease and fashionable fetters of city life, have laid the foundation of new States in the unexplored regions of the giant West, and dashed onward in search of new fields of enterprise, leaving the great results to be gathered by the settlers that came slowly after him." [15]

Since Mrs. Stephens's Waltermyer owes something to Boone of Kentucky, while Seth Jones hails from Vermont, we are forced to recognize two distinct although not inharmonious strains of influence which impinge upon Leatherstocking's upstate New York tradition. The new forces correspond to the two great cycles of frontier humor in the first half of the nineteenth century, the Down East tradition and the Southwestern tradition. Either could be merged with the Leatherstocking *persona* to repair that neglect of comic possibilities which is so marked in Cooper. Seth Jones has much of the comic stage Yankee, including the cracked voice. Waltermyer can hardly be comic in the unbuttoned Davy Crockett manner as long as he rides the high horse of the noble savage's rhetorical dignity, but there are other Beadle Leatherstockings who do embody traces of the Southwestern half-horse, half-alligator mode of humor. We are told that Ellis's Oregon Sol, in *Nathan Todd; or, The Fate of the Sioux' Captive*, who originated in Boonslick County, Missouri, a year before Kit Carson's birth in the same neighborhood, is "whimsical and eccentric," [16] but Ellis was not at home in the Crockett tradition and does not give any samples of humorous dialogue. Other writers are better able to equip their aged hunters with suitable tall tales. Joseph E. Badger, Jr.'s old scout Pete Shafer, in *The Forest Princess; or, The Kickapoo Captives. A Romance of the Illinois*, is rather elaborately developed in this manner.[17] But Badger's comic triumph — and it is not a negligible one — is Mustang Sam, of the Far Southwest, who despite a fantastic velvet-and-silk costume that belongs to the theater or the recesses of adolescent longing rather than to any actual West, delivers himself of a noble frontier boast beginning, "I'm Mustang Sam, the *high muck-a-muck* of E Pluribus

Unum. I was got by a bull whale out o' a iceberg." [18] This is not
the definitive achievement of Mark Twain's "I was sired by the
Great American Eagle and foaled by a Continental dam," [19] but
it is worthy to stand just below the master's perfection.

Unfortunately, the tradition of backwoods humor was not
always handled with so much feeling for its true nature. Edward
L. Wheeler, whom we shall encounter presently as the celebrated
creator of Deadwood Dick, used it a great deal, but he exaggerated the eccentric aspect of Southwestern exuberance to the point
of imbecility. Wheeler's character Old Avalanche, unwarrantably
described as "a genuine northern mountain man," who makes
his first appearance turning handsprings and accompanied by a
pet black goat named Florence Nightingale,[20] is allowed to talk
endlessly in a dialect that Wheeler intended to be outrageously
funny, but it is now unreadable even under the urging of scientific
curiosity. This character appears repeatedly in the Deadwood
Dick series and does not improve on longer acquaintance.[21] But
Wheeler's most audacious use of the Crockett tradition is his
creation of a frontier boast for an alarming young woman named
Rowdy Kate, who announces, "I'm a reg'ler old double-distilled
typhoon, you bet," and so on.[22]

Either in the rather solemn traditional form preferred by Ellis,
or with a comic elaboration of dialect, the *persona* of Leatherstocking was endlessly repeated in the Beadle stories. Of seventy-
nine dime novels selected as a sample of those dealing with the
West between 1860 and 1893, forty contain one or more hunters
or trappers whose age, costume, weapons, and general functions
entitle them to be considered lineal descendants of the great
original. Such characters cling to the flintlock rifle long after their
companions are using breech-loading Winchesters and six-
shooters; and they take reluctantly to horseback, although they
are in the end forced to this innovation as they are to repeating
weapons. By preference they pursue their specialty of rescuing
beautiful heroines from the Indians. When the Indians begin to
yield place in the dime novel to road agents or counterfeiters as
the standard enemy, the hunters of the Leatherstocking type
lend a hand in fighting the newer foes. Generally speaking, however, the traditional hunter and trapper is so closely linked in

imagination with the redskins, living with them in a kind of symbiosis, that he follows the Indian off the stage at a certain chronological distance. It should be added that Leatherstocking's notorious virtue was a hereditary trait. A hunter wearing moccasins and carrying a long rifle is almost certain — although not absolutely certain, since nothing is impossible for a Beadle author — to be benign.

In contrast with the relative stability of the *persona* of the aged scout, the younger hunter produced by doubling the character of Leatherstocking was less predictable. Under the name of Kit Carson he had already proved himself capable of dominating the action of Averill's early tales, and he, rather than the original Leatherstocking, was the ancestor of later Wild Western heroes like Deadwood Dick and Buffalo Bill — the literary Buffalo Bill, that is. If we are to make out a continuity of development in the Wild Western hero from Leatherstocking to the two-gun man of the 1890's, we shall have to establish the nature of this transformation with some care.

Young, handsome, and actually or potentially genteel trappers and hunters are almost as numerous as the older hunters descended directly from Leatherstocking. We may note some of them in Ellis's works. The titular hero of *Nathan Todd; or, The Fate of the Sioux' Captive*,[23] for example, is of this younger group. The Leatherstocking types are Oregon Sol, already mentioned, and Bill Biddon, both natives of Boonslick County, Missouri. Todd originated in Maine and has some coloring of the Down East tradition that Ellis had exploited in Seth Jones. Although he sometimes speaks a dialect that ought to consign him irretrievably to a nonheroic status, he has become a trapper because of a disappointment in love, he carries with him a locket that experienced readers will recognize as an incontrovertible badge of upper-class standing, and in the presence of the heroine he speaks in the elevated rhetoric appropriate for a hero of romance.[24] Further evidence is furnished by Todd's eloquent discourse to Biddon on religion and immortality. The relation of the characters to one another is placed quite beyond doubt when Biddon sacrifices himself so that Todd and Irene Merment may be saved and eventually wed.[25]

Lewis Dernor in Ellis's *The Riflemen of the Miami* appears as a hunter in the company of no less than three woodsmen developed from the Leatherstocking *persona*. His right to mate with Edith Sudbury after her rescue from the Indians is authenticated by the pangs of sensibility he experiences when he clasps the heroine's almost fairy hand. The touch of this delicate member on the horny palm of the hunter is a moment charged with meaning in the development of the Western hero.[26] It shows Ellis confronting the possibility that an upper-class heroine might love a man of the Wild West, as Cooper could never quite bring himself to do. In Ellis's *The Hunter's Cabin. An Episode of the Early Settlements*, George Ferrington, "a young hunter, or, more properly, a soldier," [27] is mated with Annie Stanton without perceptible tenseness over status; perhaps because in this tale Annie's father Sylvester Stanton seems to fill the place normally occupied by the Leatherstocking *persona*. He is represented as a former associate of Daniel Boone [28] and likewise has some of the traits of the Indian hater who had been a recognizable figure since the time of James McHenry's *The Spectre of the Forest* (1823). Ferrington uses a conventional rhetoric but the potential conflict between forest roughness and the heroine's gentility is delicately acknowledged in a passage that demands quotation. Ferrington and Annie are in a cabin besieged by the Indians. Noticing a bush that moves suspiciously, Ferrington exclaims:

"It is a devilish Indian contrivance —"
" 'Sh, George; do not speak thus," she interrupted, noticing the expression, in spite of the tumultuous feelings that reigned in her breast.
"I beg pardon. It is an Indian contrivance, and there are Shawnees hid behind that same bush."

Fortunately, the friendly Huron Oonomoo is at hand to aid in the rescue of the beleaguered pair, so that the hero is not fatally hampered by the restrictions under which he must work.[29]

In Edward Willett's *The Five Champions; or, The Backwoods Belle*, the problem of status is brought to the center of the stage. Henry Denton, who "occupied a humble but useful position" as the son of a blacksmith in one of the Cumberland settlements in early Kentucky "but possessed a laudable ambition to rise above his present station," loves Lucy Simms, daughter of the founder of the settlement.[30] William Simms, her aristocratic, wealthy, and arrogant cousin, a rival suitor for Lucy's hand, denounces Henry's "presumption." Lucy is captured by the Indians, and despite the machinations of William Simms, Henry rescues her with the aid of an old scout Ben Smiles who has all the Leatherstocking stigmata. It is made plain that this mating is a triumph of love over the humble origins and poverty of the suitor. But the story exemplifies an interesting principle which often operates in the Beadle series — and which indeed has its precedents in Cooper: namely, that both the sons and daughters of parents who speak a pronounced dialect are themselves free of dialect if they are involved in a love affair.[31] The belief that no one is suitable to conduct a sentimental courtship unless he speaks a pure English is very strong; strong enough, in fact, to upset the normal processes by which children acquire the speech of the families and communities in which they grow up.

Joseph E. Badger's *The Forest Princess; or, The Kickapoo Captives. A Romance of the Illinois* presents an almost perfect pattern of the paired hunters, of whom the elder, Pete Shafer, speaks a strong dialect (here developed with genuine comic feeling, as has been indicated earlier), while Uriah Barham, the young hunter of presumably similar origins, has no trace of dialect, and marries the heroine Myra Mordaunt.[32] Badger uses a similar formula in *The Border Renegade; or, The Lily of the Silver Lake.*[33] Of three scouts operating in the vicinity of Detroit in 1812, Andy Goochland and Sam Hill have a strong dialect, while the young and handsome Oscar Jewett, who wins the hand of Agnes Letcher, speaks in conventionally stilted rhetoric. A fourth hunter, represented as old and devoted to his flintlock rifle, is a particularly faithful replica of Leatherstocking. Eventually he turns out to be the renegade George Girty in disguise. The *persona* tended to persist with unusual rigidity when it was literally a mask.

This rapid survey of examples chosen mainly from the first decade of the Beadle novels makes it plain that the development of the Western hero did not proceed in a straight line. If a trend can be discerned, it is toward creating a hero-type based on the

CERES IN THE GARDEN OF THE WORLD (1819)

THE EARLIEST GRAPHIC REPRESENTATION
OF LEATHERSTOCKING (1823)

SETH JONES, DIME-NOVEL DESCENDANT
OF LEATHERSTOCKING (1860)

LEW DERNOR CONDUCTS EDITH SUDBURY TO SAFETY (1862)

DEADWOOD DICK BUYS SALAMANDER SAM'S DAUGHTER AT AUCTION (1880)

UFFALO BILL, THE KING OF BORDER MEN (1869)

BEADLE'S

Dime

New York Library

Copyrighted, 1882, by Beadle and Adams.   Entered as Second Class Matter at the New York, N. Y., Post Office.   September 13, 1892.

No. 777.   Published Every Wednesday.   *Beadle & Adams, Publishers,*   Ten Cents a Copy. $5.00 a Year.   Vol. LX.
98 WILLIAM STREET, NEW YORK.

BUFFALO BILL'S SPY-SHADOWER

OR,

The Masked Men of Grand Canyon.

A Romance of the Dread Driver of the Colorado.

BY COLONEL PRENTISS INGRAHAM,
AUTHOR OF THE "BUFFALO BILL" NOVELS, ETC.

CHAPTER I.
THE HERMIT OF THE GRAND CANYON.

A HORSEMAN drew rein one morning, upon the brink of what is one of the wonders of the world, yet seen by very few—the Grand Canyon of the Colorado.

A mighty abyss, too vast for the eye to take in in its grand immensity; a mighty mountain rent asunder and forming a chasm which is a valley of grandeur and beauty, through which flows

BUFFALO BILL FOUND A RETREAT UPON THE CLIFF GIVING HIM A VIEW IN BOTH DIRECTIONS.

BUFFALO BILL IN THE GRAND CANYON (1892)

THE EMIGRANT'S DREAM OF KANSAS (1873)

CORA RICHTER ABDUCTED BY AN INDIAN (1864)

WILD EDNA, THE GIRL BRIGAND (1878)

DENVER DOLL, THE DETECTIVE QUEEN (1882)

THIRD EDITION.

Copyrighted, 1885, by Beadle and Adams. Entered at the Post Office at New York, N. Y., as Second Class Mail Matter. Sept. 16, 1885.

Vol. VII. $2.50 a Year. Published Weekly by Beadle and Adams, No. 98 William St., New York. Price, Five Cents. No. 88.

Deadwood Dick in Leadville; Or, A Strange Stroke for Liberty.

BY EDWARD L. WHEELER.

CALAMITY JANE HELD A PAIR OF COCKED REVOLVERS, WHICH SHE HAD LEVELED TOWARD RALPH GARDNER, THREATENINGLY.

CALAMITY JANE (1885)

Leatherstocking *persona* but made younger and more genteel. This trend, however, is accompanied by frequent returns to Cooper's standard practice of providing an indisputably upper-class hero who comes into the Wild West from the East. A decade of experiment had not established a revised Western hero. This state of confusion lasted well down into the 1870's. But in 1877 Edward L. Wheeler created a character who despite the author's lack of imaginative coherence was impressive enough to deserve a place with Leatherstocking in the short roster of distinctive Western heroes. Wheeler's character bore the name Deadwood Dick, derived from the mining town which sprang up with the gold rush to the Black Hills in Dakota Territory, in the middle 1870's. Later Deadwood Dick operated throughout the West, although a certain fondness for mining camps reminds the reader of his origins. His filiation with the young Wild Western heroes produced by the doubling of the *persona* of Leatherstocking might seem tenuous at first glance, for he resembles these characters only in his youth, his beauty, his mastery of the various manly arts of defense and offense that are necessary to survival in the mining camps, and his power of attracting women. But the genealogy becomes clearer when we analyze Deadwood Dick in connection with Duke Darrall, hero of W. J. Hamilton's *Old Avoirdupois; or, Steel Coat, the Apache Terror,* who preceded him upon Beadle's stage by several years.

Duke, young and handsome, appears on the plains in the company of several clearly Wild Western characters, including the Kentuckian hunter Big Sam, and is introduced by the author as "the *beau ideal* of the hunter and scout." [34] He seems to have originated in the West — at any rate, no outside origin is mentioned. He is dressed in the buckskin that had clad so many descendants of Leatherstocking, but his garments are tailored with a theatrical and implausible elegance. He is master of the skills of a plainsman, and of others besides. When a herd of stampeding mustangs is about to overrun the party, Duke leaps from the ground to a standing position on the backs of the closely packed horses and with the assistance of Big Sam succeeds in turning the herd.[35] Yet Duke does not speak in dialect, and is destined to marry the beautiful Wilna, a white girl reared by the Indians. Indeed, it is now the heroine who needs touching up to make her a suitable bride. She is sent to a seminary in St. Louis for two years before her marriage. At the end of that time she is "changed as only education and the society of refined people can change; but still the same frank, loving nature." [36] Then she is ready to take the hand of Duke Darrall, whose education has not been mentioned at all.

This is a rather confused story and not much can be built on it, but at least it offers us a hero without hereditary upper-class rank, a hunter and trapper by vocation, who functions as a skilled craftsman of the wilderness and aids in the rescue of a heroine from the Indians according to ancient prescription. Yet he is at the same time a romantic lover of unquestioned status. The same can be said of Moccasin Mat, the less fully developed hero of Harry St. George's *Roaring Ralph Rockwood, The Reckless Ranger*. Mat is a former Texas Ranger with a horse named Storm Cloud that answers his whistle.[37] He speaks what is intended as correct English and is united at the end with his long-lost sweetheart Hattie Farley. The promotion of the Western hero to a part in the love story is the significant stage in his elevation. Averill's Kit Carson had been young and handsome, and had spoken a conventional English, but he had not been allowed to marry the heroine.

The most important traits of Deadwood Dick are that he too is without the upper-class rank which belongs exclusively to Easterners or Englishmen; that he possesses to a high degree such characteristic skills as riding and shooting; and that at the same time he is eligible for romantic attachments. Indeed, his life is cluttered with beautiful women pining for his love. Deadwood Dick fully illustrates the principle that Merle Curti found to be central in the dime novel. Overcoming his enemies by his own efforts and courage, he embodies the popular ideal of the self-made man. Such a hero, presumably humble in his origins and without formal education or inherited wealth, "confirmed Americans in the traditional belief that obstacles were to be overcome by the courageous, virile, and determined stand of the individual as an individual." [38] Deadwood Dick, in fact, has achieved fortune as well as fame; he has an income of five thousand dollars a year from mining properties.[39]

But after these simple points of departure have been established, the case of Deadwood Dick grows very complex. His amours are hopelessly confused. He has been married several times: one recorded wife sells herself to the devil and becomes unfaithful to him, another is killed, he is menaced by lovesick female villains, he fruitlessly courts Calamity Jane, he is subsequently the object of her hopeless devotion, and in the end he marries her. Furthermore, he shows traces not only of the Leatherstocking *persona* and of the traditional genteel hero, but likewise of the traditional villain: we learn that he has formerly been a bandit and on at least one occasion he reverts to banditry, in consequence of his wife's infidelity. Although he began life as a stage driver, in the dime novels considered here, he figures usually as a detective. And there are disquieting hints that at bottom he is a culture-hero of the Orpheus-Herakles type, for after being hanged as a bandit, as he remarks, "I was cut down and resuscitated by a friend, and thus, while I hung and paid my debt to nature and justice, I came back to life a free man whom no law in the universe could molest for past offenses."[40] This Proteus claiming to be both immaculate and immortal has yet a further function: he exhibits a concern with social problems that is, as far as my knowledge extends, unique in the dime novels. In the avatar of "Deadwood Dick, Jr.," a character indistinguishable from Deadwood Dick, Sr., who figures in many stories written by others using Wheeler's name after his death in 1885, the hero leads a miners' union and as superintendent of a mine raises wages. He is, however, no socialist; he bitterly opposes an organization called the Lion Legion which is trying to seize the mine and operate it "on the commonweal plan."[41] And on a visit to Chicago soon after the Haymarket Riots of 1886, Deadwood Dick, Jr., denounces the anarchists who are on trial because they are an undesirable foreign element. He declares that all the accused persons deserved to be hanged.[42]

It may be that Deadwood Dick's appeal to readers of the Beadle novels depended on Wheeler's eclecticism, the device of ascribing to the hero all the skills, functions, graces, and successes that had ever fallen to the lot of any Western character, plus other powers derived from folk heroes of a forgotten past, and still other accomplishments prophetic of the coming reign of the dime novel detectives, Old Sleuth and Old Cap Collier. Deadwood Dick is certainly not an integrated construction of the imagination, and his fame reflects the kind of sensationalism that increased so markedly in the later 1870's.[43]

II. BUFFALO BILL AND BUCK TAYLOR

The literary character of Buffalo Bill, most famous of dime novel heroes, is in many respects similar to that of Deadwood Dick. As the central figure of a long series of tales (more than two hundred by Prentiss Ingraham alone were still in print in the 1920's) [1] Buffalo Bill performs exploits at least as various and as prodigious as those of his rival. Although he is not so deeply involved with women as Deadwood Dick, he is young, handsome, well-tailored in a spectacular Western mode, and adept at all manly arts. In the 1890's he sometimes takes over Deadwood Dick's role of detective. The Buffalo Bill of literature, however, presents a different problem from that of Deadwood Dick because he was supposed to have as his original an actual man, the Honorable William F. Cody, former member of the Nebraska Legislature, who was constantly and flamboyantly in the public eye as principal actor in his Wild West show. It is true that a pretended original of Deadwood Dick, one Richard Clark, the first stage driver into Deadwood, has been mentioned by the scholiasts,[2] but the man was too inconspicuous to be compared for an instant with the world-famous Cody, and Wheeler makes nothing of a possible factual basis for his character. On the other hand, the authors of the dime novels about Buffalo Bill constantly stress their claim to be writing chapters in the biography of a living celebrity.[3]

This fact gives a special character to the Buffalo Bill of literature. From the time of Daniel Boone, the popular imagination had constantly transformed the facts of the westward movement in accordance with the requirements of myth. Boone himself lived to resent the popular image of him as an anarchic fugitive from civilization, and successive biographers tried in vain to correct what they considered a libelous distortion of the hero's real character. Davy Crockett of Tennessee, made the hero of a quite different cycle of Southwestern humor, was likewise completely transformed.[4]

The literary development of the Wild Western hero in the second half of the nineteenth century made the divergence between fact and fiction even greater. Where Kit Carson had been represented as slaying his hundreds of Indians, the dime novel hero slew his thousands, with one hand tied behind him. But the *persona* created by the writers of popular fiction was so accurate an expression of the demands of the popular imagination that it proved powerful enough to shape an actual man in its own image. At the age of twenty-three Cody was a young plainsman like hundreds of others who had grown up beyond the Missouri. He had learned to make a living in the ways dictated by his environment — bull-whacking, serving as "office boy on horseback" for Alexander Majors of the famous overland freighting firm of Russel & Majors, driving stagecoaches, and scouting with detachments of troops fighting the plains Indians. His title of Buffalo Bill he had earned by hunting buffalo to feed construction crews of the Kansas Pacific Railroad. His actual life on the plains before he became a figure of the theater is almost completely obscured by the marvelous tales circulated later by talented press agents, but he does not seem to have been more skillful or daring than many of his companions. It was an accident, plus a natural gift for dramatizing himself, that made him the most highly publicized figure in all the history of the Wild West.

The accident was Cody's first meeting with Edward Z. C. Judson, alias Ned Buntline, the patriarch of blood-and-thunder romancers. Beginning as a contributor to Lewis Gaylord Clark's *Knickerbocker Magazine* in the late 1830's, Buntline had poured forth for decades an endless stream of sea stories, articles about field sports, tales of the Mexican War, temperance tracts, and Know-Nothing attacks on foreigners. By the time of his death in 1886 he had written more than two hundred stories of the dime novel type.[5] In 1869 he signed a contract to write exclusively for the *New York Weekly*, published by Francis S. Street and

Francis S. Smith; his fee was said to be $20,000 a year.[6] Although Buntline's specialty had been sea stories, he evidently decided that it was time to turn systematically to the plains for materials: the nation at large was discovering the West. The editors of the *New York Weekly* announced that he had been traveling for two years in order to prepare himself to write a new series of works.[7]

Buntline had heard of Major Frank North, commander of three companies of Pawnee scouts who had been enlisted in the regular army to fight the Sioux, and late in 1869 sought out North at Fort McPherson, Nebraska, with the intention of making him into a dime novel hero. But North declined. "If you want a man to fill that bill," he said, according to Cody's biographer Richard J. Walsh, "he's over there under the wagon." The man sleeping under the wagon was Cody, then a relatively obscure scout attached to North's command. Buntline talked with him, accompanied the Pawnees on a scouting expedition, and bestrode Cody's horse Powder Face.[8] Then he went back to New York and introduced an apotheosized Cody to the readers of the *New York Weekly* in a serial entitled "Buffalo Bill, the King of the Border Men," which the editors characterized as "The Greatest Romance of the Age!"[9] The story was subsequently brought out in book form, was reprinted again and again, and was still being sold by Sears, Roebuck at twenty-two cents in 1928.[10]

Although both Buntline and his publishers made much of the supposed authenticity of the novel, it has a very slight basis in biographical fact — no more, indeed, than might have been gathered in a somewhat hasty interview. That Buntline was using oral data exclusively is suggested by his phonetic spelling of proper names — "M'Kandlas" for "McCanles," "Bill Hitchcock" for "Bill Hickok," and "Cantrell" for "Quantrell." For our purposes it is important to notice that the character of Buffalo Bill in this first fictional appearance is in the main line of descent from Cooper. The action consists of a series of abductions of genteel females — principally Bill's twin sisters — and rescues according to the time-honored pattern. Wild Bill Hitchcock and Sim Geary, worthy companions of the hero, speak in the dialect of the Leatherstocking *persona*, and Geary is represented as being appropriately aged. Buffalo Bill, an example of the younger hunter created by doubling the *persona*, and not speaking dialect, has Leatherstocking's skills in trailing and creeping silently past sentries. It is notable also that although he rides a horse, as Leatherstocking did not, he carries a rifle.[11] He even retains a trace of Leatherstocking's humility — a quaint archaism testifying to Buntline's membership in a pre-Beadle generation. After Buffalo Bill rescues the beautiful Louisa La Valliere of St. Louis from a gang of drunken soldiers, he tells her grateful and wealthy father they must never meet again: "If I see *her* any more, I shall love her, and love above my station would be madness and folly." [12]

Buntline's knowledge of the geography of the Far West is hazy and there is almost no authentic Wild Western coloring in the narrative. A great deal is made of the Cody household in Kansas, which boasts a comic Irish servant girl and four farm hands. Bill's mother and his two sisters are excruciatingly genteel. The latter half of the novel deals with guerrilla fighting in Missouri during the Civil War and reaches a climax in the Battle of Pea Ridge. Three straight heroes, including Buffalo Bill but not including any of the scouts who speak dialect, are wounded in the battle, taken to a privately established hospital by the father of Bill's fiancée, and there married to their respective ladies. The grain of truth in this narrative consists of the fact that Cody had served as a private in the Union Army and married Louisa Frederici of St. Louis in 1866.

Buntline and the editors of the *New York Weekly* publicized Buffalo Bill so enthusiastically that he became something of a fad. James Gordon Bennett, editor of the *New York Herald,* who had been on one of General Sheridan's hunting trips for which Cody served as guide and had written him up lavishly as "the beau ideal of the plains," invited him to visit New York, and Sheridan encouraged Cody to make the trip. Buntline may well have planned the visit for purposes of his own; it coincided with the opening of a play *Buffalo Bill, the King of Bordermen* written by Fred G. Maeder on the basis of Buntline's serial in the *New York Weekly.*[13] The scout was guest of honor at dinners given by Bennett and by August Belmont, although because of drink or naïveté he failed to appear at the Belmont dinner. On the eve-

ning of February 20, 1872, Buntline took him to the Bowery
Theater to see the play. The climax, in the third act, was a
hand-to-hand fight between Buffalo Bill and Jake McCanles in
which they used knives reported to be three feet long, and in
the stage version Bill married the Irish serving girl. The spotlight
was turned on Cody and he was introduced to the audience.
Later the manager of the theater offered him five hundred dollars
a week to enact himself in the play. But Cody was too timid to
accept the offer.[14]

Nevertheless, he had not heard the last of Buntline, who continued writing to him at intervals urging him to come back East
and go on the stage. At last Cody agreed to meet the novelist in
Chicago, bringing his friend Texas Jack Omohundro and twenty
Indians. When they arrived, December 12, 1872, they had forgotten the Indians but Buntline hired supers and with his sublime
nonchalance set about writing a script. In four hours he produced a piece entitled "The Scouts of the Plains" that consisted
mainly of shooting Indians, and the play opened four days later.
Buntline, who had wisely arranged to be on the stage himself
most of the time, managed to improvise a rambling conversation
when his two scouts forgot all their lines. Then there was a great
deal of shooting and the curtain came down.[15] After three years
of association with Buntline, Cody and Omohundro organized
their own show, with John M. Burke as press agent and business
manager, and Buffalo Bill was on his way to world-wide fame.[16]

To Burke, apparently, belongs the credit for carrying through
the major revision of the character of Buffalo Bill as Buntline had
originally conceived it. Buntline had been content to exploit the
rudimentary values of Indian fighting and stock romance; even
the publicity writers for the *New York Weekly* had not claimed
that Buffalo Bill was anything more than "the most daring scout,
the best horseman, the best informed guide, and the greatest
hunter of the present day." [17] But Burke determined to enlarge the
frame within which his client was to be viewed by the public.
Buffalo Bill was to become an epic hero laden with the enormous
weight of universal history. He was to be placed beside Boone and
Frémont and Carson in the roster of American heroes, and like
them was to be interpreted as a pioneer of civilization and a stand-

ard bearer of progress, although of course no showman would forget the box-office appeal of black powder and trick riding. This conception Burke dinned into Cody's ears so constantly that the hero himself took up the clichés, and in his old age used to say, "I stood between savagery and civilization most all my early days." [18] The actual phrasing of the slogan may have been due to Prentiss Ingraham, the dime novelist, who had become virtually a staff writer for Cody by 1878, and possibly earlier. Ingraham wrote that Buffalo Bill was

one of America's strange heroes who has loved the trackless wilds, rolling plains and mountain solitudes of our land, far more than the bustle and turmoil, the busy life and joys of our cities, and who has stood as a barrier between civilization and savagery, risking his own life to save the lives of others.[19]

Ingraham composed the play that Cody used during the season 1878–1879, and presumably also the "autobiography" published in 1879.[20] It will be recalled that before his death in 1904 he produced more than two hundred stories about Buffalo Bill, in addition to his probable authorship of a large number of dime novels signed by Cody.[21]

From his earliest youth Ingraham's Buffalo Bill is associated with the spectral apparitions, the chain-mail shirts that can stop bullets, and the beautiful transvestite maidens seeking revenge that are normal in the later dime novels. The novelist's personal idiosyncrasy — which Cody's own tastes encouraged — was his delight in splendor of attire. The costume which he designed for Buffalo Bill's first appearance as a Pony Express Rider in the tale *Gold Plume, the Boy Bandit* was described as

a red velvet jacket, white corduroy pants, stuck in handsome top boots, which were armed with heavy gold spurs, and . . . upon his head a gray sombrero, encircled by a gold cord and looped up on the left side with a pin representing a spur.

He also wore an embroidered silk shirt, a black cravat, gauntlet gloves, and a sash of red silk, in which were stuck a pair of revolvers and a dirk-knife.[22]

In his autobiography Cody — or Ingraham — describes a costume which the hunter wore when he acted as guide for Sheridan, Bennett, and other celebrities. He says that since "it was a nobby and high-toned outfit," he determined to put on a little style himself.

So I dressed in a new suit of light buckskin, trimmed along the seams with fringes of the same material; and I put on a crimson shirt handsomely ornamented on the bosom, while on my head I wore a broad *sombrero*. Then mounting a snowy white horse — a gallant stepper — I rode down from the fort to the camp, rifle in hand. I felt first-rate that morning, and looked well.[23]

Several years later, in the summer of 1876, when Cody fought his much publicized duel with Yellow Hand and took "the first scalp for Custer" under the eyes of newspaper correspondents, he wore a costume that must have been taken from the wardrobe of his theatrical company. It consisted of a Mexican suit of black velvet, slashed with scarlet and trimmed with silver buttons and lace.[24] These costumes, fictional and actual, illustrate the blending of Cody with his theatrical role to the point where no one — least of all the man himself — could say where the actual left off and where dime novel fiction began.

As if to exhaust all the possible relationships between fact and imagination, Cody's press-agents caused many stories to be issued under his own name. Although he himself does not figure in the plots of these stories, they closely resemble those in which he does. *Deadly-Eye*, issued with *The Prairie Rover* in 1877 in the short-lived Beadle & Adams 20 Cent Novel series, relates the exploits of the Unknown Scout, alias Deadly-Eye, alias Alfred Carleton, young, handsome, and of such sartorial splendor that the story must be by Ingraham.[25] Like the young Buffalo Bill in Buntline's first story, the Unknown Scout is motivated by a thirst for vengeance upon the slayer of his parents. Since he has been educated in the East and speaks the straight rhetoric of the genteel hero, the Unknown Scout represents the Seth Jones use of the *persona* as a disguise and can marry the heroine Sibyl Conrad without impediments.[26] Gold Spurs, hero of *Gold Bullet Sport; or, The Knight of the Overland*, is even more elegant than the Unknown Scout; he has a velvet jacket and gold-plated spurs and weapons that again strongly suggest Ingraham's authorship. He is assisted by a benign hunter and trapper named Buckskin Ben who speaks in dialect and is viewed with the patronizing approval tradition-

ally reserved for replicas of Leatherstocking.[27] Since the Gold
Bullet Sport wears many disguises in the course of his pursuit of
the villain, and is represented as having served a prison term after
a false conviction of bank robbery, he has some of the criminal
flavor that clings to Deadwood Dick.[28] In view of these similarities
one is not surprised to find the Buffalo Bill of later Ingraham
stories appearing as a detective and as a stage driver.[29] And one
recalls that the Deadwood Coach was always a part of Buffalo
Bill's Wild West show.

The Wild Western hero as cowboy, who in the twentieth century has become the dominant type, first appeared in the wake of
Buffalo Bill in the late 1880's. American readers of the national
magazines had long been familiar with Mexican *rancheros* and
vaqueros in California and Texas, but the American hired man on
horseback did not become a celebrated figure until the range
industry spread northward from Texas over the Great Plains in
the early 1870's. In this decade the term "herder" was as likely to
be used as the classic name of "cowboy," and it usually called up
the image of a semibarbarous laborer who lived a dull, monotonous life of hard fare and poor shelter.[30] Laura Winthrop Johnson, writing for *Lippincott's* in 1875, saw no glamor in the "rough
men with shaggy hair and wild, staring eyes, in butternut trousers
stuffed into great rough boots" whom she described at a round-up
in Wyoming.[31]

Toward the end of the decade, however, Henry King, a writer
for *Scribner's*, was able to detect a touch of the picturesque in the
ranch life of western Kansas. Although he was depressed by the
bleak solitude of the plains, he enjoyed the exotic note of color
introduced by the costumes of the herdsmen, who affected "old
Castilian sombreros, and open-legged trowsers with rows of buttons, and jackets gaudy with many-colored braid and Indian
beads, and now and then a blood-red scarf like a matador's." [32]
King also suggested that the cowboy had some virtues despite his
violence: he was generous, brave, and scrupulously honest, with
"a strange, paradoxical code of personal honor, in vindication of
which he will obtrude his life as though it were but a toy." [33] As
late as 1881, however, the pejorative connotations of the term
"cowboy" were still uppermost. President Chester A. Arthur's First

Annual Message to Congress mentioned a disturbance of the public tranquility by a band of "armed desperadoes known as 'Cowboys,' probably numbering from fifty to one hundred men," who had for months been committing acts of lawlessness and brutality in the Territory of Arizona, and across the border in Mexico. He asked for legislation empowering the Army to intervene.[34]

But the Western point of view was different. In 1882 the citizens of North Platte, Nebraska, decided to organize a big Fourth of July celebration, an "Old Glory blowout," that would resemble what we know as a rodeo. Cody, who was already a famous theatrical figure and had bought a ranch in the vicinity, was appointed Grand Marshal. Thus was the Wild West show born. Since North Platte was in cattle country, the roping and riding and shooting contests dominated the celebration and determined the character of the show which Cody took on the road next year. His brightest cowboy star was Buck Taylor, who could ride the worst bucking horse, throw a steer by the horns or tail, and pick up a neckerchief from the ground at full speed.[35]

Probably the earliest use of a cowboy hero in the Beadle novels is an alleged biography of Taylor by Prentiss Ingraham published in 1887. In this narrative, Taylor comes as a youngster to a camp of Captain McNally's Texas Rangers, and asks to be enlisted. After his prowess as a pugilist and as a bronco rider has been tested, he is admitted to the chosen band. The principal activity of the Rangers is fighting Mexican raiders headed by one Rafael, but Taylor identifies himself with the tradition of Leatherstocking when he is captured by Comanches and freed by an Indian he has befriended, as well as when he rescues McNally's daughter from the Indians. The Rangers likewise wear a costume that belongs to the tradition — leggings and hunting coats — although they have adopted the broad sombreros of Mexican culture.[36] But Ingraham soon designed a more adequate costume for Buck Taylor, one equal to the splendor of Buffalo Bill:

He was dressed in somewhat gaudy attire, wore a watch and chain, diamond pin in his black scarf, representing a miniature spur, and upon the small finger of his right hand there was a ring, the design being a horseshoe of rubies.

About his broad-brimmed, dove-colored sombrero was coiled a

miniature lariet [*sic*], so that the spur, horseshoe and lasso designated his calling.[37]

As a press agent for the Wild West show Ingraham strove to offset the bad reputation which cowboys had with the public. In *The Cowboy Clan; or, The Tigress of Texas. A Romance of Buck Taylor and his Boys in Buckskin* he undertakes a defense of the cowboys as a class. They are indeed reckless, but light-hearted, fearless, generous, and "noble in their treatment of a friend or a fallen foe." They are feared by Indians and evil-doers but admired and respected by soldiers and people of the settlements.[38] Surgeon Hassam, of the Medical Corps of the Army, continues this defense in another story by Ingraham. Because the cowboys are a little wild, he tells Buck, they are terribly maligned by those who do not know them. Taylor agrees. "I know well," he adds, "that a great many wicked men have crept into the ranks of our cowboy bands; but there are plenty of them who are true as steel and honest as they can be." His note is somewhat plaintive: "We lead a wild life, get hard knocks, rough usage and our lives are in constant peril, and the settling of a difficulty is an appeal to revolver or knife; but after all we are not as black as we are painted." [39]

Whatever may be the merits of the dime novel cowboy, however, he apparently has nothing to do with cattle. If an occasional story (like Philip S. Warne's *Lariat Lil; or, The Cast for a Life. A Story of Love and Jealousy*)[40] describes the actual business of a round-up, most cowboy tales are hardly distinguishable from the Deadwood Dick and Buffalo Bill series. The professional duty of Beadle cowboys is to fight Indians, Mexicans, and outlaws. And the atmosphere created by wronged women seeking vengeance upon their false lovers, Mexican girls in men's clothing, and Army officers detailed for secret service is thoroughly typical of the decadent phase of Beadle fiction. The introduction of characters described as cowboys is little more than an effort to achieve an air of contemporaneity. It does not change the shape of Wild Western fiction.

CHAPTER X

The Dime Novel Heroine

The evolution of the Beadle Wild Western heroine illustrates even more impressively the increase of sensationalism in the dime novel toward the end of the century.

Everyone is aware of the awe-inspiring gentility of Cooper's heroines. Lowell's remark that they were flat as a prairie and sappy as maples [1] does less than justice to the address and energy which some of them could display on occasion, but it is nevertheless true that no lady in Cooper was capable of the remotest approach to indelicacy of thought, speech, or action. The escape of the Western story from the canons of gentility had greater consequences for the women characters than for the men, because the genteel female had been the primary source of refinement in the traditional novel. One method of transforming the heroine from the merely passive sexual object she had tended to be in the Leatherstocking tales was to introduce a supposed Indian girl able to ride and shoot who later proves to be an upper-class white girl captured long ago by the Indians. But this device, like that of disguising the genteel hero as a hunter, did not involve a fundamental change in the heroine's character. Beneath the savage costume she was almost as genteel as ever.

A much more promising means of effecting a real development in the heroine was the ancient device of introducing a woman disguised as a man, or wearing male attire. Maturin M. Ballou's *Fanny Campbell*, who appeared in 1845, was a female pirate captain; [2] and Charles E. Averill caused the two Eastern heroines of his *Life in California* to disguise themselves as boys. [3] The earliest Western heroine wearing men's clothing seems to be Eulalie

Moreau in Frederick Whittaker's *The Mustang-Hunters; or, The Beautiful Amazon of the Hidden Valley*, apparently published in the late 1860's.[4] Eulalie is possibly derived from Emilie in Charles W. Webber's *Old Hicks, The Guide*, who is likewise French and inhabits a Hidden Valley in the Far Southwest. If this surmise is correct, it would suggest that Webber's experiment in cultural primitivism exerted some influence on the creation of the ferocious women who came finally to people the Beadle stories. Whittaker, like Webber, may have felt that violation of propriety was less shocking in a French girl than in an American one.

Eulalie, for that matter, is virtuous enough. She does not invariably wear male attire, but pays obeisance to her literary ancestors by appearing on occasion in the costume of an Indian princess.[5] She lives with her father, an exiled "Red Republican" of 1848, in a luxurious establishment three weeks' journey northwest of Austin, Texas. With the "marvelous mixture of feminine gentleness and masculine firmness that marked her character" she easily tames the splendid Black Mustang stallion that the elegant hero Frank Weston has succeeded in lassoing on the plains.[6] There is more than enough bloodshed of a somewhat sadistic flavor in this story, but Eulalie does not take part in it. At the end she is married to the hero and they go to live in New Orleans. The hunter Pete Wilkins, an authentic Leatherstocking type, continues a faithful friend of the family and this somehow makes the whole thing seem more domestic and respectable.

The first heroine who commits an act of violence is most likely Dove-Eye, alias Kate Robinette, half-breed daughter of the Indian trader Silas Wormley in Edward Willett's *Silver-spur; or, The Mountain Heroine. A Tale of the Arapaho Country*. Supposed at first to be a full-blooded Indian maiden, Dove-Eye rides astride and carries a battle axe, which she throws at the hero Fred Wilder.[7] This initial misunderstanding is soon overcome and the two are betrothed; but Fred's father Colonel Wilder opposes the match as unsuitable. Dove-Eye thereupon rescues the Colonel from a buffalo and from hostile Indians, wielding her battle axe to great effect.[8] Thus mollified, the old gentleman consents to the marriage. But Dove-Eye has to be revised somewhat before she can become a full-fledged heroine. She is given a large fortune by

opportune inheritance from her father. Colonel Wilder then suggests the standard treatment of a few years in a young ladies'
seminary. Fred, however, begins the full enfranchisement of the
nongenteel heroine by rejecting this plan:

Do you think I could allow the ducks and turkeys of the settlements to
laugh at my wild bird? Do you think I could be separated from her a
few years, or a few months? She is sufficiently polished, and no one can
educate her better than her husband.

The author assures us that Kate's "brains and will soon made
amends for the deficiencies of her education," and when she arrived at St. Louis "no one who was not acquainted with her story
would have supposed that the greater part of her life had been
spent among savages." [9]

The earliest available case of aggressiveness on the part of a
Beadle female is that of the beautiful white girl Aneola who, like
Dove-Eye, has been reared by the Indians, and who has acquired
a perfect command of English against what must have been very
great odds. When the hero Uriah Barham is captured by the
Indians and given the traditional choice of death or an Indian
wife, Aneola offers herself as a solution, confessing her passionate
love for him. On this occasion she has the decency to blush. But
he loves another, and refuses her. Despite the blush, she threatens
him with death, but relents, helps him escape, and then leaps from
a cliff.[10] Badger's Mountain Kate, the daughter of a white outlaw
in the Northern Rockies, has a better fate. She is a master of the
pistol. When the traitorous companions of the hero attack him, she
turns fiercely on the miscreants, killing three and wounding one:
"The stately thumb and forefinger worked like magic." But since
she has not been guilty of overt aggressiveness she does not have
to die. Instead, she marries the hero and achieves a home and
children in St. Louis.[11]

Frederick Whittaker, creator of Eulalie Moreau, ventured a
more pronounced Amazon a few years later in *The Jaguar Queen:
or, The Outlaws of the Sierra Madre.*[12] As in the earlier story, the
action concerns a secret valley in the Far Southwest but the coloring is noticeably more lurid. A certain Count Montriche who, like
Webber's Count Albert, has become an Apache chief, maintains
an imposing harem in a remote part of northern Mexico. The

Amazon in this story is the Wagnerian Katrina Hartstein, six feet tall, who is accompanied by seven trained jaguars. Because she loves the previously committed Gerald Leigh, Katrina must also die, and is accordingly killed in the course of an assault on Count Montriche's establishment for the rescue of the fortunate heroine Blanche Hayward.[13]

Toward the end of the 1870's the Amazons and heroines in male attire took a distinct turn for the worse, no doubt corrupted by the general increase of sensationalism. A date around 1880 might be suggested as the critical point in the transformation of the genteel heroine. Philip S. Warne's *A Hard Crowd; or, Gentleman Sam's Sister*, a tale laid in Omaha, "the 'hardest place' east of Denver," and devoted to what the author describes as the scum and dregs of society in the low groggeries and gambling hells of this railroad town,[14] has two women characters wearing men's clothing, expert in firearms, and fully at home amid the violence and bloodshed which surround them. Pepita, who sometimes appears in the guise of Nebraska Larry, is motivated by an insatiable desire for vengeance against the man who has wronged her.[15] The vengeance motive was a favorite way of accounting for the ferocious behavior of characters, especially of women. It has the advantage of affording a rationale of violence less cumbersome than the older method of staging a war between Indians and whites. But the narrowing of the frame of ethical reference involves a marked loss of social significance. Characters bent on private vengeance may owe something to the monomaniac Indian haters who had long peopled Western fiction, but their motivation seems more closely related to the melodramatic stage.

The character of Iola, Gentleman Sam's sister in Warne's story, who is "quite an Amazon," capable of shooting down instantly a man who accosted her on the street,[16] marks a drastic weakening of the long prevalent taboos against sexual passion in women. The hero of the story has been wounded and is being nursed by Iola. One day, when his convalescence has set in, he slips an arm about her waist as she straightens the pillows on his bed.

Unconsciously she yielded to the persuasive clasp of his arms, until she rested, almost fainting, on his breast, and felt the throbbing of his heart, and his warm breath on her cheek.

Their love sought no expression in words. But the woman, whose free heart had been little curbed by the conventionalities of artificial society, let her arms glide about his neck, as was most natural that she should, and clasped him closer and closer until their lips met.

Thus lip to lip they drank in the first incense of mutual love . . . .[17]

Not all writers who exploited the sensational possibilities of the woman desperado were inclined to take precisely this advantage of the decline of gentility, but there is certainly a more perceptible awareness of sex as a physical fact in the stories published after 1880 than in those published during the 1860's.

The transference of the skills and functions of the Wild Western hero to a woman, the use of the theme of revenge to motivate violence, and the promotion of the Amazon to full status as a heroine are all exemplified in Edward L. Wheeler's Hurricane Nell, who appeared in 1878 almost simultaneously with the first appearance of Deadwood Dick. At the opening of the story Nell is the conventional distressed female, victim of the ruffian Bob Woolf's cruelty in firing her house and hastening the death of her parents. She swears the customary oath of vengeance and reappears after a time in the Pike's Peak mining towns wearing men's clothing, a mistress of all the accomplishments of the Wild West. She can "outrun, out-ride, out-shoot, out-lasso, and out-yell" any man in town.[18] When the hero, a handsome Philadelphia lawyer, hires her as a guide, she lassoes a mustang for him and rescues him from the Indians in a scene that reverses a vast tradition. As the hero's horse tires, Hurricane Nell seizes the man about the waist, raises him high overhead "by the power of her wonderful arms," and deposits him on the back of the wild stallion. She also kills three men with three shots from her rifle.[19] The heroine's assumption of the functions of the Leatherstocking type is complete when the hero bets a thousand dollars on her skill in a shooting match and she wins:[20] at the very beginning of Leatherstocking's career in literature, in The Pioneers, Elizabeth Temple had backed him in a turkey shoot.

The tendency to make the Amazon athletic might seem likely to detract from her feminine charms, but Wheeler does not mean to surrender this source of interest. He takes pains to make Hurricane Nell overwhelmingly beautiful, gives to her lustrous eyes a soft, dreamy, wistful expectancy when she looks at the hero, and indulges in a touch of sadism by having her dangled over a fire by her torturers.[21] Wheeler's Wild Edna, leader of a band of high- waymen in *Old Avalanche, The Great Annihilator; or, Wild Edna, the Girl Brigand*, is likewise but a wistful ingénue beneath her formidable exterior. There is "a vacant spot in her pure virgin heart" of which she becomes painfully aware when she meets the dashing titled English hero.[22]

Wheeler's celebrated creation, Calamity Jane, the feminine counterpart of Deadwood Dick, has much in common with these preliminary studies of the softhearted Amazon. Like much of the inner structure of the Deadwood saga, the relations between Deadwood Dick and Calamity Jane are hard to make out. For one thing, the date of publication of the stories seems to bear little relation to the supposed order of events in the hero's career. In *Blonde Bill; or, Deadwood Dick's Home Base. A Romance of the "Silent Tongues,"* Calamity Jane, "the girl sport," "nobbily attired in male garb," is represented as being hopelessly in love with Deadwood Dick, who has a wife named Edith. Edith is killed in the course of the story.[23] When Dick tells Calamity Jane of this event, she turns away "lest the yearning, hungry look in her wildly beautiful eyes should pain him," [24] and matters stand more or less at this point when the story ends. In the earlier part of *Deadwood Dick of Deadwood; or, The Picked Party. A Romance of Skeleton Bend*, Jane is jealous of Deadwood Dick, but at the end of the story they are to be married.[25] Calamity Jane does not appear in No. 195 of this series, but Dick is involved with no less than three girls in men's attire, each of whom proposes marriage to him.[26] One of these young ladies, Phantom Moll, the Girl Footpad, is the first Beadle female character within my acquaintance who lights a cigarette. In trying to persuade Dick to join her band and marry her, she exclaims, " 'Tis a jolly life we outlawed sinners lead. . . ." [27] 'Shian Sal, developed at greater length than the other women characters, speaks dialect, and despite the fact that she is only eighteen or so, is proprietress of the Eureka Saloon. She confesses that she smokes, gambles, swears, drinks, "and sometimes I pop over a rough, jest to keep my hand in and let 'em know Sal is old bizness." She is also good with her fists; she knocks down one of the men with a single blow.[28]

Calamity Jane is studied most fully in Wheeler's *Deadwood Dick on Deck; or, Calamity Jane, The Heroine of Whoop-Up. A Story of Dakota*. Although Wheeler, like other dime-novel writers, knows that his readers have little interest in psychological analysis and seldom bothers to offer details about his characters' motivation, in this story he causes an oberver, Colonel Joe Tubbs, to discuss her case at some length. It appears that she belongs to the category of heroines whom great wrongs have transformed into ruthless Amazons. Deserted by her lover, she has become "the most reckless buchario in ther Hills. Kin drink whisky, shute, play keerds, or sw'ar, ef et comes ter et." But "Ther gal's got honor left wi'her grit, out o' ther wreck o' a young life." [29]

The most convincing evidence that Calamity Jane was once a lady is the fact that she can drop her dialect at will and speak a correct English.[30] Her tough appearance and manner are, in other words, a voluntarily assumed mask like that of Seth Jones. Yet a woman cannot shed such a *persona* as easily as a man. Jane's beautiful face is lined with dissipation and hard usage. It is true that even in her buckskin trousers, beaded leggings, and boiled shirt she retains visible evidences of her former appearance — her feet are clad in dainty slippers and her shirt opens to reveal "a breast of alabaster purity." But her behavior is extremely boisterous. She first appears dashing through the streets erect in the saddle, leaping sluices and other obstructions, "lighting a cigar at full motion," and uttering "a ringing whoop, which was creditable in imitation if not in volume and force to that of a full-blown Comanche warrior." [31] Jane realizes what such conduct must mean to a young lady's reputation. Concerning another girl she remarks with a delicate sense of propriety, "life here in the Hills has — well, has ruined her prospects, one might say, for she has grown reckless in act and rough in language." [32]

In this story Deadwood Dick has a wife named Leone, although she does not figure prominently in the plot. Calamity Jane loves Sandy, a handsome young Easterner who, deceived by villains into believing himself guilty of forgery, has come West to the mines. But the author says she will probably never marry. Her prospects, too, have suffered sadly from her neglect of appearances.[33]

By 1877, when Wheeler began his Deadwood Dick series, the Wild Western hero had been transformed from a Leatherstocking with an infallible sense of right and wrong and feelings which "appeared to possess the freshness and nature of the forest" [34] into a man who had once been a bandit, and who even after his reformation could not easily be distinguished from the criminals opposing him. Cut loose first from the code of gentility that had commanded Cooper's unswerving loyalty, and then from the communion with God through nature that had made Leatherstocking a saint of the forest, the Western hero had become a self-reliant two-gun man who behaved in almost exactly the same fashion whether he were outlaw or peace officer. Eventually he was transformed into a detective and ceased in any significant sense to be Western. The heroine, undergoing an even more drastic evolution when she was freed from the trammels of gentility, developed at last into an Amazon who was distinguished from the hero solely by the physical fact of her sex.

These changes in the characters reveal a progressive deterioration in the Western story as a genre. It is true that the abandonment of the artificial code of gentility was a necessary step in the development of American literature. But when a frontiersman in the Leatherstocking tradition replaced the genteel heroine as the pivotal center of plot construction, the Western story lost whatever chance it might once have had to develop social significance. For Leatherstocking was a child of the wilderness to whom society and civilization meant only the dread sound of the backwoodsman's axe laying waste the virgin forest. A genre built about such a character could not establish any real contact with society.

On the other hand, the theme of communion with nature in the West proved too flimsy to sustain a primitivistic literature of any magnitude. The spiritual meaning which a former generation had believed it found in nature became more and more inaccessible after the middle of the century. The static ideas of virtue and happiness and peace drawn from the bosom of the virgin wilderness — the ideas symbolized in Charles W. Webber's Peaceful Valley — proved quite irrelevant for a society committed to the ideas of civilization and progress, and to an industrial revolution. Devoid alike of ethical and social meaning, the Western story could develop in no direction save that of a straining and exaggeration of its formulas. It abandoned all effort to be serious, and by 1889, when Erastus Beadle retired from the firm of Beadle & Adams, it had sunk to the near-juvenile level it was to occupy with virtually no change down to our own day. The Street & Smith enterprises like the Buffalo Bill stories, the Log Cabin Library, the Jesse James stories, the Tip-Top Weekly, and the Red, White, and Blue Library, together with Frank Tousey publications like the Boy's Story Library, Frank Manley's Weekly, the New York Detective Library, the Pluck and Luck Stories, and the Wild West Weekly — the cheap series widening downward from the 1890's into the twentieth century almost baffle enumeration — lead in a straight line from the Beadle publications to the Westerns of the present day.[35] The movies and the radio have tidied up the morals, or at least the manners, of the genre, but plot construction and characterization follow an apparently unbreakable pattern.

BOOK THREE ☆ ☆ ☆

THE GARDEN OF THE WORLD

Here nature opens her broad lap to receive the perpetual accession of new comers, and to supply them with food. I am sure I cannot be called a partial American when I say, that the spectacle afforded by these pleasing scenes must be more entertaining, and more philosophical than that which arises from beholding the musty ruins of Rome.

— CRÈVECOEUR, *Letters from an American Farmer* (1782)

CHAPTER XI

The Garden of the World
and American Agrarianism

Although it was endlessly exciting for nineteenth-century Americans to contemplate the pioneer army moving westward at the command of destiny, and the Sons of Leatherstocking performing their improbable exploits in the wilderness, these themes had only an indirect bearing upon the major trends of economic and social development in American society. The forces which were to control the future did not originate in the picturesque Wild West beyond the agricultural frontier, but in the domesticated West that lay behind it.

With each surge of westward movement a new community came into being. These communities devoted themselves not to marching onward but to cultivating the earth. They plowed the virgin land and put in crops, and the great Interior Valley was transformed into a garden: for the imagination, the Garden of the World. The image of this vast and constantly growing agricultural society in the interior of the continent became one of the dominant symbols of nineteenth-century American society – a collective representation, a poetic idea (as Tocqueville noted in the early 1830's [1]) that defined the promise of American life. The master symbol of the garden embraced a cluster of metaphors expressing fecundity, growth, increase, and blissful labor in the earth, all centering about the heroic figure of the idealized frontier farmer armed with that supreme agrarian weapon, the sacred plow. Although the idea of the garden of the world was relatively static, resembling an allegorical composition like that depicted in the first illustration, its role in expressing the assumptions and aspirations of a whole society and the hint of narrative content supplied by the central figure of the Western farmer give it much of the character of a myth.

The myth of the garden affirmed that the dominant force in the future society of the Mississippi Valley would be agriculture. It is true that with the passage of time this symbol, like that of the Wild West, became in its turn a less and less accurate description of a society transformed by commerce and industry. When the new economic and technological forces, especially the power of steam working through river boats and locomotives, had done their work, the garden was no longer a garden. But the image of an agricultural paradise in the West, embodying group memories of an earlier, a simpler and, it was believed, a happier state of society, long survived as a force in American thought and politics. So powerful and vivid was the image that down to the very end of the nineteenth century it continued to seem a representation, in Whitman's words, of the core of the nation, "the real genuine America." [2]

The myth of the garden was already implicit in the iridescent eighteenth-century vision of a continental American empire, "vested," in Lewis Evans's prediction of 1775, "with all the Wealth and Power that will naturally arise from the Culture of so great an extent of good Land, in a happy Climate." [3] It was present in embryo in the mighty kingdoms which Jonathan Carver foresaw beyond the Mississippi.[4] But at this stage the vision of the future empire in the West resembles something out of Charles Rollin's *Ancient History* rather than something concretely American. It is merely the last of the familiar series of world empires and derives its coloring from them. Nathaniel Ames of Harvard, predicting in his almanac for 1758 that "Arts and Sciences will change the Face of Nature in their Tour from Hence over the Appalachian Mountains to the Western Ocean," thought of the Mississippi Valley in the future as dotted with metropolises like Rome, Paris, or London. "Shall not . . . those vast Quarries," he asked, "that teem with mechanic Stone, — those for Structure be piled into great Cities, — and those for Sculpture into Statues to perpetuate the honor of renowned Heroes . . .?" [5] In their poem written for the

Princeton commencement of 1771 young Freneau and Brackenridge drew similar parallels: new states, new empires, they prophesied, would arise in America,

> and a line of kings,
> High rais'd in glory, cities, palaces,
> Fair domes on each long bay, sea, shore or stream . . .
> .   .   .   .
> Hoarse Niagara's stream now roaring on
> Thro' woods and rocks and broken mountains torn,
> In days remote far from their antient beds,
> By some great monarch taught a better course,
> Or cleared of cataracts shall flow beneath
> Unnumbr'd boats and merchandize and men . . . .[6]

It is true that these predictions of an urban commercial society
were reasonably accurate concerning the remote future of the
Middle West. But before the palaces appeared beside the rivers
and lakes of the interior there was to intervene a long period of
development during which the West was overwhelmingly devoted
to agriculture. This fact, on the plane of rational and imaginative
interpretation, emerged as an agrarian social theory.

As has been noted earlier, the materials for such a theory were
present in the writings of Franklin from the 1750's onward. They
became increasingly prominent after the United States had
achieved independence from Britain. When he surveyed the society of the new nation, the aging statesman consoled himself for
the idleness and extravagance of the seaboard cities with the
reflection that the bulk of the population was composed of laborious and frugal inland farmers. Since the hundreds of millions of
acres of land still covered by the great forest of the interior would
every year attract more and more settlers, the luxury of a few
merchants on the coast would not be the ruin of America.[7] "The
great Business of the Continent," he declared with satisfaction in
the late 1780's, "is Agriculture. For one Artisan, or Merchant, I
suppose, we have at least 100 Farmers, by far the greatest part
Cultivators of their own fertile Lands. . . ."[8] The body of the
nation consisted of the "industrious frugal Farmers, inhabiting the
interior Part of these American States. . . ."[9]

Such ideas were widely current in late eighteenth-century

America, as Chester E. Eisinger has pointed out. He uses the term
"freehold concept" to designate a complex of general notions arising from the effort of many writers to interpret the new society
that was coming into being under the influence of an abundance
of land awaiting settlement.[10] He finds repeated reference to the
doctrines that agriculture is the only source of real wealth; that
every man has a natural right to land; that labor expended in cultivating the earth confers a valid title to it; that the ownership of
land, by making the farmer independent, gives him social status
and dignity, while constant contact with nature in the course of
his labors makes him virtuous and happy; that America offers a
unique example of a society embodying these traits; and, as a general inference from all the propositions, that government should
be dedicated to the interests of the freehold farmer. The concrete
imaginative focus for these abstract doctrines was the idealized
figure of the farmer himself, called variously "husbandman," "cultivator," "freeman," or — perhaps most characteristically — "yeoman." [11]

The best known expositors of the agrarian philosophy in the
generation after Franklin were St. John de Crèvecœur and Thomas
Jefferson. But one must remember that these men were uttering
ideas shared by many of their contemporaries.

Crèvecœur, a Norman of good bourgeois family who served as
a cartographer with the French forces during the French and
Indian War, later married an Anglo-American wife and settled on
a farm of 371 acres twenty-five miles west of the Hudson in Or-
ange County, New York.[12] His *Letters from an American Farmer*,
written for the most part before the Revolution, were published at
its close and achieved great popularity in this country during the
1780's and 1790's.[13] Like Franklin, Crèvecœur took it for granted
that American society would expand indefinitely westward.

Many ages [he exclaimed] will not see the shores of our great lakes
replenished with inland nations, nor the unknown bounds of North
America entirely peopled. Who can tell how far it extends? Who can
tell the millions of men whom it will feed and contain? for no European
foot has as yet travelled half the extent of this mighty continent! [14]

The process of westward expansion would create three main divisions of the society: a remote fringe of backwoods settlements, a

central region of comfortable farms, and, to the East, a region of growing wealth, cities, and social stratification. Crèvecœur believed that both the beginning and the end of the process brought about undesirable social conditions. But the middle condition offered a unique opportunity for human virtue and happiness.

In dedicating his *Letters* to the Abbé Raynal, a former Jesuit whose widely read *Philosophical and Political History of the Settlements and Trade of the Europeans in the East and West Indies* (1770) summed up many ideas of the French Encyclopedists,[15] Crèvecœur declared, "you viewed these provinces of North America in their true light, as the asylum of freedom, as the cradle of future nations, and the refuge of distressed Europeans."[16] He found abundant confirmation in his own experience for Raynal's opinion that in the simple agricultural communities comprising the bulk of the American colonies "a certain equality of station, a security that arises from property, a general hope which every man has of increasing it" fostered "one general sentiment of benevolence."[17] These conditions, Crèvecœur believed, were unknown either among the half-barbarous hunters of the most advanced frontier or in the cities of the seacoast. But in the great body of American society, as it spread westward across the continent, would prevail an ideal simplicity, virtue, and contentment.

Here [he wrote in his celebrated letter entitled "What Is an American?"] are no aristocratical families, no courts, no kings, no bishops, no ecclesiastical dominion, no invisible power giving to a few a very visible one; no great manufacturers employing thousands, no great refinements of luxury. The rich and the poor are not so far removed from each other as they are in Europe. Some few towns excepted, we are all tillers of the earth, from Nova Scotia to West Florida. We are a people of cultivators, scattered over an immense territory, communicating with each other by means of good roads and navigable rivers, united by the silken bands of mild government, all respecting the laws, without dreading their power, because they are equitable. We are all animated with the spirit of an industry which is unfettered and unrestrained, because each person works for himself. If he travels through our rural districts he views not the hostile castle, and the haughty mansion, contrasted with the clay-built hut and miserable cabbin, where cattle and men help to keep each other warm, and dwell in meanness, smoke, and indigence. A pleasing uniformity of decent competence appears throughout our habitations. The meanest of our log-houses is a dry and comfortable habitation. Lawyer or merchant are the fairest titles our towns afford;

that of a farmer is the only appellation of the rural inhabitants of our country. . . . We have no princes, for whom we toil, starve, and bleed: we are the most perfect society now existing in the world.[18]

Jefferson was primarily interested in the political implications of the agrarian ideal. He saw the cultivator of the earth, the husbandman who tilled his own acres, as the rock upon which the American republic must stand. "The small land holders," he wrote, "are the most precious part of a state." [19] Such men had the independence, both economic and moral, that was indispensable in those entrusted with the solemn responsibility of the franchise. Thus the perception of Franklin and Crèvecœur that the waiting West promised an indefinite expansion of a simple agricultural society became the most certain guarantee that the United States would for a long age maintain its republican institutions. Not for many centuries would the vacant lands be filled and an overcrowded population fall into the depravity of crowded Europe.[20] The policy of the government should obviously be to postpone this unhappy day as long as possible by fostering agriculture and removing all impediments to westward expansion. Jefferson's program for the state of Virginia included the abolition of entails and primogeniture and the proposal that every landless adult should be given fifty acres from the public domain.[21] Although he was not able to persuade the Virginia legislature to adopt this early homestead proposal, Jefferson did succeed in establishing a federal policy favoring westward expansion. He framed the Northwest Ordinance that opened the trans-Allegheny to settlement and provided for the eventual admission of new western states; he devised the system by which the public lands were to be conveyed to individual owners; and later he consummated the Louisiana Purchase, which more than doubled the area awaiting settlement in the West.

The agrarian doctrines of Jefferson and his contemporaries had been developed out of the rich cluster of ideas and attitudes associated with farming in European cultural tradition: the conventional praise of husbandry derived from Hesiod and Virgil by hundreds of poetic imitators, the theoretical teaching of the French Physiocrats that agriculture is the primary source of all wealth, the growing tendency of radical writers like Raynal to make the farmer a republican symbol instead of depicting him in pastoral terms as a peasant virtuously content with his humble status in a stratified society.[22] The restatement and revision of these ideas in America during the period of the Revolution gave them a nationalistic coloring by insisting that the society of the new nation was a concrete embodiment of what had been in Europe but a utopian dream. The second stage in the development of American agrarian theory began with the perception that settlement beyond the Alleghenies promised an even more perfect realization of the agrarian ideal on a scale so vast that it dwarfed all previous conceptions of possible transformations in human society.

Crèvecœur had stated the theme in his account of a journey to the upper Ohio River which he probably made in 1767:

I never before felt myself so much disposed for meditation: My imagination involuntarily leaped into futurity; the absence of which was not afflicting, because it appeared to me nigh — I saw those beautiful shores ornamented with decent houses, covered with harvests and well cultivated fields. . . . I consider . . . the settling of the lands, which are watered by this river, as one of the finest conquests that could ever be presented to man . . . . It is destined to become the source of force, riches, and the future glory of the United States.[23]

But this was prophecy. The actual character of the society created by agricultural occupation of the interior was only gradually realized. The writers who described the earliest trans-Allegheny settlements in Kentucky were too much preoccupied with the beauty and fertility of the land and with the stereotypes of political theory to concern themselves with the details of social change. Thus John Filson presents in *The Discovery, Settlement and Present State of Kentucke* (1784) a rapturous picture of luxuriant Nature — a country "like the land of promise, flowing with milk and honey, a land of brooks of water, . . . a land of wheat and barley, and all kinds of fruits." In Scriptural accents he proclaims that in this central part of the extensive American empire, "you shall eat bread without scarceness, and not lack any thing in it," under mild skies where no infectious fogs nor pestilential vapors spread disease. The West is, grandly and abstractly, a place where afflicted humanity raises her drooping head; where conscience ceases to be a slave, and laws are no more than the security of happiness. In the great wilderness "nature makes reparation for having created man; and government, so long prostituted to the most criminal purposes, establishes an asylum . . . for the distressed of mankind." [24]

Gilbert Imlay's widely read *Topographical Description of the Western Territory of North America* develops these political ideas at greater length. Imlay was a New Jersey surveyor and veteran of the Revolution who went out to Kentucky in the 1780's, presently migrated to London, and then proceeded to Paris, where he moved in the circle of Tom Paine and formed a temporary liaison with Mary Wollstonecraft.[25] The *Topographical Description* appeared in London in 1792, the year before the publication of William Godwin's *Enquiry Concerning Political Justice*, and was probably written there, although it is cast in the form of letters from Kentucky to a correspondent in England. The book abounds in the clichés of contemporary European radicalism. Imlay announces that his purpose is to contrast "the simple manners, and rational life of Americans, in these back settlements, with the distorted and unnatural habits of the Europeans," who are oppressed by priestcraft and gothic tyranny.[26] The beauty of the landscape reinforces his political enthusiasms. "Every thing here," he writes, "assumes a dignity and splendour I have never seen in any other part of the world." Flowers decorate the smiling groves, as if a florist had cultivated them.

Soft zephyrs gently breathe on sweets, and the inhaled air gives a voluptuous glow of health and vigour, that seem to ravish the intoxicated senses. The sweet songsters of the forests appear to feel the soft influence of this genial clime, and, in more soft and modulated tones, warble their tender notes in unison with love and nature. Every thing here gives delight; and, in that mild effulgence which beams around us, we feel a glow of gratitude for the elevation which our all bountiful Creator has bestowed upon us. Far from being disgusted with man for his turpitude or depravity, we feel that dignity which nature bestowed upon us at the creation; but which has been contaminated by the base alloy of meanness, the concomitant of European education . . . .[27]

Imlay's infrequent passages of direct observation of the life of frontier settlers are colored by literary convention and a stilted rhetoric. An example is his account of making maple sugar:

The business of the day being over, the men join the women in the sugar groves where inchantment seems to dwell. — The lofty trees wave their spreading branches over a green turf, on whose soft down the mildness of the evening invites the neighbouring youth to sportive play; while our rural Nestors, with calculating minds, contemplate the boyish gambols of a growing progeny, they recount the exploits of their early age, and in their enthusiasm forget there are such things as decrepitude and misery. Perhaps a convivial song or a pleasant narration closes the scene.[28]

Most of the other observers who visited Kentucky in the early days tended to see the region, as Imlay did, through a haze of rhetoric. A "European Traveler" whose supposed letters to a friend in London were serialized in Matthew Carey's *American Museum* in 1788 related that when he stopped at a log cabin in a remote clearing in the western wilds, built only six years previously, he was enchanted by the virtuous contentment of the settlers:

I fancied myself to have fallen upon a discovery, after which the sages of antiquity had sought in vain; and that here in the wilderness, I had found in what the greatest happiness in life consisted: for here was religion without colour of superstition — here was civil and religious liberty in perfection — here was independence, as far as the nature of human life would admit — here fulness was enjoyed without retirement — and the whole shut out from the noise and bustle of the world.[29]

Similar sentiments are expressed in anonymous verses entitled "The Banks of Kentucke," in the same magazine, which may not have been based on firsthand observation. There is a liberal sprinkling of genius, virtue, truth, and other abstractions dear to the Age of Reason. The spirit of freedom prevails on the banks of Kentucke; tyrannical power and the foul banner of bigotry will forever be absent from them. The nearest approach to a record of things said and done is a single allusion to "honest industry" and "heart-cheering mirth." [30] The *Kentucky Gazette* of Lexington reprinted all five stanzas — forty lines — of this poem, no small tribute when newsprint and space were at such a premium;[31] and the original efforts of Western settlers sound just like it. In 1797 a Kentuckian celebrated the end of a series of bloody Indian fights in the Treaty of Greenville by announcing a new era for the state:

Our soil so rich, our clime so pure,
Sweet asylum for rich and poor —
Poor, did I say! — recall the word,
Here plenty spreads her gen'rous board;
But poverty must stay behind,
No asylum with us she'll find —
Avaunt, fell fiend! we know thee not,
Thy mem'ry must forever rot;
Dame Nature, by a kind behest,
Forbade you ever here to rest.[32]

The country north of the Ohio, settled somewhat later than Kentucky, was described in virtually the same terms by early observers. The Reverend James Smith, a Methodist minister from Virginia, wrote in his journal in 1797 at Deerfield (now South Lebanon), Ohio:

O, what a country will this be at a future day! What field of delights! What a garden of spices! What a paradise of pleasures! when these forests shall be cultivated and the gospel of Christ spread through this rising republic, unshackled by the power of kings and religious oppression on the one hand and slavery, that bane of true Godliness, on the other.[33]

This passage employs familiar conventions, but the writer has clear intimations of the future. He knows that the pioneers with their axes and plows will convert the forest to farmlands; and his allusion to slavery points significantly toward the sectional conflict which the westward movement was eventually to bring to a head.

CHAPTER XII

The Yeoman and the Fee-Simple Empire

The rapid settlement of the trans-Allegheny region during the thirty years following the Revolution revealed a crucial ambiguity in the conception of agriculture held by Jefferson and Crèvecœur. Although both these men were slaveowners, they both accepted the ideal of a society composed predominantly of freemen tilling their own acres. But the expansion of the plantation system into the Deep South during the first quarter of the nineteenth century, under the stimulus of apparently limitless world markets for cotton, created a slave power which was agricultural and yet quite unlike the free Northwest.

By 1830 there were thus two agrarianisms in the place of one, and their inherent opposition to one another was to become clearer with each passing decade until it reached a climax during the 1850's in the contest for control of the territories beyond the Mississippi. Each of these new agrarianisms found expression in imaginative and symbolic terms: that of the South in a pastoral literature of the plantation, that of the Northwest in the myth of the garden of the world with the idealized Western yeoman as its focal point. The Southern social ideal owed nothing to Western experience. Its emphasis was upon the settled patterns of life in the older slave states along the Atlantic seaboard rather than upon the newer, rawer Southwest. The main tradition of Western agrarianism was developed north of the Ohio River and thence transported into the trans-Mississippi region as a consequence of the Northern victory over the South in the Civil War.

The conflict between the ideal of a society composed of yeoman farmers and the plantation slave system came to dramatic formulation in the debate over slavery in the Virginia legislature in 1832, only six years after the death of Jefferson. Charles J. Faulkner, delegate from Berkeley County in the Shenandoah Valley and leading spokesman for the small farmers who were being pushed into obscurity, demanded that slavery be abolished in the state. The bold and intrepid forester of the West, he declared, should not be forced to yield to "the slothful and degraded African." If the plantation system continued to expand, the Western valleys which had until then reëchoed with the songs and industry of freemen would be blighted by the withering footsteps of slavery. Virginia was faced with a choice between two social patterns: the plantation system, with its masters and slaves, and the Jeffersonian ideal of a society of small landowners tilling their own soil. Faulkner's praise of his constituents shows that the figure of the yeoman had become the focus of a developed agrarian philosophy:

Sir, our native, substantial, independent yeomanry, constitute our pride, efficiency and strength; they are our defence in war, our ornaments in peace; and no population, I will venture to affirm, upon the face of the globe, is more distinguished for an elevated love of freedom — for morality, virtue, frugality and independence, than the Virginia peasantry west of the Blue Ridge.[1]

The same clichés had been applied to Roman, French, and English farmers down through the centuries, but they had no doubt been at least partly true all along, and they were true enough in 1832 to constitute an accurate prediction of the intellectual history of the free-soil West for the next half-century. Contrasting Ohio and Kentucky, Faulkner described the blighting effects of slavery in a region that had once seemed to hold such a brilliant promise of freedom and prosperity. The true meaning of the West must now be sought in the free states north of the Ohio River, where happiness and contentment, the busy and cheerful sound of industry, rapid growth in population, and the development of education showed to what heights of social well-being America might aspire. When the Virginia legislature, at the close of the debate, voted down abolition, it spoke for a South that had abandoned Jefferson's ideal of a republic based on small subsistence farmers.[2]

The yeoman ideal that was henceforth to dominate the social thinking of the Northwest had emerged as a fusion of eighteenth-century agrarian theory with the observation of American experience beyond the Alleghenies. But the process had been slow. Only gradually had the Western farmer become a distinct figure for the imagination and his role in an essentially classless society recognized. The old attitude of upper-class condescension toward the plowman made it difficult for even sympathetic observers to become fully aware of the social revolution that was taking place in the interior. As late as 1819, the surveyor and gazetteer Edmund Dana, who knew his subject first hand, remarked casually in his *Geographical Sketches* that "The main business of common laborers, constituting the great mass of population in the west, will be the cultivation of the lands." [3] Faulkner himself, whose allusions to independent yeomen are a far cry from the unconscious snobbery of Dana's phrase "common laborers," could nevertheless refer to the "peasantry west of the Blue Ridge" in a way that would have been inconceivable ten years later. The Western yeoman had to work as hard as a common laborer or a European peasant, and at the same tasks. Despite the settled belief of Americans to the contrary, his economic status was not necessarily higher. But he was a different creature altogether because he had become the hero of a myth, of *the* myth of mid-nineteenth-century America. He no longer resembled even the often-praised English yeoman, darling of poets and social theorists. The very word had changed its meaning in American speech.[4] The Western yeoman had become a symbol which could be made to bear an almost unlimited charge of meaning. It had strong overtones of patriotism, and it implied a far-reaching social theory. The career of this symbol deserves careful attention because it is one of the most tangible things we mean when we speak of the development of democratic ideas in the United States.

The beginnings of it can be observed in James K. Paulding's early poem *The Backwoodsman*, published in 1818. Paulding's story begins in Crèvecœur's country, the Hudson Valley, but a single generation has brought a lamentable change there in the condition of the agricultural laborer. Instead of the Arcadian bliss which Crèvecœur had described on the eve of the Revolution, poverty and even starvation threaten Paulding's hero, the worthy but unfortunate Basil. The hardest toil and the most unremitting frugality cannot now earn independence for the agricultural laborer without inherited capital. There is no longer any land for him. After a week of desperate exertion in the fields — another man's fields — he spends his Sundays trying to find game or fish to keep his family from starvation, but to no avail, and when he falls ill the household faces absolute despair. If Paulding has darkened the shadows for dramatic effect, the picture still stands in impressive contrast with that presented in the *Letters from an American Farmer*.

Paulding's theme is the opportunity waiting in the West for such unfortunates. The crux of the matter is the ownership of land, which constitutes independence.[5] As long as he must till another's land, Basil can never rise above grinding poverty. This will forever be the miserable destiny of "old Europe's hapless swains," but in America the great virgin West offers land for all who will cultivate it:

> Hence comes it, that our meanest farmer's boy
> Aspires to taste the proud and manly joy
> That springs from holding in his own dear right
> The land he plows, the home he seeks at night;
> And hence it comes, he leaves his friends and home,
> Mid distant wilds and dangers drear to roam,
> To seek a competence, or find a grave,
> Rather than live a hireling or a slave.[6]

Basil accordingly gathers his family together and joins the throngs heading westward.

Settled beyond the Ohio on land bought from a benevolent landlord with liberal terms of credit, Basil is transformed. He now has that blessed independence which is the basis at once of physical comfort and moral virtue. Where free or virtually free land is available Crèvecœur's Utopia can flourish again. It is worth noting, incidentally, that Paulding's version of an ideal society in the West likewise has a strong tinge of that delight in the village which distinguished the stream of New England influence (as expressed for example in Dwight's *Greenfield Hill*) from the Southern frontier pattern of settlement in scattered clearings. Basil and his family had wept to leave behind the village church and

tolling bell and the smoke of rural hamlets in their old home, but
the backwoodsmen immediately create "a little rustic village" on
the bank of the Ohio:

> To cultivated fields, the forest chang'd,
> Where golden harvests wav'd, and cattle rang'd;
> The curling smoke amid the wilds was seen,
> The village church now whiten'd on the green,
> And by its side arose the little school,
> Where rod and reason, lusty urchins rule,
> Whose loud repeated lessons might be heard,
> Whene'er along the road a wight appear'd.[7]

The white church and the school are of New England but we must
also make allowance for British influence. Paulding's acknowledged master, Thomas Campbell, had already transplanted a very
literary village to the Pennsylvania frontier in his *Gertrude of
Wyoming* (1809). And back of Campbell was, among others, the
Goldsmith of *The Deserted Village* (1770).

The sturdy plowman, it will be recalled, is the mainstay of his
country in war as well as in peace. The mettle of the Ohio emigrants is soon tested by Indian troubles arising from the War of
1812. Paulding points out that the hardy peasantry in Germany
and Spain had stood to defeat Napoleon after kings and nobles
had fled: Freedom's band, the militia of the West, are warriors
even more formidable than the downtrodden slaves of the Old
World.[8] When Basil and his companions confront the Indians at
Tippecanoe they have become "our bold yeomen." [9]

At this stage of Basil's development Paulding's failure to grasp
the implications of his material is strikingly evident. Like many
later writers who dealt with the settlement of the West, he means
to depict the "rise of the common man." But there are two ways of
thinking about this rise. The political ideology of the 1830's and
1840's assumed that the common man had risen to dominate, or at
least to share control of the government without ceasing to be the
common man; it was a process whereby power in the state passed
from one class to another. If this theory were analyzed rigorously,
it would probably appear that the transfer of power to a new class
was believed to have been accompanied by a decided weakening
of all lines between classes. Certainly the myth of the garden as it

had matured by the middle of the century interpreted the whole vast West as an essentially homogeneous society in which class stratification was of minor importance.

But *The Backwoodsman* was written before these changes had become apparent. Furthermore, Paulding was a prisoner of literary convention. Although Campbell, closer to the centers from which technical innovation was radiating, had written of the American frontier in Spenserian stanzas, the provincial Paulding was not up to this revolutionary daring and felt incapable of managing anything beyond the heroic couplet. But this choice of a measure committed him to linguistic and social conventions thoroughly unsuited to his theme. There was a basic impropriety in trying to write about the fluidity of classes in a measure which proclaimed with every caesura that order was Heaven's first law. In this dilemma Paulding resorted to irony:

> My humble theme is of a hardy swain [he began],
> The lowliest of the lowly rural train . . . .
> Simple the tale I venture to rehearse,
> For humble is the Muse, and weak her verse;
> She hazards not, to sing in lofty lays,
> Of steel-clad knights, renown'd in other days,
> For glorious feats that, in this dastard time,
> Would on the gallows make them swing sublime . . . .[10]

We are to understand that the theme seems humble only when looked at from the standpoint of an indefensible code of aristocracy; the hardy swain appears degraded to those who venerate the knight, but a true scheme of values would make the swain the hero and consign the knight to the gallows.

Yet Paulding is not prepared either intellectually or technically for the reversal of social values which his irony implies; he is not really convinced that the hardy swain is superior to the upper classes. The rise of the common man is for him not a destruction of the class system but the rise of an individual member of the lower class in a social scale which itself is not changed. It is therefore not enough that Basil should be elevated to the rank of a bold and independent yeoman; he must be promoted out of his class. At the end of the poem he is something quite different from either a backwoodsman or a yeoman:

> Old BASIL — for his head is now grown gray —
> Waxes in wealth and honours every day;
> Judge, general, congressman, and half a score
> Of goodly offices, and titles more
> Reward his worth, while like a prince he lives,
> And what he gains from heav'n to mortals gives . . . .[11]

Timothy Flint's efforts to depict Western life in fiction are even more instructive than Paulding's. A Massachusetts clergyman who went West in 1816 as a missionary and became a leading Western man of letters, he was in theory committed to the dream of a democratic agrarian Utopia. If his New England background led him to emphasize the recreation of the pattern of the village in the West, the villages of his imagination were very close to the soil and represented no alien element in a basically agricultural economy. In his *Recollections of the Last Ten Years*, published in 1826, he apostrophizes the Missouri River in prophecy of an ideal Western society much like Paulding's:

>   anticipation, rapt away,
> Forestalls thy future glory, when thy tide
> Shall roll by towns, and villages, and farms,
> Continuous, amidst the peaceful hum
> Of happy multitudes, fed from thy soil;
> When the glad eye shall cheer at frequent view
> Of gilded spires of halls, still vocal with the task
> Of ripening youth; or churches sounding high,
> Hosannas to the Living God.[12]

On occasion Flint could do full justice to a very Jeffersonian yeoman, and like Jefferson he saw the problem of American society as a choice between an agrarian and an industrial order. He defined his position in attacking the apologists for industry who were developing a theory of protective tariffs. Reviewing Alexander Hill Everett's *America* in 1827, Flint refused to accept either the Boston Brahmin's glowing description of New England mill towns or the pathetic picture of the sufferings of farmers who had escaped to the West:

Thousands of independent and happy yeomen [he declared], who have emigrated from New England to Ohio and Indiana, — with their numerous, healthy and happy families about them, with the ample abundance that fills their granaries, with their young orchards, whose branches must be propped to sustain the weight of their fruit, beside their beautiful rivers, and beech woods, in which the squirrels skip, the wild deer browse, and the sweet red-bird sings, and with the prospect of settling their dozen children on as many farms about them, — would hardly be willing to exchange the sylvan range of their fee simple empires, their droves of cattle, horses, and domestic animals, and the ability to employ the leisure of half of their time as they choose, for the interior of square stone or brick walls, to breathe floccules of cotton, and to contemplate the whirl of innumerable wheels for fourteen hours of six days of every week in the year. . . . While there are uncounted millions of acres of fertile and unoccupied land, where farmers can rear their families in peace, plenty and privacy, under the guardian genius of our laws, we hope, that farms will continue to spread to the bases of the Rocky mountains. Farmers and their children are strong, and innocent and moral almost of necessity. Compare the cheeks of the milk maid with the interesting, but pale faces in the great manufactories. The rigid laws, the stern rules of young associations, the extreme precautions that regulate the intercourse, the moral schools of discipline in these establishments, prove, after all, what the wise and provident superintendents think of the natural tendency of things in them. It is only a besieged city, that requires martial law, and the constant guard of armed sentinels.[13]

The fee-simple empire on this familiar pattern appears again and again in Flint's nonfictional writings. He describes Ohio, for example, as a perfect realization of the ideal, which for him means that it reproduces the bucolic New England of the age before the coming of the cotton mills — a land of small farms, as he had described it in 1815 before he left, cultivated by independent and virtuous owners; of frequent and neat schoolhouses; of village churches standing as emblems of law, justice, order, industry, and temperance.[14] Ohio, Flint wrote admiringly in 1833, "seems to have invited a hardy and numerous body of freeholders to select themselves moderate and nearly equal-sized farms, and to intersperse them over its surface." [15] Like Faulkner of Berkeley County he points the contrast between this picture of social happiness and the landscape presented by the slave states. Under the plantation system, flourishing villages and a compact population of small farmers cannot develop. Isolated mansions inhabited by intelligent and hospitable families rise here and there, at great distances from one another, but the mansions are surrounded by squalid Negro cabins, and "the contrast of the hovels and the mansion can never cease to be a painful spectacle to the eye." [16]

Yet if Flint took pleasure in the yeoman society of the free Northwest, he was unable to use the yeoman in fiction. His only novel laid in the Mississippi Valley shows that he was even more handicapped by ingrained class feeling than Paulding had been. *George Mason, The Young Backwoodsman,* published in 1829, is in part autobiographical. The Reverend George Mason, father of the hero, like Flint resigns his pastorate in a New England village because of factional strife in his congregation, and takes his family to the Southwest. They settle on a small claim in the forest — probably a reminiscence of Flint's experiences near Jackson, Missouri, although the setting of the story is ostensibly Mississippi. After great hardships which stand in marked contrast to Flint's generalizations about peace and plenty in the West, the father dies, but the eldest son George succeeds in becoming owner of a steamboat and at the end of the book the Mason family is installed with a comfortable income in a village on the Upper Ohio. The son and the eldest daughter Eliza have meanwhile been provided with suitable mates.

Flint's feeling about this material is confused. He announces at the outset that he will deal with "the short and simple annals of the poor," who comprise nine-tenths of the human race. His thesis is that a noble heart can swell in a bosom clad in the meanest habiliments, and that "incidents, full of tender and solemn interest, have occurred in a log cabin in the forests of the Mississippi." [17] Certain slaveowners are depicted as illiterate and rude, the coarse and vulgar rich.[18] But no instance of nobility in natives of the West is exhibited except in the benevolent slave Pompey. The Masons, although destitute, encounter no person in the backwoods whom Flint considers their social equal. The mates provided for the son and daughter are as wealthy as Cooper would have made them. One is a New Englander, the other a Pennsylvanian. Near the end of the book George's prospective wife turns pale at the thought of having to travel on the deck of the river steamboat with the poor families, instead of in the cabin with the first-class passengers.[19]

The lesson of Flint's novel — and of other novels about the West to be considered later — is that the literary imagination moved very slowly toward acceptance of the democratic principles so glowingly embodied in agrarian theory. This was doubtless due in part to the fact that even bad fiction comes out of a deeper level of the personality than conceptual thought. It owes something also to the inertia of literary forms, a force we have seen operating in the Leatherstocking tales. But the agricultural West in literature presents problems quite distinct from agrarian theory and will be treated in a later chapter.

The abstractions of the agrarian tradition were applied with little change to successive areas in the Northwest as settlement advanced into them. James B. Lanman, for example, a native of Connecticut who lived in Michigan for two years in the late 1830's at the height of the land boom, contributed articles to the influential *Hunt's Merchants' Magazine* celebrating the intelligent plowman who, as he followed his harrow over the mellow land, his own land, was filled with "the spirit of independence, always arising in the mind of every freeholder." [20] In a later article Lanman invokes the memory of Jefferson and recites all the themes of the myth of the garden:

If, as has been remarked by a distinguished statesman, cities are the sores of the political body, where the bad matter of the state is concentrated, what healthful habitudes of mind and body are afforded by agricultural enterprise! The exhilarating atmosphere of a rural life, the invigorating exercise afforded by its various occupations, the pure water, the abundance of all the necessaries of subsistence, leading to early and virtuous marriages, all point to this pursuit as best adapted to the comfort of the individual man. Its beneficial bearing upon the state is no less obvious. The agriculturist, removed from the pernicious influences that are forever accumulated in large cities, the exciting scenes, which always arise from large accumulations of men, passes a quiet and undisturbed life, possessing ample means and motives thoroughly to reflect upon his rights and duties, and holding a sufficient stake in the soil to induce him to perform those duties both for himself and his country. It is to the true-hearted and independent yeomen of a nation that we look, in times of national danger, to uphold its institutions, and to protect themselves in preserving the principles of the state. It is to them that we refer for the support of sound legislation, and from their ranks that we derive the best soldiers when the horrors of war overspread a land. While other branches of human enterprise are protected in their due measure, it can scarcely be denied that agricultural enterprise, the basis of almost every form of human pursuit, should be encouraged as the safeguard of a country, the promoter of its virtue, and the solid foundation of its permanent happiness and most lasting independence.[21]

As the vision of a Western utopia of yeoman farmers acquired stronger and stronger antislavery overtones, Southern writers undertook an aggressive critique of it. An unidentified writer in the *Southern Literary Messenger* seized upon the publication of Horace Greeley's *Hints Toward Reforms* in 1851 to examine the proposals of the National Reformers with whom Greeley had become associated. The Southerner assailed the very foundations of agrarian theory. He called in question the ecumenical dogma "that all real production is from the soil, and that land possesses some mysterious quality which guaranties to its occupants a more certain abundant, and permanent support than other employments." He also objected to the notion that agricultural labor has a peculiar sanctity. Agriculture was not an end in itself but merely a way of making a living. The small farm which Greeley and his fellows wished to give to every settler, while it might provide the bare necessities of an ordinary family, was not large enough to provide for its cultivated and refined maintenance. Indeed, the agricultural unit should be large enough to provide an adequate support for each of the children when the estate should be divided at the death of the original patentee. The limitation on individual holdings of land should therefore not be placed very low; certainly not lower than a section and a half or two sections — 960 to 1280 acres. In other words, the limit should not be brought down below a conceivable size for a plantation employing slave labor.[22] The ultimate value assumed in this line of reasoning is not the virtuous labor of the farmer, but the leisure of the landowning class.

Other Southern critics of what was now clearly a Northwestern free-soil ideal joined in the attack on the notion that farming was a pleasant occupation. This traditional idea, said another writer for the *Messenger* in 1856, is nothing but a dream of theorists and poets. The actual, manual operations of farming he described as irksome and repulsive to the great mass of mankind. Adam Smith's doctrine that cultivation of the soil promotes keenness of mind is contradicted outright; agricultural laborers "have little opportunity to cultivate either the exercise of their intellects or the accomplishments, tastes, and habits, which alone could build up agreeable social communities. . . ." The Southern critic denied even the favorite agrarian doctrine that manual labor in the earth fostered political insight. The arduous toil of the farmer restricted his mental range and prevented him from acquiring a comprehension of the principles on which free government must depend.[23] (It was indeed true that the yeoman of the Northwest had proved inadequately grounded in the doctrines of Calhoun.) Sound political principles, in the view of this apologist for the plantation system, could be developed and preserved only by a leisure class freed from the necessity of physical toil. George Fitzhugh of Virginia, the most ingenious among the proslavery theorists, summed up the Southern repudiation of the Western agrarian ideal in his *Cannibals All!*:

Agricultural labor is the most arduous, least respectable, and worst paid of all labor. Nature and philosophy teach all who can to avoid and escape from it, and to pursue less laborious, more respectable, and more lucrative employments. None work in the field who can help it. Hence free society is in great measure dependent for its food and clothing on slave society.[24]

The most suggestive aspect of this Southern critique of the myth of the garden is the extent to which it anticipates the disillusioned view of farm life that was to be taken a generation later by pioneer Middle Western "realists" like E. W. Howe and Hamlin Garland.

CHAPTER XIII

The South and the Myth of the Garden

By the 1850's the South had become actively hostile to the yeoman ideal which had been developed as a rationale of agricultural settlement in the Mississippi Valley. But this break with the Northwest came only after a long struggle on the part of Southern leaders to maintain economic and political ties with all the interior basin.

The first advance beyond the Alleghenies, in the last quarter of the eighteenth century, had been decidedly Southern in coloring. Virginia and North Carolina had been the bases for the settlement of Kentucky and Tennessee. Even the earliest Anglo-American penetration north of the Ohio, in the wake of George Rogers Clark's expedition during the Revolution, was largely a Southern venture. The history of Western exploration is filled with Southern names, from Boone and Lewis and Clark to James Clyman of Virginia and John Charles Frémont of South Carolina. Through Jefferson, Virginia had provided the geographical insight and the strategic planning for the first half-century of westward advance. So marked was the Southern dominance of this process that as late as 1846 the Pennsylvanian William Gilpin could, to be sure with an element of exaggeration, ascribe the entire impulse to the South. "The progeny of Jamestown," he declared, "has given to the Union twelve great agricultural States; has created that mighty production and generating capacity on which are based the grand power and prosperity of the Nation." Among Southern accomplishments he listed not only the settlement of Kentucky, Tennessee, Missouri, and the Southwest, but also that of Ohio, Indiana, Illinois, and Iowa.[1] Even after the Civil War Whitman declared in his poem "Virginia — The West" that Virginia had given to the nation the stalwart giant of the West whose plenteous offspring had put on uniforms of blue and preserved the Union against the rebellious Confederacy.[2]

The association between South and West had been reflected in national politics. Many representatives of the Middle States and New England had feared from the beginning that the development of the trans-Allegheny would unduly strengthen the South. In August, 1786 James Monroe wrote to Patrick Henry from New York, where Congress was sitting, that the Northerners meant to break up the settlements on the western waters in order to "keep the States southward as they now are." [3] In the Constitutional Convention of 1787 Gouverneur Morris of Pennsylvania proposed inserting into the Constitution a provision "That the number of representatives in ye first branch from the States hereafter to be established shall not exceed the representatives from the States already confederated." [4] Delegates to the Convention regarded this proposal as a clear test of strength between North and South. It was rejected by the close vote of four states to five, with Pennsylvania divided. The states favoring the measure were Massachusetts, Connecticut, Delaware, and Maryland (which, having no claim to Western territory, was jealous of Virginia). Those opposing it were New Jersey, Virginia, North Carolina, South Carolina, and Georgia.[5]

During the next twenty years the alignment of South and West against North and East persisted through a series of crises, of which the most spectacular arose from Federalist opposition to the Louisiana Purchase in 1803 and to the War of 1812, especially in its Western phase. As Benton picturesquely summarized the attitude of New England Federalists, the cry was, "The Potomac the boundary; the negro States by themselves! The Alleghanies the boundary, the western savages by themselves! The Mississippi the boundary, let Missouri be governed by a Prefect, or given up as a haunt for wild beasts!" [6] The alliance of West and South continued into the 1850's as a political force to be reckoned with. It was the basis of the careers of Jackson, Benton, Douglas, and other Democratic leaders; and even after the Northwest had been won for the Republican Party in the election of 1860, Western sympathy with the South found expression in the powerful Copperhead movement of disaffection during the Civil War. But the changes in the structure of American society recorded in the Republican victory of 1860 had begun soon after the War of 1812. Although the introduction of steamboats on the western waters for a time strengthened the sway of New Orleans throughout the Mississippi Valley, the Erie Canal, steam transportation through the Great Lakes, and the east-west trunk line railways eventually tied the Northwest to New York rather than to the Gulf of Mexico.

The changes which had begun to take place in the relations among the sections were fully explored in the famous Webster-Hayne debate of 1829–1830, noted in the history books for its bearing on constitutional theory, but originating in a Southern bid for Western support. The doctrine of nullification which Hayne, acting as the mouthpiece for Calhoun, announced in the course of this debate, and which South Carolina put into effect two years later in its declaration that the tariff of 1832 would not be enforced in ports of the state, expressed the Southern fear that a coalition of North and West would soon outweigh the strength of the South within the Union. From this time on the South wavered between two strategies. One was to surrender its long-standing but now weakening dominance of the West and fall back on constitutional minority rights. The other was to try to regain control of the West through development of trade routes from the south Atlantic coast to the Ohio Valley. Southern spokesmen in Congress resisted federal aid in the construction of canals and other means of bringing the Northwest and New England closer together, and tried to protect the position of New Orleans as queen of the trade on the western waters.

Benton stated the doctrine underlying such efforts: ". . . every canal, and every road, tending to draw the commerce of the Western States across the Alleghany mountains, is an injury to the people of the West." His desire for a continued economic alliance of South and West clouded his vision of the impending revolution in transport. Here, as in his discussion of a transcontinental trade route, he insisted that the steamboat would always outweigh the railway in importance. The bulky products of Western farms and packing houses would continue to make their way to market downstream through New Orleans. "As to the idea of sending the products of the West across the Alleghanies, it is the conception of insanity itself! No rail roads or canals will ever carry them, not even if they do it gratis!" Commercial routes from East to West could be useful only for carrying manufactured goods of relatively small bulk. If Westerners bought these goods they endangered their own market at New Orleans; for New Orleans could not buy if she were not allowed to sell. Besides, decline of the trade with New Orleans threatened to destroy the immensely important steamboat system of the West, which already, in 1829, had grown to three hundred thousand tons.[7]

The desire to strengthen economic ties with the West accounts for one of the strangest moments in the career of Calhoun, archchampion of the strict construction of the Constitution which most Southerners believed forbade federal aid for internal improvements. Having reluctantly accepted an invitation to attend the Memphis Commercial Convention of November, 1845,[8] Calhoun was elected president of the meeting and delivered the opening address. This discourse shows what a strong attraction was being exerted by the West on Southern constitutional theory. Calhoun begins with the assumption that the Western and the Southern states occupy a single physiographic region, consisting of the Mississippi Valley and the Gulf Plains from the Atlantic to the Rio Grande — a patent translation of political desire into geographical terms. He dwells on the need for free and ready transit for persons and merchandise among the various portions of this vast region of the world. Integration of the South with the West obviously depended upon the utmost possible development of the river systems, especially of the Mississippi, whose current drew the produce of every part of the valley to the Southern metropolis of New Orleans.[9]

The crucial importance to the South of maintaining this commercial connection along the channels of the inland waterways demanded every effort to foster navigation, including federal appropriations to remove snags, dredge channels, install lighthouses, and so on. Calhoun Democrats had opposed such appropriations for twenty years as unconstitutional. But before an astonished and delighted audience Calhoun himself now proceeded to perform the mental gymnastics necessary to reach the conclusion "that the invention of Fulton has in reality, for all practical purposes, converted the Mississippi, with all its great tributaries, into an inland sea. Regarding it as such," he continued, "I am prepared to place it on the same footing with the Gulf and Atlantic coasts, the Chesapeake and Delaware Bays, and the Lakes, in reference to the superintendence of the General Government over its navigation." [10] Indeed, under the influence of this new exaltation, Calhoun even found himself celebrating the passage to India. In words that might almost have come from the lips of William Gilpin he announced in conclusion:

you occupy a region possessing advantages above all others on the globe, of the same extent, not only for its fertility, its diversity of climate and production, but in its geographical position; lying midway between the Pacific and Atlantic Oceans, in less than one generation, should the Union continue, and I hope it may be perpetual, you will be engaged in deliberations to extend your connection with the Pacific, as you now are with the Atlantic; and will ultimately be almost as intimately connected with the one as the other. In the end, you will command the commerce . . . of the world, as well as that of our great Union, if we preserve our liberty and free popular institutions.[11]

But Calhoun's effort was in vain. The South failed in the end to maintain its hold on the developing Northwest, and the failure was a turning point in American history. When the break between North and South came in 1860, the Northwest went with the Union. The weakening of the South's hold on the area north of the Ohio can be traced in the history of the now familiar symbols which expressed the ultimate purposes of the two sections. The richest vein of Southern materials bearing on this subject is the file of *DeBow's Review*, established in New Orleans in 1846 and devoted to the promotion of commercial relations between the South and the West along the lines endorsed by the Memphis Convention. DeBow and his contributors constantly urged the development of trade routes connecting New Orleans with the upper Mississippi Valley. They warned the South of the ominous increase in trade from the Great Lakes through the Erie Canal.[12]

They urged New Orleans to waken from her complacent reliance on the Mississippi and build railways.[13] In accordance with the geographical conception advanced by Calhoun, which regarded the South and the Mississippi Valley as forming one region, DeBow celebrated the progress of the Great West as enthusiastically as Benton himself.[14] This policy led him to publish contributions from Western spokesmen developing the theme of the garden of the world. As late as 1858 DeBow included in his *Review* two characteristic essays by William Gilpin.[15] He also published articles by Jessup W. Scott of Ohio, who had long been a contributor to *Hunt's Merchants' Magazine* of New York on the development of the West. Scott, who will come up for fuller discussion in another connection, elaborated for DeBow's readers the familiar ideas of manifest destiny, predicting that the Star of Empire would "shine for ages and ages from the zenith on our central plain." [16]

DeBow's commitment to the theme of Western progress, which implied national unity if it was to benefit the South, early came into conflict with his enthusiastic support of slavery. As early as 1851 he was speaking of secession as a step the South might have to take if Northern attacks continued.[17] Southern leaders were eventually forced to recognize that the notions of the course of empire and of the coming dominance of the West were implicitly free-soil. By 1860 Senator Louis T. Wigfall of Texas could put this awareness into words in an attack on Andrew Johnson's expansionism:

The Senator from Tennessee [declared Wigfall] supposes that we have a sort of blatherskiting Americanism that is going to spread over the whole continent, and cross the Pacific, and take in the Sandwich Islands; and that, in the area of freedom, we are going to take in the whole world, and everybody is going to benefit us. The whole of that is false doctrine. I think it is a doctrine that no Democrat should ever entertain.

There was no manifest destiny, Wigfall insisted, in the Kentucky and Virginia Resolutions. "We ought to begin and repudiate and trample on this national idea," he exclaimed. The notion of colonizing and extending the area of freedom was nothing but "Red Republicanism; it is Federalism; it is nationalism; it is an ignoring of history." [18] Wigfall's instinct was sound. The very men to whom DeBow turned in the late 1850's for celebration of the imperial destinies of the Mississippi Valley were free-soilers, soon to enter the Republican party. The hero of their expansionism was Gilpin's soldier of the pioneer army, the axe man, the industrious farmer, the independent yeoman of the Western agrarian tradition. And this man was free.

Nothing could stand in greater contrast to the symbols which had meanwhile been created to express the ideal ends of the slave system. These symbols were grouped in the powerful and persuasive myth of the Southern plantation. Originating within the nostalgic and sentimental mode of Washington Irving, and first applied to the South in John P. Kennedy's *Swallow Barn* (which was published in 1832 at the turning point of Southern history), the picture of aristocratic masters, brilliant and charming heroines, and devoted slaves reached full development in the historical fiction of the Virginian John Esten Cooke in the middle 1850's. So compelling to the imagination was this group of symbols, bathed as they were in the charm of pastoral tradition and feudal romance, that they long survived the destruction of the plantation system itself. In the hands of such Southern writers as Thomas Nelson Page after the Civil War the idealized image of the plantation proved to have a strong appeal to Northern as well as to Southern audiences, and indeed to this day forms an apparently indestructible part of the national store of literary themes.[19]

But the briefest glance at the plantation in literature shows why it could not compete with the myth of the garden of the world as a projection of American experience in the West, and therefore why men like DeBow had no imaginative weapons to supplement their geographical and economic arguments for maintaining the Mississippi Valley under the hegemony of the South. The fiction dealing with the plantation emphasizes the beauty of harmonious social relations in an orderly feudal society. It presupposes generations of settled existence and is inimical to change. Literary plantations are almost always in the older South, and when they are situated in the new, developing Southwest, they are unhistorically depicted as duplicates of the Virginia and Carolina estates on which the convention was first based. Such symbols could not be adapted to the expression of a society like that of the West, either South or North, where rapidity of change, crudity, bustle, heterogeneity were fundamental traits.

It is true that during this same period the Southwest produced its own striking symbols, embodied in the newspaper sketches and oral tales which were called, collectively, Southwestern humor. These symbols were also destined to survive the Civil War and to have important consequences for American literature. They formed the tradition out of which developed Mark Twain. But Southwestern humor was of little or no use politically because while it depicted a society containing slaves, it dealt with slavery only incidentally and had no case to make for the institution. The boisterous mood of this writing veers toward satire rather than toward apologetics; it makes no appeal to sentiment, which proved to be the most powerful weapon of both defenders and attackers of slavery.

During the 1830's and early 1840's the case for westward expansion of the plantation system was the case for the annexation of Texas. The fertility of this enormous region beyond the Sabine, the mildness of its climate, its unexampled resources of every kind were presented so enthusiastically by travelers and settlers that an epidemic of "Texas fever" raged in the South.[20] Despite Mexican laws, slavery had been established in Texas from the earliest days of Anglo-American settlement, and it was generally recognized that the region offered a vast area suitable for the cultivation of cotton and other plantation crops. Yet proslavery advocates of annexation failed entirely to create symbols comparable to the free-soil symbol of the yeoman. They were prepared to defend slavery as such with the standard doctrines, and to state the familiar propositions of manifest destiny, but they were not able to endow the westward expansion of the slave system with imaginative color. One of the most celebrated statements of the case for annexation is a letter written by Robert J. Walker of Mississippi for circulation as campaign literature in 1844. Asserting that the reannexation of Texas is "the greatest question, since the adoption of the constitution, ever presented for the decision of the American people," [21] Walker makes the standard appeal to the need for restoring the integrity of the Mississippi Valley. The Creator, he declares, has planed down the whole valley, including Texas, and united every atom of the soil and every drop of the waters of the mighty whole. He has linked their rivers with the great Mississippi, and marked and united the whole for the dominion of one government and the residence of one people; and it is impious in man to attempt to dissolve this great and glorious Union.[22]

The oratory moves with assurance toward the images that had become a part of the folk heritage:

Who will desire to check the young eagle of America, now refixing her gaze upon our former limits, and repluming her pinions for her returning flight? . . . Who will oppose the re-establishment of our glorious constitution, over the whole of the mighty valley which once was shielded by its benignant sway? Who will wish again to curtail the limits of this great republican empire, and again to dismember the glorious valley of the West? . . . Who will refuse to heal the bleeding wounds of the mutilated West, and reunite the veins and arteries, dissevered by the dismembering cession of Texas to Spain?[23]

But in his treatment of the problem of slavery Walker falls back upon the defensive, picturing the economic ruin of the North and the social chaos of the South that would follow emancipation.[24] The annexation of Texas, he argued, would drain Negro population away from the older Southern states. A large and increasing number of Negroes, attracted by a congenial climate, would cross the Rio Grande and mingle with the population of the Latin-American republics to the South on a basis of social equality. Indeed, this process would eventually bring about universal emancipation. Slavery, announced the prophet with the emphasis of italics, "will certainly disappear if Texas is reannexed to the Union. . . ."[25] Providence would open Texas "as a safety valve, into which and through which slavery will slowly and gradually recede, and finally disappear into the boundless regions of Mexico, and Central and Southern America."[26]

Although this is ingenious, it is not an ideology of slavery expansion. The only Southern expansionist dream which had imaginative depth led in a different direction. This was the notion of a Caribbean slave empire, which found its most spectacular expression in the Ostend Manifesto of 1854. The Southern diplomats who in this remarkable document threatened forcible conquest of Cuba if Spain refused to sell the island to the United

States, were trying to put into effect a geopolitical conception developed in part from the general notion of manifest destiny and in part from the idea of the passage to India. The oceanographer Mathew F. Maury, leading Southern scientist of his day, had called the Gulf of Mexico the American Mediterranean. Into this sea emptied the Mississippi, and the archaic Southern tendency to emphasize the primacy of natural waterways allowed Southern thinkers to conceive of the Gulf as dominating the whole interior valley. On the east the Gulf merged into the Caribbean, which touched the Isthmus of Panama, gateway to the Pacific; control of the Gulf was said to mean mastery of the dominant commercial route to the Indies. Southward the Caribbean led to South America, where the slave empire of Brazil in the fabulous basin of the Amazon offered the world's most promising theater for expansion of the plantation system.[27] The key to all this potential empire was Cuba: ". . . if we hold Cuba," wrote an editorialist in the Richmond *Enquirer*, "in the next fifty years we will hold the destiny of the richest and most increased commerce that ever dazzled the cupidity of man. And with that commerce we can control the power of the world. Give us this, and we can make the public opinion of the world." [28]

Well might a Southerner point out that the South had a manifest destiny different from that of the North.[29] The conception of a tropical empire occupying the basins of the Amazon and the Mississippi and controlling the trade of the Pacific, populated by Negroes brought from Africa through a reopened slave trade — "the purple dream," as Stephen Vincent Benét calls it,

> Of the America we have not been,
> The tropic empire, seeking the warm sea,
> The last foray of aristocracy, —* [30]

offers a glaring contrast with the myth of the garden of the world which expressed the goals of free-soil expansion into the Mississippi Valley. But the dream was powerful enough to inflame a young printer and newspaperman in Keokuk, Iowa, Sam Clemens by name, who set out down the Mississippi in 1856 on his way to found a coca plantation on the Amazon.[31]

* Copyright, 1927, 1938, by Stephen Vincent Benét.

CHAPTER XIV

The New Calculus of Western Energies

The very fertility of the Northwest posed a dilemma with respect to the agrarian ideal. The hardy yeoman came out into the wilderness seeking land, and his search was rewarded: he acquired title to his farm and reared his numerous children amid the benign influences of forest and meadow. But the land was so fertile and the area under cultivation increased so rapidly that a surplus of grain and livestock quickly appeared, and the Western farmer was no longer content within the primitive pattern of subsistence agriculture.

Timothy Flint noted this problem as early as 1827: everyone who was willing to work had an abundance of the articles which the soil produced, far beyond the needs of the country, and it was a prevalent complaint in the Ohio Valley that this abundance greatly exceeded the chances of profitable sale.[1] A farmer who wants access to markets becomes interested in internal improvements. He agitates for highways and canals, for improved navigation of the rivers, and later for railways. Developing commerce creates depots like Cincinnati and Louisville — cities in the wilderness. The cities have banks and at least rudimentary manufactures such as the packing industry, and eventually it is they rather than the farming communities that set the tone of the West.

The rapid growth of cities and the development of an elaborate transportation system presaged a time when the West — at least the older West of the Ohio Valley and the Great Lakes — would no longer be predominantly agricultural. This process led to a greater and greater disparity between the agrarian ideal cherished by the society and the changing facts of its economic organization. The agrarian ideal had supplanted mercantilist theory in the latter part of the eighteenth century because at that time it had corresponded more closely to the actual state of affairs in the North American interior and had provided a much more reliable basis for charting the course of Western history in the immediate future. One index to its adequacy was the vigor and persuasive power of the symbol of the yeoman that had been developed from its premises. But by the 1830's a new calculus and new symbols were required to interpret the new West that was being created by forces wholly foreign to the agrarian assumptions. The greatest of the new forces was the technological revolution which set loose the power of steam — in boats on the western waters, somewhat later in railways, and eventually in factories. Steam power hastened the transition from subsistence to commercial agriculture, caused the accumulation of capital in units of unprecedented size, transformed the older western cities, and created new cities on a metropolitan scale like Cleveland and Chicago. These changes spelled the end of the simple economy which in the first stages of settlement had corresponded at least approximately to the agrarian ideal. In the long run the virtuous yeoman could no more stand his ground against the developing capitalism of merchant and banker and manufacturer in the Northwest than he could against the plantation system in the Southwest.

But the disparity between the static agrarian ideal and the drive of economic change was by no means clear to contemporary observers. Amos Stoddard, for example, the Massachusetts lawyer and veteran of the Revolution whom Jefferson appointed first governor of Louisiana, was equally enthusiastic over the future agricultural development of the vast regions on the Mississippi and the splendid tokens of industry and commerce which they would exhibit.[2] The prophetic picture of the West drawn in 1815 by Daniel Drake, a Cincinnati physician with an interest in social science, has much in common with Stoddard's:

the opinion that these states cannot support even a denser population than any in the East, is altogether groundless; the associations of wildness and ferocity — ignorance and vice, which the mention of this distant land has hitherto excited, must ere long be dissolved; and our

Atlantic brethren will behold with astonishment, in the green and untutored states of the West, an equipoise for their own. Debarred, by their locality, from an inordinate participation in foreign luxuries, and consequently secured from the greatest corruption introduced by commerce — secluded from foreign intercourse, and thereby rendered patriotic — compelled to engage in manufactures, which must render them independent — secure from conquest, or even invasion, and therefore without the apprehensions which prevent the expenditure of money in solid improvements — possessed of a greater proportion of freehold estates than any people on earth, and of course made industrious, independent and proud; — the inhabitants of this region are obviously destined to an unrivalled excellence in agriculture, manufactures and internal commerce; in literature and the arts; in public virtue, and in national strength.[3]

The West, in other words, can have everything; it does not need to choose among good ends.

The contemporary attitude toward the introduction of steam transportation upon the western waters illustrates the general failure to comprehend the magnitude of the new forces. Timothy Flint, for example, saw in the internal commerce of the valley merely a means of extending the society of virtuous yeomen over a wider area.[4] He depended on the old agrarian calculus, for which the technological novelties of canals and steamboats and railways had no real meaning. Few of his contemporaries were able to see into the future more clearly than he did. It is true that John Filson in the 1780's and Gilbert Imlay in the 1790's had understood that the experimental steamboat of James Rumsey of Virginia might be highly valuable for Kentucky.[5] And beneath the dazzled awe with which backwoodsmen greeted the first snorting river monsters there was a dim intimation of what these machines might do to the shape of society in the West. Morgan Neville of Pittsburgh and Cincinnati wrote in James Hall's *Western Souvenir* in 1829:

The rudest inhabitant of our forest . . . is struck with the sublime power and self-moving majesty of a steamboat; — lingers on the shore where it passes — and follows its rapid, and almost magic course with silent admiration. The steam-engine in five years has enabled us to anticipate a state of things, which, in the ordinary course of events, it would have required a century to have produced. The art of printing scarcely surpassed it in its beneficial consequences.[6]

Yet it was natural to be impressed most of all, as Flint was, by the sheer picturesqueness of the steamboat. In 1827 he wrote:

An Atlantic cit, who talks of us under the name of backwoodsmen, would not believe, that such fairy structures of oriental gorgeousness and splendor, as the Washington, the Florida, the Walk in the Water, the Lady of the Lake, &c. &c., had ever existed in the imaginative brain of a romancer, much less, that they were actually in existence, rushing down the Mississippi, as on the wings of the wind, or plowing up between the forests and walking against the mighty current "as things of life," bearing speculators, merchants, dandies, fine ladies, every thing real, and every thing affected, in the form of humanity, with pianos, and stocks of novels, and cards, and dice, and flirting, and love-making, and drinking, and champaigne, and on the deck, perhaps, three hundred fellows who have seen alligators, and neither fear whiskey, nor gunpowder.[7]

Flint had a literary interest in the way such an apparition brought a little of Paris, a section of Broadway, a slice of Philadelphia to the backwoods, troubling the minds of the young, and no doubt of their elders as well.

Other observers, however, were beginning to perceive that the steamboat had more important functions than these. As Henry S. Tanner remarked in his clear-headed *View of the Valley of the Mississippi*, "No other country on earth will be benefitted to an equal extent by this wonderful invention." [8] For one thing, the steamboat would tend to weld the nation into unity. Caleb Atwater of Ohio had pointed out as early as 1829 that the river system seemed designed by God to make the Americans one people.[9] James Hall declared that

the name of Fulton should be cherished here with that of Washington: if the one conducted us to liberty, the other has given us prosperity — the one broke the chains which bound us to a foreign country, the other has extended the channels of intercourse, and multiplied the ties which bind us to each other.[10]

Hardly to be distinguished from the function of the steamboat in fostering unity was its impetus to commercial prosperity, for trade was the force that was expected to bind the parts of the nation together. The genius of man was never more nobly employed, wrote the Mississippi historian John W. Monette in the middle of the 1840's, than when Fulton applied the force of steam to the

navigation of the western waters. This was all that the West required to make it the noblest and richest country on earth. Nature
and a great man had collaborated in the Mississippi Valley to
exhibit the triumph of steam in the exaltation of the American
Republic. Monette declared that the revolution wrought in the
West by this magical power was equal to any recorded in the
annals of history.[11]

Yet even when such men called the advent of steam a revolutionary force, they hardly seem to have realized what drastic
changes it was destined to work. The steam engine was not only
to subordinate the yeoman farmer to the banker and merchant of
the new Western cities; eventually it transformed him into a pro-
ducer of staple crops for distant markets and thus placed him at
the mercy of freight rates and of fluctuations in international com-
modity prices. One of the most significant facts of American intellectual history is the slow and inadequate fashion in which the
momentum of the new forces was appreciated, or, to put the
matter another way, the astonishing longevity of the agrarian ideal
as the accepted view of Western society. In 1846 an Illinois newspaper editor declared, "The West is agricultural; it has no manufactures and it never will have any of any importance." [12] This
opinion persisted long after it ceased to correspond to the facts.
Writers reporting on the World's Columbian Exposition at Chicago in 1893 for Eastern magazines note with naïve surprise that
the West had grown up into urbanism and industrialism while the
world's back was turned.[13] An observer as shrewd as Henry Adams
found it difficult to assimilate what had happened in the interior.
"That the Exposition should be a natural growth and product of
the Northwest," he wrote, "offered a step in evolution to startle
Darwin. . . ." [14]

Despite the educational impact of the Exposition, most Americans long continued to think of the West as a primitive agricultural region. The persistence of this idea throws into bold relief
the prescience of a solitary Western analyst who had begun fifty
years earlier to assess the industrial revolution in the Mississippi
Valley. This man was Jessup W. Scott, Whig editor of the Toledo
(Ohio) *Blade*. Between 1843 and the outbreak of the Civil War,
Scott contributed almost a score of articles to *Hunt's Merchants'*

Magazine of New York and *DeBow's Review* of New Orleans, discussing the probable future development of the West. In Scott's analysis agriculture had all but sunk out of sight. He fixed his attention on the forces of trade and industry that were rapidly becoming dominant, and protested against the prevalent notion that the destiny of the Mississippi Valley had "fixed it down to the almost exclusive pursuit of agriculture, ignorant that, as a general rule in all ages of the world, and in all countries, the mouths go to the food, and not the food to the mouths." [15] Scott likewise pointed out how outmoded was the doctrine of the primacy of maritime commerce.

Old ideas [he remarks], whether hereditary, or the fruit of early education, are hard to eradicate or supplant. The salt sea, and commerce, and great cities, are naturally associated together in the minds of Western Europeans, and their descendants in America. As naturally is the interior of a broad continent associated, in their minds, with gloomy forests, desert prairies, and slow movements in all the channels of business.

Both these old beliefs ceased to be valid when steam transportation came to the Mississippi Valley. Although the fact had been slow to register itself on the public mind, internal commerce had developed to such a point that it now rivaled foreign trade in importance.[16] Future changes resulting from the use of steamboats, locomotives, and Macadam highways would be even greater, for

these machines are but just being brought into use; and he is a bold man who, casting his eye 100 years into the future, shall undertake to tell the present generation what will be their effect on our North American valley, when their energies shall be brought to bear over all its broad surface.[17]

Scott used his new calculus to predict the course of Western society. He saw first of all that it would be urbanized. The use of machines in transportation and industry fostered "The increasing tendency to reside in towns and cities, which is manifested by the inhabitants of all countries, as they make progress in the arts and refinements of civilization." [18] Vast cities would grow up at points determined by transportation routes and the availability of raw materials and fuel for factories. In 1843 Scott declared that the dominant Western city would be near the Great Lakes, although he was not certain just where: it might be Cleveland, or Maumee, Ohio (where he had once lived), or Detroit, or Chicago.[19] But regardless of the exact location, "No logical induction, no mathematical demonstration can be clearer to our mind, than that here will come together the greatest aggregation of men in cities, — outrivalling in splendor as in magnitude, all which past ages have produced."[20]

The growth of huge cities would hasten the inevitable shift of dominance from the Atlantic seaboard to the interior: the central power of the continent was certain to move to the border of the Great Lakes and remain there permanently. For industrial developments sooner or later control the political element, so that the economic analyst need not concern himself with political forms.[21] Economic forces unrecognized a generation earlier gave new meaning to the old theme of the westward course of empire. The climactic moment in universal history which Gilpin had prophesied as a consequence of American access to the trade of Asia, Scott foresaw as the outcome of the economic development of the Mississippi Valley.

The westward movement of the Caucasian branch of the human family [he declared] from the high plains of Asia, first over Europe, and thence, with swelling tide, pouring its multitudes into the New World, is the grandest phenomenon in history.

The entrance of this tide into America was its climax: the whole process began to find its true meaning when population streamed into the great valley of the West.

While . . . we contemplate with patriotic pride [Scott asked in conclusion] the position which, as a nation, we hold in the world's affairs, may we not indulge in pleasant anticipations of the near approach of the time when the commercial and social heart of our Empire will occupy its natural place as the heart of the continent, near the centre of its natural capabilities.[22]

Scott shared with other writers about the West the belief that the Mississippi Valley guaranteed the continuance of the Union. The natural network of rivers and lakes, together with ten thousand miles of railways certain to be built within twenty years and a corresponding maze of telegraph wires, he wrote in 1852, would give to the entire population of thirty millions a community of ideas and interests which must soon mold them into homogeneousness of character, and "make us one country in heart as in government." [23] A year later he put the idea more epigrammatically: steam on the western waters and on the railways "has made our commerce one and our people a brotherhood." [24] As late as 1859 he was insisting that the iron bands of the railways, accentuating the physical unity of the great western plain, were daily strengthening the Union.[25] If Scott failed to appreciate the political and social forces that were about to bring on a Civil War in defiance of the growing forces of economic integration, his analysis has been triumphantly vindicated in the long run.

Nature and technology had combined in the Mississippi Valley to underwrite the American Union and to render all efforts to break it not only criminal but futile: on the eve of the crisis of 1860, the agrarian myth of the garden and the newer calculus of technological change led to the same conclusion. The idea of national unity was as clear a part of manifest destiny as had been the earlier doctrine of an inevitable expansion to the Pacific. A basic Western article of faith, it came out in pleas for the Union uttered by the two great Westerners, Douglas and Lincoln. In an unscheduled speech delivered in April 1861 at Bellaire, Ohio, not far from Wheeling, Douglas asked the question that secession raised for the West. He was appealing to the Virginians west of the Blue Ridge whose fathers had been Faulkner's constituents and whose great-grandfathers had stormed at John Jay for surrendering the American right to navigate the Mississippi. If the few states upon the Gulf could secede and close the Mississippi, how long would it be before New York would do the same, taxing every dollar's worth of Western produce that went out through her port, and every dollar's worth of imports that came in for the Western market? With "a great wave of emotion checking his utterance," he proclaimed the Western faith as if it were an incantation:

This great valley must never be divided. The Almighty has so arranged the mountain and the plain, and the watercourses as to show that this valley in all time shall remain one and indissoluble. Let no man attempt to sunder what Divine Providence has rendered indivisible.[26]

A few days later, in a speech at Springfield which moved one witness to write, "I do not think that it is possible for a human being to produce a more prodigious effect with spoken words," Douglas made his plea for the Union on the same grounds: "I ask every citizen in the great basin — between the Rocky Mountains and the Alleghanies . . . to tell me whether he is ever willing to sanction a line of policy that may isolate us from the markets of the world, and make us dependent provinces upon the powers that thus choose to isolate us?" [27]

After more than a year of war Lincoln invoked the idea of a geographical unity confirmed by technology in a last solemn effort to frame a compromise that would avert a fight to the finish. For him, as for Douglas, the physical fact of the valley of the Mississippi had an almost transcendent importance. "One generation passeth away," he quoted, "and another generation cometh. But the earth abideth forever."

It is of the first importance to duly consider and estimate this ever-enduring part [of the nation]. That portion of the earth's surface which is owned and inhabited by the people of the United States is well adapted to be the home of one national family, and it is not well adapted for two or more. Its vast extent and its variety of climate and productions are of advantage in this age for one people, whatever they might have been in former ages. Steam, telegraphs, and intelligence have brought these to be an advantageous combination for one united people. [28]

The "great interior region bounded east by the Alleghenies, north by the British dominions, west by the Rocky Mountains, and south by the line along which the culture of corn and cotton meets" would have fifty millions of population within fifty years if not prevented by political folly or mistake. The Interior Valley, especially the Northwest, was the great body of the Republic; the other parts were but marginal borders to it. Without searching the future to guess what industrialization would make of the valley, Lincoln was content to take it as it was, a region still predominantly agricultural — one of the most important in the world, yet no more than well launched toward its ultimate development. "Ascertain from statistics," he went on, in words that echo a hundred earlier statements, "the small proportion of the region which has yet been brought into cultivation, and also the large and rapidly increasing amount of products, and we shall be overwhelmed with the magnitude of the prospect presented." [29] Speaking directly to the men of this agricultural Northwest he argued that because of their need for outlets to markets they could not conceivably accept a negotiated peace and the independence of the Confederacy:

this region has no seacoast — touches no ocean anywhere. As part of one nation, its people now find, and may forever find, their way to Europe by New York, to South America and Africa by New Orleans, and to Asia by San Francisco; but separate our common country into two nations, as designed by the present rebellion, and every man of this great interior region is thereby cut off from some one or more of these outlets, not perhaps by a physical barrier, but by embarrassing and onerous trade regulations. . . . These outlets, east, west, and south, are indispensable to the well-being of the people inhabiting and to inhabit this vast interior region. *Which* of the three may be the best is no proper question. All are better than either, and all of right belong to that people and to their successors forever. True to themselves, they will not ask *where* a line of separation shall be, but will vow rather that there shall be no such line. [30]

Seen in the vast perspective of the geography of the continent, the civil strife was but an incident. It did not spring "from our permanent part, not from the land we inhabit; not from our national homestead." [31] The continent itself demanded union and abhorred separation. In the end it would force reunion, however much of blood and treasure the separation might have cost.

CHAPTER XV

The Agrarian Utopia
in Politics: The Homestead Act

During the crisis that preceded the Civil War the ideal of a yeoman society in the West exerted a powerful, perhaps even a decisive influence on the course of American history by shaping the policy of the Republican party.

The Republican platform of 1860, on which Abraham Lincoln was elected president, was a more cautious document than the platform on which Frémont had been defeated four years earlier. The abolitionist fervor of 1856 was cooling. The platform of 1860 opposed extension of slavery into the territories and criticized the proslavery Dred Scott decision of the Supreme Court, but it declared against any interference with slavery in states where it already existed. The position with regard to slavery, in fact, had been weakened to such a degree that it was quite unsatisfactory to radical abolitionists.[1]

These changes were in large part concessions to Western opinion, especially that of the southern Ohio Valley as contrasted with the northern lake region, to which much New England radicalism had been transplanted. Horace Greeley, who played a dominant role in writing the platform, had doubted in 1859 whether the Republicans could get a hundred electoral votes on a square slavery issue.[2] Everyone knew that the party could not succeed unless it carried the formerly Democratic Northwest. And in the Northwest, among recent German immigrants as well as among the descendants of pioneer settlers, the most important issue was the Homestead Bill, which had been vetoed by Democratic President Buchanan in 1858. "This Homestead measure overshadows everything with us, and throughout the West," wrote a Minnesota politician in 1860.[3]

The Republicans had been relatively slow to take up the issue of "land for the landless." It is true that when the future leaders of the party first turned their attention to the West they had translated their repudiation of slavery on abstract moral grounds into the slightly more concrete doctrine of "free soil." But this doctrine was not associated in their minds with agrarian tradition. They had related it to the older themes of the American empire and the passage to India. Such, for example, was the basis on which William H. Seward of New York demanded the admission of California in 1850.

The Atlantic States [he declared, in the accents of Benton and Gilpin], through their commercial, social, and political affinities and sympathies, are steadily renovating the Governments and the social constitutions of Europe and Africa. The Pacific States must necessarily perform the same sublime and beneficent functions in Asia. If, then, the American people shall remain an undivided nation, the ripening civilization of the West, after a separation growing wider and wider for four thousand years, will, in its circuit of the world, meet again and mingle with the declining civilization of the East on our own free soil, and a new and more perfect civilization will arise to bless the earth, under the sway of our own cherished and beneficent democratic institutions.[4]

Speakers attacking Stephen A. Douglas's Kansas-Nebraska bill in 1854 still linked the issue of free soil with the passage to India. Edward Everett of Massachusetts pointed out that the proposed territories beyond the Missouri

occupy a most important position in the geography of this continent. They stand where Persia, Media, and Assyria stood in the continent of Asia, destined to hold the balance of power — to be the centres of influence to the East and to the West. . . . The commerce of the world, eastward from Asia, and westward from Europe, is destined to pass through the gates of the Rocky Mountains over the iron pathways which we are even now about to lay down through those Territories. Cities of unsurpassed magnitude and importance are destined to crown the banks of their noble rivers.[5]

Such a strategic area, he believed, must not be allowed to come under the domination of the slave power. Predicting that within two decades a million freemen from Asia would be pouring into the trans-Mississippi every year, Seward declared in 1854 that the territories must be kept open for them.[6]

These arguments, like the free-soil doctrine itself, were essentially negative with regard to the internal development of the West. The position was simply that slavery must be kept out of areas where it was not already established. There was some positive meaning in the notion that the way must be kept clear for Asiatic trade and immigration, but it was not a very compelling argument because the theme of the passage to India had lost much of its fascination after the acquisition of Oregon and California. The position of Seward and Everett in 1854 was weak also because it emphasized maritime trade according to the assumptions of an archaic mercantilism instead of invoking the agrarian calculus that had been the basis of Western social thought for almost half a century. Seward showed an even more striking failure to understand the attitude of the West when he said that Douglas's squatter-sovereignty doctrine made "the interested cupidity of the pioneer" the arbiter of national policy.[7] This unflattering description of the Western yeoman and of the land-hunger which Douglas meant to gratify in his Kansas-Nebraska bill was a condemnation of the very impulses which advocates of homestead legislation proposed to foster. If the Republican Party was to challenge the Democratic Douglas's hold on the Northwest, it would have to develop a critique of squatter sovereignty in Western terms.

Benjamin F. Wade of Ohio moved toward this strategic goal when he declared that Douglas's doctrine invited the Western yeoman to occupy the territories beyond the Missouri in company with slaves from the South.

Gentlemen know that the high-minded free man of the North, although not blessed with property, has nevertheless a soul, and that he cannot stoop to labor side by side with your miserable serf. He has never done it — he never will do it. It was an unlucky word from the gentleman from Kentucky when he said, if he cannot labor in that way, let him go somewhere else. Is that the democracy of the Chairman of the Committee on Territories [Douglas]? Let him tell the yeomanry of Illinois — the hard-fisted laboring man of that great State — that this is the principle upon which he acts; that this Territory is to be covered over with slaves and with masters, and that his proud constituency are to go out there and work side by side, degrading themselves by working upon a level with your miserable slaves.[8]

The anti-Negro feeling of such remarks was hardly compatible with the moral principles of abolitionism, and Senator Archibald Dixon of Kentucky tried to impale Wade on the horns of a dilemma by asking him whether the Negro slave was not equal to the white farmer.[9] But the farmers of the Northwest were not as a group pro-Negro. Free-soil for them meant keeping Negroes, whether slave or free, out of the territories altogether. It did not imply a humanitarian regard for the oppressed black man.

Merely criticizing Douglas was still not formulating a positive program for the territories. Although individuals like Galusha A. Grow who were prominent in the formation of the Republican party had taken up the homestead principle before 1856, and although homestead bills had been twice passed by the House, the Republican platform of that year was silent on the subject. "Free soil, free labor, and Frémont" was conceived as an antislavery slogan rather than as a program for the West. But between 1856 and 1860 the homestead principle with its utopian blueprint for developing the trans-Mississippi region became official Republican doctrine. This change represented a victory for the conservative wing of the party. It was a bid for votes that could not be attracted to the antislavery cause. The platform of 1860, demanding free homesteads for actual settlers, showed that the Republicans meant to capture the myth of the garden and the symbol of the hardy yeoman, and thus to command the imaginations of Northwestern farmers. It was to this end also, in large part, that they abandoned the stern moral condemnation of slavery in general that had characterized the original policy of the party, and merely opposed the extension of slavery into the territories. Although John R. Commons went too far in saying, "Only because slavery could not live on one-hundred-and-sixty-acre farms did the Republican party come into conflict with slavery," his overstatement contains more than a half-truth.[10]

The basic demand for more liberal treatment of settlers on the public domain, of which the Homestead Act was the ultimate expression, had originated in slave states of the Southwest. During the 1820's and 1830's its principal spokesmen were Benton and

James A. Walker of Mississippi; in the 1840's they were joined by Andrew Johnson of Tennessee. All these men were Democrats, and all were, in varying degrees, proslavery, although Benton eventually opposed slavery extension. As late as the session of 1852–1853 the issue regarding homestead legislation was drawn, not between proslavery and antislavery groups, but between West and Northeast — between Western Democrats and Eastern Whig capitalists. It was only after the passage of the Kansas-Nebraska Act, when the Republican party cohered about aggressive free-soil principles, that Southern opinion became unified in opposition to the homestead policy. The Southwest, motivated by fear of the Republican party, now abandoned alliance with the Northwest and joined the Southeast in opposing the Homestead Bill; in 1859 thirty Southwestern Congressmen voted against the measure.[11] A realignment of forces also took place in the Northeast, which down to 1854 had been almost evenly divided on the homestead proposal but in 1859 voted seventy to one in favor of it.[12] The Republican party had established a working coalition between Northeast and Northwest, and a clear North-South cleavage had replaced the equally clear East-West cleavage of prior decades.

The intellectual framework of the Republican homestead program, the theory that rationalized the almost instinctive land-hunger of the West, was the National Reform doctrine propounded by George Henry Evans and his followers. As a leader in the New York Workingmen's party and an associate of Robert Dale Owen and Frances Wright, Evans represented the Eastern labor movement and currents of international radicalism. His contention was that free land in the West would attract unemployed or underpaid laborers from industrial cities and thus "prevent such a surplus of workmen in factories as would place the whole body (as now) at the mercy of the factory owners."[13] National Reform influenced Republican theory through such leaders as Greeley, who had been converted to Evans's program in 1846, and Galusha Grow.[14]

Aside from its theory about free land and the labor surplus, National Reform relied heavily on the idea that the only valid title to land was that of the man who applied his own physical labor to its cultivation. Derived from John Locke and the conception of

natural rights, and carefully expounded by Jefferson,[15] this argument offered strong intellectual support to the defense of free
labor against the slavery system, and gave defenders of the homestead principle a basis for denying that their proposal called for
donations of land as outright charity.[16] The settler who perfected
his title by five years' cultivation of the soil had paid for his land
in the only currency which theorists of this school regarded as
valid. A corollary of the National Reform platform was a stout
resistance to land monopoly by speculators, whose titles were
quite invalid from the standpoint of the labor theory of property.
Attacks on land monopoly touched an ancient bitterness in the
West. The practical expression of the antimonopoly creed was the
proposal, often made but always voted down, to limit the total
holdings which any one person might accumulate.[17] The principle
should have dictated also a repeal of all existing provisions through
which public land might be acquired by any means except actual
settlement. But this likewise proved politically impossible, and the
Homestead Bill was enacted in 1862 without the repeal of the pre-
emption provision or other procedures for what amounted to the
sale of public land.[18]

Opposition to slavery, the safety-valve theory, and the labor
theory of property were still but subsidiary parts of the case for
the Homestead Bill as it was presented to Western voters. These
arguments, although likely to appear in any speech favoring the
bill, were largely Eastern in origin. The strongest appeal of
the homestead system to the West, an appeal which touched the
deepest levels of American experience in the nineteenth century,
lay in the belief that it would enact by statute the fee-simple empire, the agrarian utopia of hardy and virtuous yeomen which had
haunted the imaginations of writers about the West since the time
of Crèvecœur. This theme Western representatives in the 1850's
developed with a rhetoric which overlays but cannot entirely
smother a real conviction. Besides Andrew Johnson, the pioneer
agitator, the leading spokesmen for what was already becoming
the older West were Representatives George W. Julian and Cyrus
L. Dunham, of Indiana; and Galusha A. Grow, whose constituency in the up-country of northern Pennsylvania had strong ties
with the Ohio Valley. These men were intellectual heirs of Thomas

Jefferson and Andrew Jackson, whom they quoted as conclusive authorities on the nature of the American tradition. Grow had an especially close tie with the Jackson tradition through intimate association with the aging Benton during his first term in Congress.[19]

In view of the wide currency of the ideal of the yeoman society the question of these men's immediate sources is hard to settle, if indeed it is important. We need merely note that the time-honored themes of the agrarian tradition functioned with unimpaired vigor for such a man as Representative Julian in his speeches in favor of offering free land to settlers.

The life of a farmer [Julian declared in 1851] is peculiarly favorable to virtue; and both individuals and communities are generally happy in proportion as they are virtuous. His manners are simple, and his nature unsophisticated. If not oppressed by other interests, he generally possesses an abundance without the drawback of luxury. His life does not impose excessive toil, and yet it discourages idleness. The farmer lives in rustic plenty, remote from the contagion of popular vices, and enjoys, in their greatest fruition, the blessings of health and contentment. . . . The pleasures and virtues of rural life have been the theme of poets and philosophers in all ages. The tillage of the soil was the primeval employment of man. Of all arts, it is the most useful and necessary. It has justly been styled the nursing father of the State; for in civilized countries all are equally dependent upon it for the means of subsistence.[20]

Most of the ideas advanced by Julian and his colleagues, in fact, had been long familiar in discussion of the West. Representative Dunham's speech supporting a homestead bill in 1852 sounds like Filson or Imlay:

I believe, Mr. Chairman, that we were placed here for wise and glorious purposes — to restore poor, downtrodden humanity to its long-lost dignity; to overthrow despots, and shed abroad the genial influence of freedom; to break the bonds of the oppressed, and bid the captive go free; to liberate, to elevate and restore . . . by the sword of the spirit, by the genius of our institutions. And this very bill will do more to extend the influence of those institutions and make them popular; more to break the chains of tyranny, and give an impetus to freedom, than anything else you possibly could do.[21]

Another traditional idea invoked by Western spokesmen was the conception of nature as a benevolent guardian of man. Dunham makes a surprising allusion to Tecumseh in this connection:

I have often admired that lofty expression of the great Tecumseh — for he was great, though a savage; he was one of Nature's great men, made in God's own image, he spoke God's own language — the voice of nature — who, when General Harrison . . . was negotiating a treaty with him . . . , [and] ordered his interpreter to set the great chief a chair, and to tell him that his father desired him to take a seat . . . drew himself up, only as can he who feels the dignity of a man, and replied: "My father! The Great Spirit is *my* father, the earth is my mother, and upon her bosom will I repose." And he stretched himself upon the bosom of our common mother.[22]

This fragment from the saga of the noble savage was urged as an argument for the Homestead Bill, which would allow the Western farmer to repose on the bosom of the American earth and draw sustenance from it. There was even a mystical conception of nature hidden beneath the rhetoric of Seward's declaration before an Ohio audience in 1848: "Slavery demands a soil moistened with tears and blood — Freedom a soil that exults under the elastic tread of man in his native majesty." [23]

But the cult of nature was of minor importance beside the symbol of the yeoman for whom the official homestead of 160 acres was designed. The seizure of this symbol by Republican orators in the campaign of 1860 enlisted in their cause the undefined but powerful force which the imagination of the masses of voters always exerts in political crises. Advocates of the Homestead Bill sincerely believed that the yeoman depicted in the myth of the garden was an accurate representation of the common man of the Northwest, and this belief was evidently shared by thousands of voters. As a pivot on which turned momentous issues, the yeoman had been — in theory — entirely freed from the stigma of inferiority. North of the Ohio, declared Julian in 1851,

The owners of the soil are in general its cultivators, and these constitute the best portion of the population. Labor, instead of being looked upon as degrading, is thus rendered honorable and independent.

The inference for public-land policy was clear:

Donate the land lying within our territories, in limited plantations, to actual settlers whose interest and necessity it will be to cultivate the soil with their own hands, and it will be a far more formidable barrier against the introduction of slavery than Mr. WEBSTER's "ordinance of nature," or even the celebrated ordinance of Jefferson. Slavery only thrives on extensive estates. In a country cut up into small farms, occupied by as many independent proprietors who live by their own toil, it would be impossible — there would be no room for it. Should the bill now under discussion become a law, the poor white laborers of the South, as well as of the North, will flock to our territories; labor will become common and respectable; our democratic theory of equality will be realized . . . and thus physical and moral causes will combine in excluding slavery forever from the soil. The freedom of the public lands is therefore an anti-slavery measure.[24]

Julian was right. Although the demand for a more liberal land policy had originally had nothing to do with the slavery question, and although supporters of the Homestead Bill could be quite indifferent to the rights of the Negro,[25] the image of the yeoman with which the farmers of the Northwest identified themselves was a free-soil symbol. The classless society of the fee-simple empire had no place for the Negro. If in this respect it was deficient in moral grandeur, it at least excluded slavery from its vision of the future. The point was made throughout the 1850's by free-soil spokesmen, and amply warranted the charge of Senator James M. Mason of Virginia that the homestead principle was "the Emigrant Aid Society's policy upon a wider scale . . . purchased at the price of the public domain gratuitously given."[26] The ideal society which Julian described, with its division of the soil into small farms tilled by their owners, the husbandmen's virtuous attachment to their firesides and their country, the rapid advance of population, the great number of churches and schoolhouses, depended upon a single basic principle which was true at once to agrarian tradition and to antislavery doctrine: "The distribution of landed property, and its cultivation by freemen."[27]

CHAPTER XVI

The Garden and the Desert

At the end of the Civil War the time came at last for the realiza-tion of the dream of an agrarian utopia in the West on the basis of the Homestead Act.[1] In 1865 the frontier of agricultural settle-ment ran roughly along the ninety-sixth meridian in eastern Kan-sas and Nebraska. The surge of westward advance which followed the war soon pushed the frontier out upon the subhumid plains. By the middle 1870's, lands were being taken up in areas where the rainfall was likely to decline every few years below the level necessary for the traditional type of farming on which the myth of the garden had been based. The undependable rainfall posed a problem that for two decades and more proved insoluble. Time and again, between 1870 and 1890, settlement advanced far out upon the plains in periods of relatively high rainfall, only to be forced back by the dry period which always followed.[2] Not until special seeds were developed and special methods of cultivation devised — the techniques of "dry farming" — was agriculture fea-sible on a large scale beyond the one hundredth meridian.[3] And even with these new weapons the Western farmer has continued to fight a drawn battle with an inhospitable terrain. After a half century of struggle, the drought of the 1930's turned much of the settled portion of the plains into a dust bowl and raised the ques-tion whether the region had not been seriously overpopulated.[4]

But in the decade following the Civil War the impetus of the westward movement and the implied pledge of the victorious Republican party to develop the West were uncontrollable forces urging the agricultural frontier onward. On the level of the

imagination it was therefore necessary that the settler's battle
with drought and dust and wind and grasshoppers should be supported by the westward extension of the myth of the garden. In
order to establish itself in the vast new area of the plains, however, the myth of the garden had to confront and overcome another myth of exactly opposed meaning, although of inferior
strength — the myth of the Great American Desert.

The conception of the Great Plains that had prevailed generally in this country during the first half of the nineteenth century did full justice to, if indeed it did not grossly exaggerate, the
aridity which settlers encountered there after the Civil War.[5] The
existence of an uninhabitable desert east of the Rocky Mountains
had first been announced to the American public in 1810, when
Zebulon M. Pike published the journal of his expedition across the
plains to the upper Rio Grande Valley. His assertion that the vast
treeless plains were a sterile waste like the sandy deserts of Africa
was an impressive warning to the prophets of continuous westward advance of the agricultural frontier.[6] Americans were used
to judging the fertility of new land by the kind of trees growing on it;[7] a treeless area of any sort seemed so anomalous that
settlers were long reluctant to move out upon the fertile and well-
watered prairies of Illinois. The absence of trees over great ex-
panses of the plains was regarded as proof that the area was unsuited to any kind of agriculture and therefore uninhabitable by
Anglo-Americans. Henry M. Brackenridge, the son of the novelist,
who had made a trip up the Missouri River with a fur trading
brigade, wrote in his *Views of Louisiana* in 1817 that

the prevailing idea, with which we have so much flattered ourselves,
of these western regions being like the rest of the United States, suscep-
tible of cultivation, and affording endless outlets to settlements, is
certainly erroneous. The [Indian] nations will continue to wander over
those plains, and the wild animals, the elk, the buffaloe, will long be
found there; for until our country becomes supercharged with population, there is scarcely any probability of settlers venturing far into
these regions. A different mode of life, habits altogether new, would
have to be developed.[8]

The existence of the desert was confirmed by the narrative of
the Stephen H. Long expedition, published in 1823,[9] and it was

mentioned again and again by writers about the West during the next three decades. When the sudden upswing in travel toward the Pacific Coast began in the late 1830's, the supposed desert, given brilliant but sinister coloring by the accounts of overland travelers' sufferings from hunger and thirst, received even wider publicity. Thomas J. Farnham, who went out from Illinois to Oregon in 1839, wrote that the Great American Desert, stretching three hundred miles east of the Rocky Mountains, was a scene of desolation scarcely equaled on the continent, a "burnt and arid desert, whose solemn silence is seldom broken by the tread of any other animal than the wolf or the starved and thirsty horse which bears the traveller across its wastes." [10] Or, to take only one other example of what the reading public might learn of the region beyond the Missouri, Francis Parkman described the plains as a barren, trackless wilderness extending more than four hundred miles east of the mountains. Sketching the dreary and monotonous scene as his party approached the valley of the Platte River in present central Nebraska, he wrote:

Before us and behind us, the level monotony of the plain was un-broken as far as the eye could reach. Sometimes it glared in the sun, an expanse of hot, bare sand; sometimes it was veiled by long coarse grass. Huge skulls and whitening bones of buffalo were scattered every where. . . .[11]

Such travelers, coming from the familiar well-watered regions east of the Mississippi, were likely to be more vividly impressed by the sterility of the plains than were seasoned Westerners, who had learned that the short-grass country and even the true desert beyond the Rockies were not entirely without resources for sustaining life. Thus Edwin Bryant, a Kentucky newspaperman who went out to California in 1846, noted in his journal that the aridity and desolation of western Nebraska proclaimed it to be uninhabitable by civilized man.[12] The important word in Bryant's statement is "civilized." We have had occasion earlier to notice the prevalent belief that civilization depended upon agriculture. Although regions too dry for farming could be inhabited by migratory tribesmen following their flocks and herds, such peoples were considered uncivilized. They could not be integrated with American society and were therefore perpetual outlaws. The analogues were often mentioned — the Bedouins of the Arabian desert, the Tartars of Asiatic steppes.[13] Even if American frontiersmen should push out upon the plains and take up the pastoral life imposed upon them by the environment, they would become nomadic brigands, a menace to settled agricultural communities farther to the East.

The belief in the menacing Asiatic character of the plains had its origin in eighteenth-century English discussion of the Ohio Valley. Despite the unsuitability of the dense forests of Ohio and Kentucky for maneuvers on horseback, Edmund Burke had warned the House of Commons in 1775 that if the British government tried to prevent settlement in the trans-Allegheny, the American frontiersmen "would wander without a possibility of restraint; they would change their manners with the habits of their life; . . . would become hordes of English Tartars, and, pouring down upon your unfortified frontiers a fierce and irresistible cavalry, become masters of your governors and your counsellors. . . ." [14] Such ideas were much better suited to the Great American Desert; and in his *Astoria* Washington Irving developed them quite elaborately. On the plains, he wrote, beyond the limits of possible civilization,

may spring up new and mongrel races, like new formations in geology, the amalgamation of the "debris" and "abrasions" of former races, civilized and savage; the remains of broken and almost extinguished tribes; the descendants of wandering hunters and trappers; of fugitives from the Spanish and American frontiers; of adventurers and desperadoes of every class and country yearly ejected from the bosom of society into the wilderness.[15]

If the "civilized" Indians of the old Southwest were transported beyond the Mississippi, Irving foresaw they too would be gradually transformed by the environment into pastoral hordes like the rude peoples, half shepherd and half warrior, who roamed the steppes of Central Asia. Some would certainly form predatory bands, mounted on the fleet steeds of the plains — "A great company and a mighty host, all riding upon horses, and warring upon those nations which were at rest, and dwelt peaceably, and had gotten cattle and goods." [16]

This prediction concerning the desert was taken seriously by other writers. James D. B. DeBow, referring to Irving, wrote in 1846 that brigands and robber chieftains might grow into power on the plains, and ally themselves with the Indians to carry death and dismay to the agricultural frontier.[17] An anonymous writer for the unsentimental *Hunt's Merchants' Magazine* in 1851, prophesying the condition of the Far West in 1900, when he believed millions of civilized persons would be living on the Pacific slope, foresaw a continued state of barbarism in the interior basin. It would be overrun by a strange mixture of half-civilized, pastoral nomadic tribes, "A mixture of races, creeds, habits and customs, fusing into one people, and contending for the supremacy of language and tradition." [18] A milder version of the idea was presented by a writer for the *Southern Quarterly Review* in 1849, who predicted that the arid plains east of the Rocky Mountains would be inhabited only by trappers and miners, and those whom misanthropy or outlawry might lead into the remote desert.[19]

Entirely apart from such half-literary fantasies, the settled conviction that an uninhabitable desert stretched for hundreds of miles east of the Rockies was a matter of course in official circles until the eve of the Civil War. Lieutenant Gouverneur K. Warren, an explorer sent out upon the plains beyond the Missouri by the federal government, reported in the late 1850's that the ninety-seventh meridian was the western limit of ordinary agriculture.

> The people now on the extreme frontiers of Nebraska [he wrote] are near the western limit of the fertile portions of the prairie lands, and a desert space separates them from the fertile and desirable region in the western mountains. They are, as it were, upon the shore of a sea, up to which population and agriculture may advance, and no further.

If white men tried to live beyond the line of aridity, Warren asserted, they would have to lead a life similar to that of the Indian, depending upon their herds and flocks for support.[20] A substantially similar estimate of the plains was embodied in the elaborate reports of the Pacific Railway Surveys in the same decade;[21] and when the Union Pacific was chartered in 1862 it was conceived as a means of connecting the agricultural settlements of the Mississippi Valley with the settled portions of the Pacific Coast by offering a way through the imposing barrier of the desert and the mountains.[22]

The pressures of expansion, however, were certain to give rise eventually to an effort to occupy the plains. Such an undertaking would demand a revision of the forbidding image of an American Sahara. The imaginary figure of the wild horseman of the plains would have to be replaced by that of the stout yeoman who had for so long been the protagonist of the myth of the garden. As settlement moved up the valleys of the Platte and the Kansas rivers, the myth of the desert was destroyed and in its stead the myth of the garden of the world was projected out across the plains. The crux of the matter was rainfall, since it was rainfall alone that distinguished the abundantly fertile prairies of eastern Kansas and Iowa from the bleak uplands farther west. The imaginative conquest of the desert accordingly took the form of a proliferation of notions about an increase of rainfall on the plains.

The first move toward a revision of the myth of the desert came with the earliest systematic penetration of the plains in the overland trade from Independence, Missouri, to Santa Fé. Josiah Gregg, a Missourian, was engaged in the trade from 1831 to 1840. His *Commerce of the Prairies*, published in 1844, contains a passage that perfectly illustrates how the imagination of the American frontiersman went to work transforming the image of the desert:

> The high plains [wrote Gregg] seem too dry and lifeless to produce timber; yet might not the vicissitudes of nature operate a change likewise upon the seasons? Why may we not suppose that the genial influences of civilization — that extensive cultivation of the earth — might contribute to the multiplication of showers, as it certainly does of fountains? Or that the shady groves, as they advance upon the prairies, may have some effect upon the seasons? At least, many old settlers maintain that the droughts are becoming less oppressive in the West. The people of New Mexico also assure us that the rains have much increased of latter years, a phenomenon which the vulgar superstitiously attribute to the arrival of the Missouri traders. Then may we not hope that these sterile regions might yet be thus revived and fertilized, and their surface covered one day by flourishing settlements to the Rocky Mountains?[23]

It was superstition to attribute the increase of rain to the arrival of the Missouri traders, but the folk belief of the New Mexicans had a deep truth nevertheless. The traders announced the westward movement of the frontier. Not they perhaps, but the more numerous settlers who were coming after them were bearers of a force that was committed to the occupation of all the West, and that in the end enacted its purpose. If the Americans could not cause more rain to fall, they could build irrigation systems, and devise the techniques of dry farming: and these were, functionally, equivalent to increasing the rainfall. The myth of the garden was contrary to empirical possibility on the plains but it was true to the course of history.

The folk belief recorded by Gregg received little notice outside remote and inarticulate frontier areas until the surge of westward advance following the Civil War. Then, when the attention of the nation was brought to bear upon the plains by the construction of the Union Pacific and the settlement of Kansas and Nebraska, traveling journalists began picking up intimations that the rainfall might somehow be increased and sent back notices to newspapers in the East, especially to Horace Greeley's New York *Tribune*.[24] The idea of an increase in rainfall was given further currency by the earliest continuing scientific survey of the plains under the auspices of the federal government. This was the Geological and Geographical Survey of the Territories, which began work in Nebraska in 1867 under the directorship of Ferdinand V. Hayden. In his first report to the Secretary of the Interior Hayden adopted a theory resembling that which Gregg had set down more than two decades earlier; namely, that settlement of the country would cause an increase in the timber through artificial planting and protection against prairie fires.

It is believed [wrote Hayden] . . . that the planting of ten or fifteen acres of forest-trees on each quarter-section will have a most important effect on the climate, equalizing and increasing the moisture and adding greatly to the fertility of the soil. The settlement of the country and the increase of the timber has already changed for the better the climate of that portion of Nebraska lying along the Missouri, so that within the last twelve or fourteen years the rain has gradually increased in quantity and is more equally distributed through the year. I am confident that this change will continue to extend across the dry belt to the foot of the Rocky Mountains as the settlements extend and the forest-trees are planted in proper quantities.[25]

Although Hayden professed to speak in the name of science, his writings about the plains also express a determination to further the course of empire. "It is my earnest wish at all times," he wrote in 1871, "to report that which will be most pleasing to the people of the West, providing there is any foundation for it in nature." And he voiced the faith that had sustained all American frontiers:

I have watched the growth of this portion of the West [beyond the Mississippi] year by year, from the first rude cabin of the squatter to the beautiful villages and cities which we now see scattered so thickly over that country. . . . Never has my faith in the grand future that awaits the entire West been so strong as it is at the present time, and it is my earnest desire to devote the remainder of the working days of my life to the development of its scientific and material interests, until I shall see every Territory, which is now organized, a State in the Union.[26]

From Hayden's seminal exploit of destroying the myth of the desert and legislating the myth of the garden in its stead proceeded a school of theorists localized along the eastern margin of the plains where the agricultural frontier was advancing in the 1870's out into the arid region. This group of writers developed their ideas mainly in the successive Reports of Hayden's survey, which he edited more or less as one might edit a journal forming the mouthpiece of a literary coterie. The most energetic member of the Hayden group was Samuel Aughey, who after an apprenticeship on Hayden's survey became Professor of Natural Sciences at the newly established University of Nebraska, and State Geologist. Aughey in turn was associated with a speculative town builder and amateur scientist named Charles Dana Wilber. Near the culmination of the great boom period of the eastern plains these two men joined forces in extending the myth of the garden beyond the Missouri.

The myth had behind it the momentum of fifteen hundred miles of frontier advance across the Mississippi Valley. In addition, it coincided with the economic interest of every landowner in Kansas and Nebraska, and of every business enterprise in these new states. In restating the myth and applying it to the newer West, Aughey and Wilber were speaking for their people on all the levels of imagination, ingrained habit, stereotyped response, and the most rigorous calculation of potential profit from un-earned increment.

Their task was first to nail down once and for all a "scientific" demonstration that rainfall was destined to increase on the plains, and then to restate the myth of the garden with whatever revisions might be necessary to adapt it to the short-grass country. The first of these efforts, which happened to be furthered by a series of abnormally wet years after the Civil War, was carried through with an elaborate array of pseudoscientific notions [27] and eventually summarized (by Wilber) in the terse epigram, "Rain Follows the Plough" [28] — an inspired slogan which makes the oldest and most sacred of agrarian symbols the instrument whose magical stroke calls down the life-giving waters upon the land. Although it was Aughey who furnished the technical dressing for the argument, it was Wilber who grasped its imaginative overtones:

in this miracle of progress, the plow was the avant courier — the un-erring prophet — the procuring cause. Not by any magic or enchant-ment, not by incantations or offerings, but, instead, in the sweat of his face, toiling with his hands, man can persuade the heavens to yield their treasures of dew and rain upon the land he has chosen for his dwelling place. It is indeed a grand consent, or, rather, concert of forces — the human energy or toil, the vital seed, and the polished raindrop that never fails to fall in answer to the imploring power or prayer of labor.[29]

When Wilber says this is not an incantation, he means of course that it is.

After the plow and the prayer of labor have fertilized the plains, the agrarian utopia puts down its roots there. "The question is often asked of me," said Wilber in an address before a delega-tion sent out by a group of prospective immigrants from upstate New York, "what is the most important discovery you have made in Nebraska?" His answer is a summary of the agrarian tradition:

The most important of my discoveries in Nebraska is a quarter section of land. It is a museum of wonder and value. . . . Its surface was covered with fields of grain, whose market proceeds would more than pay for the land; and near the center was a spring and a grove which encircled a happy home filled with many tokens of prosperity and the merry music of children. Half concealed from view were barns, pens, coops, granary, shed for wagons, plows and machinery, all in good order, while farther away and central in a grass plat shaded by two friendly elms was a white school house. In the distance it looked like a pearl in an emerald setting.[30]

If the reader will compare this picture of the Nebraska plains with that of Francis Parkman, he will realize the power of the myth of the garden over men's perceptions and imaginations.

On the plains, as in the Ohio Valley, the economic security and independence of the yeoman society would offer a firm basis for upward development into cultural expression. Aughey was especially persuasive on this theme.

What then [he asked] may we legitimately expect of the people in Nebraska in the future? We have a right to expect that our school system will reach the highest possible stage of advancement — that the great mass of the people will become remarkable for their intellectual brightness and quickness. Along with this natural development and synchronizing with it, there will be developed a healthy, vigorous and beautiful race of men and women. Art culture will then receive the attention which it deserves. Music, painting, and sculpture will be cherished and cultivated for their own sake. The marvelous richness of our soils will give a true and lasting basis for prosperity and wealth. For be it remembered that agriculture in all its branches, endures the tests of time better than any other industry. It is also the best school of virtue for a nation. Happy the children that are trained to industry on a farm. More men and women of high character and endowments come from the farm, than from any other station. It is nearest to the heart of nature and nature's God. Though yet in its infancy, all these agencies for the prosperity and well-being of Nebraska are steadily at work, and in fulness of time will blossom into fullfilment of its early promise.[31]

Such is the society with which the myth of the garden filled the plains, in place of the adventurers and desperadoes, the brigands and robber chieftains whom the myth of the desert had placed there. The transformation had taken approximately thirty years. It was to endure less than a decade before the angry protest of the Populist movement brought a wholly different conception of the agricultural West before the public.

CHAPTER XVII

The Empire Redivivus

A second great boom in settlement beyond the Mississippi began
with the gradual recovery from the Panic of 1873 and lasted until
the disastrous winter of 1885–1886. During this period four new
trunk railways were pushed through to the Pacific, the range cattle
industry expanded northward over the plains into Wyoming and
Montana, and bonanza wheat farming with mechanized equipment made its appearance in suitable areas like the Red River
Valley of Minnesota and the San Joaquin Valley of California.
Between 1870 and 1880 the population of Kansas, Nebraska, and
Colorado increased from a little more than half a million to one
million, six hundred thousand. By 1883 Kansas led the Union in
corn production, with a yield of more than one hundred fifty million bushels. Settlement was almost equally rapid during the early
1880's in the Dakotas, the Pacific Northwest, and the Rocky Mountain states. The northern Atlantic seaboard, both in its own right
and as financial agent for Europe, was much more deeply involved
in this surge of agricultural expansion than it had been in any
previous one. Eastern capital financed the railroads, Eastern in-
surance companies bought the mortgages upon which so much of
the development of farm lands was based, many of the great cattle
companies were owned in the East or in Europe, and a large proportion of the new migration to the West — almost half of it, in
fact — was made up of European immigrants, Scandinavians, Ger-
mans, English, who entered Atlantic ports and were taken by railroad halfway across the continent to lands in the West.

It is not surprising that enthusiasm for the development of

the West became widespread in Eastern cities. The end of recon-
struction in the South allowed the attention of the public to turn
away from postwar problems. The triumphant Republican party
was committed to support of westward expansion by its platforms,
as well as by the interest of prominent members who held stock
in such Western enterprises as the transcontinental railways. The
conquest of the wilderness acquired some of the coloring of a
moral imperative that had characterized the struggle to preserve
the Union, as is indicated in the comment of an editorial writer
for *Scribner's Monthly* in 1872 who predicted that a certain adolescent boy would soon be "winning honor and doing his duty on
Western plains, tracing iron arteries through the heart of the continent, or seeing God's wonders face to face on the dizzy crests of
the sierras." [1]

A good illustration of Eastern acceptance of the boosting spirit
of the West in this period is the encyclopedic gazetteer compiled
by Linus P. Brockett under the title *Our Western Empire: or the
New West Beyond the Mississippi*, published in Philadelphia in
1882. Brockett, a native of Connecticut, was something of an official Republican writer, author of campaign biographies of Grant
and Colfax. His work is a systematic compilation based on hundreds of printed sources and an extensive correspondence with
men who knew the West firsthand. It is a digest of what the general public knew about the West at the height of the boom.

As might have been expected from his political associations,
Brockett enthusiastically assails the myth of the desert:

Nearly the whole region lying between the Mississippi River and the
Rocky Mountains was regarded fifty years ago as a desert land, incapable of any considerable cultivation, and given over to the buffalo,
the panther, and the prairie wolf; yet in no part of the vast domain of
the United States, and certainly in no other country under the sun, is
there a body of land equal in extent, in which there are so few acres
unfit for cultivation, or so many which with irrigation or without it, will
yield such bountiful crops.[2]

Brockett will not even admit that the interior basin beyond the
Rockies is a desert. The trans-Mississippi as a whole, he concludes,
"is destined to be the garden of the world." [3]

Having demonstrated the abundant fertility that furnishes the

economic basis for Far Western development, Brockett is prepared to elaborate the ancient dream of empire. He points out that
when Bishop Berkeley prophesied the future of America,

The empire which he then saw in vision . . . was composed of the
colonies, which lay between the Appalachian range and the Atlantic.
A population of not more than 1,200,000 was the nucleus of the future
empire.

Yet in this mere handful of people scattered along the Atlantic coast
from Maine to Georgia, lay the germ of the grandest empire this world
has ever seen — an empire destined to realize . . . the dictum of the
great Roman orator, — *Imperium et Libertas*. Here is, and is to be, *the
empire*, in its vastness of extent, its teeming population, its immensity
of resources, its ripe and universal culture, and its moral power over the
nations of the earth, and united with this *the liberty* which is the right
and privilege of a great people — a liberty which is not license, but law;
a government *of* the people, *for* the people, and *by* the people. And of
this great empire, the portion largest in population, most abundant in
resources, and foremost in all great enterprises is to be the region lying
between the Mississippi river and the Western Sea. To-day, this region
has more than eleven millions of inhabitants. In A. D. 1900 it will have
fifty millions. In A. D. 1950 who shall say how many? The capacity of
the country, in point of production, to sustain human life, has never yet
been tested; but if, when our arable lands are not one-twentieth developed, and our grazing lands can feed twenty times the cattle and sheep
now there, we are feeding fifty millions at home, and nearly twenty-five
millions in Europe, what can we not do when our resources are tasked
to their full extent? [4]

With these triumphant affirmations, the desert has been effaced
from the map, and the image of the garden of the world has been
spread over every square mile of the United States to the utter-
most western margin of the fortunate land.

The final merging of the notion of an American continental
empire and the myth of the garden yields a single image of great
imaginative force. But in the process the idea of empire has lost its
transitive reference. It no longer beckons onward toward the
Pacific and the Far East, but becomes, like the myth of the garden,
an introspective, even narcissistic symbol. The intelligible field of
speculation about the destiny of America is correspondingly nar-
rowed. Always devoid of reference to the past, and indifferent to
Europe except as a foil to make America seem more glorious by
contrast, the tradition of manifest destiny in this fashion loses the

concern with Asia that had formerly given it a certain breadth of intellectual reach.

The completion of the Union Pacific in 1869 had failed to draw European trade with the Orient across the United States, largely because the Suez Canal offered a cheaper route to European shippers. American imports from Asia proved to be but a negligible part of the freight carried by the transcontinental railways — less than two per cent, for example, in 1883.[5] The renewal of interest in Asia that was to come with the Spanish-American War and the occupation of the Philippines was still in the future. Instead, a century of speculation concerning the West and the destiny of America focussed itself about Walt Whitman's question of what the Great Mother Continent meant with respect to the human race. The answer of the 1880's may likewise be expressed in Whitman's words: the continent, especially the developing West, was "a refuge strong and free for practical average use, for man and woman." [6] This is a strongly antihistorical conception, the more so for the utopian overtones that are present in most of its versions. The character of the American empire was defined not by streams of influence out of the past, not by a cultural tradition, nor by its place in a world community, but by a relation between man and nature — or rather, even more narrowly, between American man and the American West.

This relation was thought of as unvaryingly fortunate. The myths of the garden and of the empire had both affirmed a doctrine of progress, of gigantic economic development, even though the myth of the garden at the same time implied a distrust of the outcome of progress in urbanization and industrialization. Neither American man nor the American continent contained, under this interpretation, any radical defect or principle of evil. But other men and other continents, having no share in the conditions of American virtue and happiness, were by implication unfortunate or wicked. This suggestion was strengthened by the tendency to account for any evil which threatened the garden empire by ascribing it to alien intrusion. Since evil could not conceivably originate within the walls of the garden, it must by logical necessity come from without, and the normal strategy of defense was to build the walls higher and stop the cracks in them.

These inferences from the myth of the garden will be recognized as the core of what we call isolationism. The attitude toward the past and toward the outside world which the doctrine implies, its foreign policy, is related through the myth of the garden to a domestic policy. The society which is imagined as growing up in the protected West is in theory (although hardly in fact) based on a minutely specified type of agriculture — the cultivation of family-sized farms by virtuous yeomen. The society is therefore homogeneous. There are no class divisions, no employers or employees, and the manners and tastes of each of the inhabitants resemble those of all the others. The notion of class cleavage, like any notable eccentricity of outlook or behavior, can be recognized on sight as alien and therefore depraved. But by a fortunate provision of nature, that guardian of Western (and American) interests, such aberrations are quickly remedied by the sanative influence of the soil, as is set forth in the doctrine of the safety valve.

One of the most striking characteristics of the myth of the garden of the world, with its tableau of healthy and virtuous farmers laboring in fertile fields, is its vulnerability to economic disaster. Its autarchic doctrine of economic progress received fullest development at the moment when the Northwest was becoming dependent on the world grain market and thus was being involved economically in the most intimate fashion with the course of events in Europe and even in Asia. Yet the claims and promises of the myth were based on faith in the beneficence of nature in the West, without regard to disasters that might threaten other regions or other countries. Indeed, since the myth affirmed the impossibility of disaster or suffering within the garden, it was unable to deal with any of the dark or tragic outcomes of human experience. Given a break in the upward curve of economic progress for the Western farmer, the myth could become a mockery, offering no consolation and serving only to intensify the sense of outrage on the part of men and women who discovered that labor in the fields did not bring the cheerful comfort promised them by so many prophets of the future of the West. The shattering of the myth by economic distress marked, for the history of ideas in America, the real end of the frontier period.

CHAPTER XVIII

Failure of the Agrarian Utopia

During the twenty years following the passage of the Homestead
Act, the image of the garden in the West, which had triumphed
over the image of the desert, became an article of national, or
at any rate Republican, faith. It is likely that most Americans
would have said during the 1880's that the Homestead Act had
triumphantly borne out the predictions of the 1860's. These predictions had been glowing in the extreme. When the Act passed
the Senate in May, 1862 Greeley congratulated the country on the
consummation of one of the most beneficent and vital reforms
ever attempted in any age or clime. The homestead system, he
said, would greatly lessen the number of paupers and idlers and
increase the proportion of "working, independent, self-subsisting
farmers in the land evermore." [1] It marked a new era in the history
of labor. Greeley was confident that hundreds of thousands, ultimately millions of dwellers in the city slums would go West to
hew out homes for their children. There could never again be
serious unemployment in the United States. [2] John W. Forney of
the Philadelphia *Press* asserted that toiling millions of freemen
could now gain a manly livelihood in the fertile West, where they
would make the wilderness blossom as the rose. [3] With unconscious irony William Cullen Bryant declared in the New York
Evening Post that speculators in the public domain had lost their
vocation. [4] Five years later Greeley was still saying to the unemployed city laborer:

if you strike off into the broad, free West, and make yourself a farm
from Uncle Sam's generous domain, you will crowd nobody, starve

nobody, and . . . neither you nor your children need evermore beg for Something to Do.[5]

Yet the Homestead Act almost wholly failed to have the results that had been predicted. It did not lead to the settlement of large numbers of farmers on lands which they themselves owned and tilled. Vast land grants to railways, failure to repeal the existing laws that played into the hands of speculators by allowing purchase of government lands, and cynical evasion of the law determined the actual working of the public land system. Between the passage of the Homestead Act in 1862 and 1890, only 372,659 entries were perfected. At most, two millions of persons comprising the families of actual settlers could have benefited from the operation of the Act, during a period when the population of the nation increased by about thirty-two millions, and that of the Western states within which most of the homesteading took place, by more than ten millions.[6] Railways alone, for example, sold more land at an average price of five dollars an acre than was conveyed under the Homestead Act. When the mechanical revolution introduced steam-driven tractors and threshing machines to the wheat regions of the Northwest, the pattern of small freehold subsistence farms was in danger of being wiped out.[7] The most telling index of this change is the ratio of tenancy. Eighteen per cent of the farms in Nebraska were operated by tenants in 1880, the first year for which records are available; in 1890 the figure had risen to twenty-four per cent.[8] By 1900 more than thirty-five per cent of all American farmers had become tenants, and the ratio was increasing rapidly.[9] Many farms technically listed as cultivated by their owners were so heavily mortgaged that the ostensible owner was hardly his own master.

Some of these disappointments had been prophesied by supporters of the homestead principle in the event that no restraints on speculators were written into the law.[10] National Reformers in particular had demanded that homesteads granted to settlers should be made inalienable and that individual holdings of land should be limited by statute.[11] But even these theorists could hardly have foreseen the extent to which the land laws would promote concentration of holdings. As early as 1871 an obscure

San Francisco printer named Henry George noted that the effect of the public land system was to encourage monopoly.

Already the custom of renting land [he declared] is unmistakably gaining ground, and the concentration of land-ownership seems to be going on in our older States almost as fast as the monopolization of new land goes on in the younger ones. And at last the steam plow and the steam wagon have appeared — to develope, perhaps, in agriculture the same tendencies to concentration which the power loom and the trip hammer have developed in manufacturing.

We are not only putting large bodies of our new lands in the hands of the few; but we are doing our best to keep them there, and to cause the absorption of small farms into large estates. . . . Concentration is the law of the time. The great city is swallowing up the little towns; the great merchant is driving his poorer rivals out of business; a thousand little dealers become the clerks and shopmen of the proprietor of the marble-fronted palace; a thousand master workmen, the employés of one rich manufacturer, and the gigantic corporations, the alarming product of the new social forces which Watt and Stephenson introduced to the world, are themselves being welded into still more titanic corporations. . . . Of the political tendency of our land policy, it is hardly necessary to speak. To say that the land of a country shall be owned by a small class, is to say that that class shall rule it; to say — which is the same thing — that the people of a country shall consist of the very rich and the very poor, is to say that republicanism is impossible. Its forms may be preserved; but the real government which clothes itself with these forms, as if in mockery, will be many degrees worse than an avowed and intelligent despotism.[12]

The failure of the homestead system has been analyzed frequently since George's day, but subsequent scholarship has done little more than add detail to the picture he drew. The agrarian utopia in the garden of the world was destroyed, or rather aborted, by the land speculator and the railroad monopolist. These were in turn but expressions of the larger forces at work in American society after the Civil War — the machine, the devices of corporation finance, and the power of big business over Congress. The Homestead Act failed because it was incongruous with the Industrial Revolution.

The impotence of the land reformers in their struggle against these new forces was due at least in part to the fact that their social theory offered them no aid in analyzing the actual situation and displaying the real issues. The advocates of the homestead principle, especially its Western supporters like Julian and Dunham, were employing ideas that had little relevance to the conditions of Western agriculture or American society in general in the late nineteenth century.

The theoretical weakness of these well-meaning men is evident in an article on "Our Land Policy" which Julian wrote for the *Atlantic Monthly* in 1879. He confesses that land speculation has probably increased rather than diminished during the seventeen years since the passage of the Homestead Act, and his denunciation of the public land system, especially the railroad land grants, is unsparing: he calls it a cruel mockery, a wicked compact between the government and land speculators, a policy which serves only the interest of great corporations.[13] Furthermore, he sees that proper administration of the public domain is not a minor matter, but the overshadowing question of American politics. Yet Julian has no remedy to urge, no proposal for containing the speculators and the corporations. All he can do is to restate the agrarian dream, denouncing monopoly in land because it

tends to aggregate our people in towns and cities, and render them mere consumers, instead of dispersing them over our territory, and tempting them to become the owners of land and the creators of wealth. It fosters the taste for artificial life and the excitements to be found in great centres of population, instead of holding up the truth that "God made the country," and intended it to be peopled and enjoyed. If our institutions are to be preserved, we must insist upon the policy of small farms, thrifty tillage, compact settlements, free schools, and equality of political rights, instead of large estates, slovenly agriculture, widely-scattered settlements, popular ignorance, and a pampered aristocracy lording it over the people.[14]

The myth of the garden of the world is still so vivid for Julian that he seems to think it can be realized by incantation.

The yawning gap between agrarian theory and the actual circumstances of the West after the Civil War must have contributed greatly to the disillusionment which comes out in the farmers' crusades of the last quarter of the century. The Western farmer had been told that he was not a peasant but a peer of the realm; that his contribution to society was basic, all others derivative and even parasitic in comparison; that cities were sores on the body politic, and the merchants and bankers and factory owners who lived in them, together with their unfortunate employees, wicked and decadent. He had been told that he was compensated for any austerity in his mode of life by being sheltered against the temptations of luxury and vice, and against the ups and downs of the market. His outstanding characteristic, according to the conventional notion, was his independence, which was understood to be at once economic self-sufficiency and integrity of character. For all these reasons, the farmer had been assured, correct political theory required the government to make a particular effort to guard his interests.

But after the Civil War Republican policy obviously favored the city against the country, the banker and the merchant against the farmer, the speculator against the settler. Whatever may have been the theoretical advantages of the simplicity of rural existence, the ostentatious luxury of the newly rich in the growing cities was paraded in the press with a kind of prurient fascination as evidence of what a free society might achieve by way of the good life. And the Western farmer found that instead of being independent, he was at the mercy not only of the Chicago and New York and Liverpool grain pits, but also of the railways and elevator companies and steamship lines upon which he must rely to get his crop to market. Even the nature that had formerly hovered over the garden of the world as a benign presence, a goddess of fertility and a dispensatrix of inexhaustible bounty, seemed on the high plains to become periodically an avenging deity who sent scourges of drouth, sandstorms, and grasshoppers upon suffering humanity. The scope of this contrast between image and fact, the ideal and the actual, the hope and the consummation, defines the bitterness of the agrarian revolt that made itself felt with increasing force from the 1870's onward. Hamlin Garland declared in 1892 that the high-sounding clichés had done serious mischief by masking the plight of the poverty-stricken Western farmer. Speaking through the character Radbourn in his powerful story "Lucretia Burns," he wrote: "Writers and orators have lied so long about 'the idyllic' in farm life, and said so much about the 'independent American farmer,' that he himself has remained blind to the fact that he's one of the hardest working and poorest-paid men in America." The farmers of the Northwest live in hovels; their wives fill the insane asylums. Both men and women work like fiends, yet their reward is only "a hole to hibernate in and to sleep and eat in in summer. A dreary present and a well-nigh hopeless future." [15]

To the same period belongs the sensational vogue of "The Man with the Hoe," by Edwin Markham, of Oregon and California, who assimilated the American farmer to the downtrodden and brutalized peasant of Europe from whom agrarian theorists had so carefully distinguished him earlier in the century. In Markham's poem, as in Garland's fiction, the once proud yeoman has become but a laborer in the field, a symbol of

> humanity betrayed,
> Plundered, profaned and disinherited. . .[16]

CHAPTER XIX

The Myth of the Garden
and Reform of the Land System

Although the myth of the garden had exerted a conservative influence on the slavery controversy, it had fostered a humanitarian
concern for the white laborer and landless farmer, and had,
through the idealism of the homestead principle, contributed to
the Republican victory of 1860. But as the forces of big business
consolidated their control of the party during and after the war,
crusaders like Julian were brushed aside. The new leaders of the
party evidently cared nothing for the dream of an agrarian utopia.

The ghosts of outmoded idealisms, however, are not easily laid.
As they lose their pertinence to a changed social setting, they often
become bad influences by lending themselves to the uses of men
who wish merely to confuse issues. The myth of the garden suf-
fered this fate. By the 1870's it could already be invoked to prevent reform of the land system. Julian's article in the *Atlantic* in
March, 1879 was timed to support a greatly needed revision of the
laws governing the public domain that was being urged by men
sharing the high purposes of the original proponents of homestead
legislation. But the image of the garden, with the quality of time-
lessness which is characteristic of myth, failed to reflect the new
conditions and now served to hinder these purposes instead of
furthering them.

The effort to revise the land laws was dictated by the low rainfall of the Far West. When advocates of the Homestead Act proposed to settle farmers on the public domain, they were assuming
that an indefinitely large quantity of fertile land lay waiting beyond

the frontier. This was the meaning which the notion of free land had had throughout the hundred years since the first wedge of settlement entered the Mississippi Valley; it was the intellectual basis of the myth of the garden. But if a barrier of aridity limited the quantity of available land, the myth and the agrarian program intended to realize it would have to undergo drastic revision. Agricultural settlement in areas of insufficient rainfall could bring nothing but suffering on a vast scale, waste, and eventual defeat. As the frontier moved out over the plains a remarkable man named John Wesley Powell, director of the federal Survey of the Rocky Mountain Region, came before the public with a warning that the old methods of agricultural settlement could no longer be relied on.[1] The hundred and sixty acre homestead was entirely inadequate to support a family in subhumid regions. On the high plains, cattle or sheep grazing would be the dominant type of land utilization. The homestead unit must therefore be greatly enlarged — perhaps to 2560 acres or even more.[2]

This, however, was only one aspect of Powell's proposals. Coördinated scientific surveys of the public domain would be necessary to ascertain what were the economic potentialities of the areas still unoccupied. It could no longer be taken for granted that substantially all the trans-Mississippi had uniform fertility and was therefore open to agricultural settlement of the familiar type. Scientific surveys would in turn involve reorganization of the various offices and bureaus having to do with the public lands.[3] Powell did not say so in set terms, but everyone understood that such a reorganization would provide opportunity for a housecleaning of the notoriously corrupt and inefficient General Land Office.

Powell first announced his conclusions about the public lands and hinted at his program of reform in a hearing before the House Committee on Public Lands in 1874. "All of the region of country west of the 100th or 99th meridian," he declared, "except a little in California, Oregon, and Washington Territory, is arid, and no part of that country can be cultivated, with the exceptions I have mentioned; no part of it can be redeemed for agriculture, except by irrigation." He urged scientific classification of the remaining public lands on the basis of their economic potentialities.[4] But the atmosphere of Washington under the Grant administration was not propitious for reforming crusades, and for several years Powell was unable to make progress toward securing action on his proposals. With the inauguration of Hayes in 1877, however, the situation changed. Carl Schurz became Secretary of the Interior with what he believed was a mandate to clean up the department, which included the Land Office. Seizing the opportunity, Powell submitted to Schurz on April 1, 1878, his celebrated *Report on the Lands of the Arid Region*. In May of that year yet another unexpected event occurred with the death of Joseph Henry, president of the National Academy of Sciences. O. C. Marsh, the Yale geologist, vice-president of the Academy, succeeded automatically to the presidency.[5] Marsh was sympathetic with Powell's program and familiar with the work of the various scientific surveys of the public lands that had been operating for more than a decade.

On June 20, 1878, Representative Abram Hewitt of New York, who was to prove the most effective Congressional leader of the effort to enact Powell's program, secured passage of a resolution asking the Academy to investigate the problem of the surveys and recommend a plan of reorganization.[6] This was understood to involve a study of the whole problem of the public lands. A committee of the Academy presented a report restating all the main features of Powell's program, and it was sent to Congress at the opening of the session in December. The legislative battle which followed was highly confused. At least three distinct issues were involved: (1) the question whether the remaining portions of the public domain were in fact sufficiently arid to require a revision of the land laws; (2) a bitter, half-personal rivalry among scientists in the employ of the government for control of the surveys of the public domain; and (3) the problem of corruption and lax enforcement in the General Land Office.

But two main political groupings appeared with approximately opposite views on all three of these questions, which were after all closely related to one another. The general optimism of the West, together with the economic interests of land speculators and others who stood to profit from continued settlement of the plains, was challenged by Powell's claim that the agricultural frontier was approaching a natural barrier. Speculators and monopolists who had established comfortable working arrangements with accommodating officials of the Land Office were aware that any far-reaching change in the administration of the public lands would disturb illegal practices which had been highly profitable for them. Among the scientists of the government surveys, the Western group found a loyal spokesman in Ferdinand V. Hayden, a professional rival of Powell, who was determined to resist reorganization or consolidation of the surveys if possible, and if the change could not be prevented, to dominate the new organization. Hayden realized that his best strategy lay in opposing consolidation outright, for control of any new organization would be determined by presidential appointment, and Hayes was evidently sympathetic with the associates of Schurz.

The Western group controlled the House Committee on Public Lands so that when the recommendations of the Academy were referred to that committee they were simply allowed to die. But Powell had found a powerful ally in Representative John D. C. Atkins of Tennessee, Chairman of the House Committee on Appropriations. When legislation embodying the proposed reforms was drawn up under the supervision of Hewitt, Powell, and Schurz, Atkins conceived the ingenious though unparliamentary maneuver of attaching it to the Judicial Appropriation Bill and the Sundry Civil Expenses Bill. The measures came on the floor of the House late in the session amid a press of other business, but they gave rise to prolonged debate. Supporting the proposed reforms were Atkins, Hewitt, James A. Garfield, and Peter D. Wiginton of California. The leading spokesmen for the hostile Western group were Delegate Martin Maginnis of Montana; Representatives Dudley C. Haskell of Kansas, Thomas M. Patterson of Colorado, and Horace F. Page of California; and in the Senate, Aaron A. Sargent, regarded as Collis P. Huntington's representative in Congress. It may be said briefly that the proposed legislation was passed in the House, defeated in the Senate, and sent to conference. All change in the land system was prevented but Hewitt was able to secure two concessions — the consolidation of the existing surveys in a single United States Geological Survey which Powell eventually headed, and the authorization of a Public Land

Commission to make an investigation.[7] The proposals of this Commission were in turn killed in the next Congress.[8]

When the Powell program in the form endorsed by the Academy first came upon the floor of the House in the winter of 1878–1879, it was attacked from many angles. It was described as an effort of "new-fledged collegiates" and "scientific lobbyists" to shut off the development of the West and create sinecures for themselves on the federal payroll.[9] It was falsely represented as threatening the system whereby lands were set aside for the support of public schools.[10] But the most telling argument against Powell's proposals was their violation of the myth of the garden.

Our agricultural lands . . . are limited [Representative Patterson declared], and the number of our population following agricultural pursuits must also be limited. But to have that number as great as possible, to swell it to its maximum, the plan of disposing of the public lands in small tracts . . . must be steadily adhered to.

The enlarged homestead grants proposed for the arid plains would destroy the time-honored ideal of a society of yeoman subsistence farmers. Under Powell's program, asserted Patterson with a fantastic distortion of its provisions, the plains

would in a few years be filled with baronial estates, with an aristocratic and wealthy few, each owning lands sufficient for a European principality, to the exclusion of that hardy and industrious people who, by tilling their own farms, by owning the small tracts upon which they live, not only produce material wealth but give to the nation the sturdy yeomanry that must be its bulwark in the hour of its supremest danger.[11]

Congressmen from the Western states all but unanimously sided with Patterson. Haskell pointed out that, with only two exceptions, all representatives from the nineteen states and territories containing public lands were opposed to any change in the existing land system. Those who favored it were mainly "from the New England States, from New York, from the older-settled portions of the country." [12] Yet not only Julian's and Henry George's contemporary exposés, but a mass of historical evidence accumulated since that time substantiates Julian's characterization of the land system in the 1870's as a cruel mockery, humane in its pretensions but in practice a speculator's dream. Were the Western representatives ignorant of these facts at a time when Easterners

like Hewitt and Atkins understood them? Or, if they did understand how completely the land system had failed to foster the
yeoman ideal cherished by its authors, are we to accuse them of
deliberately cynical misrepresentation?

One can hardly believe that any Western Congressman was
unaware how the land system operated. Yet it is also unlikely that
all of them were simply tools of the speculative interests which
were profiting from the operation of the system. Some outright
corruption certainly existed. But the unimpaired survival of the
dream of a yeoman society, with its idealism only slightly tar-
nished as yet by the sordid collapse of the homestead system,
threw over the facts an imaginative veil which furnished the pretext for a sincere, if shallow, opposition to so drastic a reforming
program as Powell's. He was asking a great deal. He was demanding that the West should submit to rational and scientific revision
of its central myth, and indeed that the nation at large should
yield one of the principal underpinnings of its faith in progress,
in the mission of America, in manifest destiny. This demand was
too stringent; the myth could not be transformed so easily. And
so long as it survived in its increasing irrelevance to the facts, it
could be manipulated by cynical men for selfish purposes.

CHAPTER XX

The Garden as Safety Valve

The Homestead Act failed to help the Eastern urban laborer as woefully as it failed to help the farmer in the West. This failure was less important than the frustration of the frontier farmer's effort to acquire land, but it shows equally well how poor a tool the agrarian tradition was for dealing with nineteenth-century industrial society. American agrarians had long maintained that the West, the free lands beyond the frontier, would operate as a safety valve to keep down social and economic conflict in the East. The best known exponent of this notion was Horace Greeley. His constant emphasis on it, in the New York *Tribune* and on the lecture platform, is the basis for his great but not wholly deserved reputation as a spokesman for the westward movement. Greeley's famous slogan, "Go West, young man, go forth into the Country" dates from 1837, when he turned to the plan of encouraging emigration westward as means of relief from the poverty and unemployment caused by the Panic.[1] In 1846, when he adopted Evans's National Reform program, he showed his loyalty to agrarian tradition by prophesying that the operation of the safety valve would establish an independent, substantial yeomanry on the public domain.[2] A typical explanation of Greeley's theory appeared in the *Tribune* in 1854:

> Make the Public Lands free in quarter-sections to Actual Settlers and deny them to all others, and earth's landless millions will no longer be orphans and mendicants; they can work for the wealthy, relieved from the degrading terror of being turned adrift to starve. When employment fails or wages are inadequate, they may pack up and strike westward to enter upon the possession and culture of their own lands

on the banks of the Wisconsin, the Des Moines, or the Platte, which have been patiently awaiting their advent since creation. Strikes to stand still will be glaringly absurd when every citizen is offered the alternative to work for others or for himself, as to him shall seem most advantageous. The mechanic or laborer who works for another will do so only because he can thus secure a more liberal and satisfactory recompense than he could by working for himself.[3]

The general notion embodied in this paragraph is very old and at various times has been invoked by writers of every possible political orientation. Frederick Jackson Turner found a version of it in a statement made by Governor John Winthrop of Massachusetts Bay in 1634.[4] It appeared in the eighteenth century in discussions of British colonial policy, to persuade the authorities that there was no danger of a significant development of manufacturing in the American colonies. The London merchant Joshua Gee, for example, wrote to the Council of Trade and Plantations in 1721 that colonists would not be attracted into manufacturing even though abundance of good workmen had emigrated to America.

The reason is plain [he argued], there is so much an easier subsistence to be made, where land is of so smal a value, by a little farme and a smal stock of cattle, that most of them slight manufacturies, and even in New England (the poorest of all the Colonies and the fullest of people) those few that do work will have near five times as much for manufacturing nails and other things, as is given for manufacturing in England . . . .[5]

Sir William Keith, royal customs official and Governor of Pennsylvania and Delaware, urged the British government in 1731 to make a grant of land for a colony beyond the Alleghenies on the ground that without such a new outlet for their energies, the colonists would be forced into manufacturing by a glut of tobacco, rice, and corn.[6] The anonymous author of the preface to the London edition of John Bartram's *Observations* (1751) used a similar argument to urge the central government to encourage frontier settlement in America.[7] In the same year Franklin stressed the idea in his *Observations Concerning the Increase of Mankind*, again with the intention of influencing British policy. "Labour will never be cheap here," he wrote, "where no Man continues long a Labourer for others, but gets a Plantation of his own. . . ."[8]

With the establishment of American independence the bearing of this kind of economic analysis was altered. The criterion of policy was no longer the interests of British merchants. Instead, a developing American nationalism embraced the humanitarian conception of the West as a refuge for the oppressed of all the world. George Washington wrote with unaccustomed playfulness to Lafayette at the end of the Revolution:

I wish to see the sons and daughters of the world in Peace and busily employed in the . . . agreeable amusement of fulfilling the first and great commandment — *Increase and Multiply*: as an encouragement to which we have opened the fertile plains of the Ohio to the poor, the needy and the oppressed of the Earth; anyone therefore who is heavy laden or who wants land to cultivate, may repair thither & abound, as in the Land of promise, with milk and honey . . . .[9]

A similar conception of the function of the West furnished Jefferson with a perfectly logical basis for revising his theoretical hostility to the growth of industry in the United States. In 1805, when he was contemplating a new edition of the *Notes on Virginia*, he wrote that he planned to qualify several expressions in the nineteenth chapter which attacked manufacturing. These expressions, he said, applied only to "the manufacturers of the great cities in the old countries, at the time present." In Europe the poverty of urban laborers had begotten a depravity, a dependence and corruption which would make them undesirable citizens in a republic. But America had not yet reached the condition of Europe, because of the fortunate influence of free land:

As yet our manufacturers [that is, industrial workers] are as much at their ease, as independent and moral as our agricultural inhabitants, and they will continue so as long as there are vacant lands for them to resort to; because whenever it shall be attempted by the other classes to reduce them to the minimum of subsistence, they will quit their trades and go to laboring the earth.[10]

Such a hopeful conception of the role of the West is one of the principal foundations of the myth of the garden. It occurs on every hand, and in a wide variety of forms through most of the nineteenth century. New England industrialists, for example, were accused of trying to restrict westward emigration in order to maintain a surplus of laborers and keep down wages. It was such

a charge by Senator Robert Y. Hayne in 1829 that led to the
famous Webster-Hayne debate.[11] Hayne's colleague in this foren-
sic encounter, Thomas H. Benton, developed the charge against
New England at length, inveighing against

the horrid policy of making paupers by law — against the cruel legislation which would confine poor people in the Northeast to work as
journeymen in the manufactories, instead of letting them go off to new
countries, acquire land, become independent freeholders, and lay the
foundation of comfort and independence for their children.

Eastern mill owners, he declared,

are now realizing what was said by Dr. Franklin forty-five years ago,
that they need great numbers of poor people to do the work for small
wages; that these poor people are easily got in Europe, where there was
no land for them, but that they could not be got in America until the
lands were taken up. . . . This resolution, which we are now consider-
ing, is the true measure for supplying the poor people which the
manufactories need.[12]

Twenty years later Congressman Josiah Sutherland of New
York opposed the Homestead Bill for reasons exactly like those
Benton had attributed to factory owners. The bill, he said, would
take labor from the manufacturing states to the land states, increasing the cost of labor and thus the cost of manufactures.[13]

Karl Marx accepted the same theory about the relation between the status of American laborers and free land.[14] It formed
an important part of the radical tradition in this country, especially through the influence of George Henry Evans and his National Reform movement.[15] Evans's safety-valve theory became
official Republican doctrine in the 1850's when the party adopted
the homestead principle. One of the earliest groups that used
the name "Republican" was formed at Ripon, Wisconsin, in 1854
by Alvan E. Bovay, who had been a close associate of Evans
before he moved West.[16] Horace Greeley made strenuous efforts
to publicize the safety-valve doctrine as an argument in favor of
the party. In 1859 he published a stirring appeal in the *Tribune*:
"Laboring men! remember that the Republican is the only national party committed to the policy of making the public lands
free in quarter-sections to actual settlers, whereby every worker
will be enabled to hew out for his family a home from the virgin

soil of the Great West." [17] To cite only one other Republican spokesman, Senator James R. Doolittle of Wisconsin declared in 1860: "I sustain this [homestead] measure . . . because its benign operation will postpone for centuries, if it will not forever, all serious conflict between capital and labor in the older free States, withdrawing their surplus population to create in greater abundance the means of subsistence." [18]

But the Homestead Act did not make an end of unemployment and social problems. On the contrary, the three decades following its passage were marked by the most bitter and widespread labor trouble that had yet been seen in the United States. Recent scholars have accordingly raised the question whether the public domain ever operated as a safety valve for eastern laborers, and the trend of the discussion has been strongly toward the conclusion that the theory, at least in the form endorsed by Greeley and his associates, had very little foundation.[19] Unemployed workmen in eastern cities were not ordinarily able to go West and succeed as farmers. They seldom had the money needed to transport their families to the free public lands and to feed and shelter them until a crop could be made; and even if such a worker managed to establish himself on a western farm, he was not likely to succeed without skills that could be obtained only through long apprenticeship. Franklin had seen the West as a refuge for the laborer "that understands Husbandry" [20] — a simple matter perhaps in the fertile Ohio Valley during the eighteenth century but a very difficult one after the Civil War on the subhumid plains. Frontier settlers usually were farmers of some experience from nearby states. Except for European immigrants who were taken to the West by railway companies and other agencies with lands to sell, few settlers on the agricultural frontier came directly from eastern industrial centers.

But if the theory of the safety valve was largely false, how can we account for its almost universal acceptance during the nineteenth century? The question is a difficult one if we take into account only the facts of frontier settlement. The prevalence of the belief is easier to account for, however, if we realize that it was an important part of the myth of the garden of the world. The doctrine of the safety valve was an imaginative construction which masked poverty and industrial strife with the pleasing suggestion that a beneficent nature stronger than any human agency, the ancient resource of Americans, the power that had made the country rich and great, would solve the new problems of industrialism. Just as the theory that rain follows the plow was the myth of the garden expanded to include meteorology, the safety-valve theory was the form taken by the myth on the plane of economic analysis.

True or not, the theory was a two-edged weapon. Useful in the hands of humanitarian reformers who wished to open up opportunities for the poor and the exploited, or for Westerners who wished to foster the rapid development of their region, the theory had the disadvantage of implying that the future pros- perity of the nation depended on the availability of land open to settlement. So long as the supply of land could be considered practically limitless, the theory of the safety valve could be in- voked without risk to prove the uniquely fortunate destiny of America. But if opportunity, happiness, social harmony, and even liberty itself depended on the presence of free land beyond the frontier, what became of these values in the event that the available land should after all prove to be limited in extent? The doctrine of the safety valve implied that in these circumstances American society would become like crowded Europe. The ills of the Old World, which had been depicted with an invidious energy by men who insisted on the unprecedented good fortune of the United States, would become the ills of the New. The growth of population that had once seemed the surest omen of a glorious future for the American empire would become a curse on this side the Atlantic as Malthus had declared it was in Europe.[21]

Jefferson had hinted at such an outcome. The people of the United States will remain virtuous, he wrote to James Madison from Paris in 1787, as long as they are primarily agricultural, and this will be the case while vacant lands are available in any part of America. But when the lands are exhausted, Americans will "get piled upon one another in large cities, as in Europe, and go to eating one another as they do there."[22] Jefferson of course thought that day was comfortably remote. The first Americans who considered the closing of the safety valve imminent were Southern apologists for slavery searching for flaws in the Northern cult of free labor. As early as 1836 Thomas R. Dew of William and Mary College raised the question of what would happen when the supply of free land ran out:

the time must come [he said] when the powerfully elastic spring of our rapidly increasing numbers shall fill up our wide spread territory with a dense population — when the great safety valve of the west will be closed against us — when millions shall be crowded into our manufactories and commercial cities — then will come the great and fearful pressure upon the engine . . . .

This pressure would lead to class war:

then will the line of demarkation stand most palpably drawn between the rich and the poor, the capitalist and the laborer — then will thousands, yea millions arise, whose hard lot it may be to labor from morn till eve through a long life, without the cheering hope of passing from that toilsome condition in which the first years of their manhood found them, or even of accumulating in advance that small fund which may release the old and infirm from labor and toil, and mitigate the sorrows of declining years. . . .

When these things shall come [Dew inquired of the propertied men of the North] — when the millions, who are always under the pressure of poverty, and sometimes on the verge of starvation, shall form your numerical majority, (as is the case now in the old countries of the world) and universal suffrage shall throw the political power into their hands, can you expect that they will regard as sacred the tenure by which you hold your property? I almost fear the frailties and weakness of human nature too much, to anticipate confidently such justice.

The probable result was indeed lurid:

First comes disorganization and legislative plunder, then the struggle of factions and civil war, and lastly a military despotism, into whose arms all will be driven by the intolerable evils of anarchy and rapine.[23]

With its allusion to the example of Rome and its gloomy realism, this is hardly in the key of the optimism that was the official American attitude in the period of manifest destiny. The Southerners were a minority of dissent from the doctrine of progress which underlay so much Northern and Western thought. In 1857 the Virginian George Fitzhugh asserted in his *Cannibals All!* that the social tensions resulting from population increase as the West was settled would force the North to resort to slavery as a means of controlling an insubordinate and menacing laboring class.[24] A writer for the *Southern Literary Messenger* in the following year predicted that increase of population, by causing pressure on the available means of subsistence, would bring to the North a chain of grisly evils — mobs and violence in the cities, pulpits defiled by fanaticism and political passions, legislation tainted by demagoguery.[25]

A celebrated letter from Lord Macaulay written in 1857 to an American biographer of Jefferson developed the same theme. Macaulay asserted that Jeffersonian democracy was feasible only in a society possessing a boundless extent of fertile and unoccupied land. When the United States should be as thickly populated as England, "You will have your Manchesters and Birminghams, and in those Manchesters and Birminghams hundreds of thousands of artisans will assuredly sometimes be out of work. Then your institutions will be fairly brought to the test." Having made the grievous error of giving the ballot to everyone, the upper classes would then be powerless to prevent legislation confiscating their property. Like the Southern apologists for slavery, Macaulay foresaw a Roman decadence for the American democracy:

Either some Caesar or Napoleon will seize the reins of government with a strong hand, or your republic will be as fearfully plundered and laid waste by barbarians in the twentieth century as the Roman Empire was in the fifth; with this difference, that the Huns and Vandals who ravaged the Roman Empire came from without and that your Huns and Vandals will have been engendered within your own country by your own institutions.[26]

In passages like these the overtones of the phrase "safety valve" become apparent. The valve affords safety for the property of the rich against the potential violence of the poor, who are withheld from their vandal attack on the possessions of others by being enticed away to the West. It is worth recalling that Greeley urged his homestead program as an alternative to strikes, which he considered foolish and unnecessary when the worker had the opportunity to settle on his own farm from the public domain.

The antidemocratic tendency of the notion of the safety valve comes out very explicitly in Melville's *Clarel* (1876). Rolfe, the "straight" American, is discussing the destiny of the United States with Ungar, the "clouded man" and "malcontent," an expatriate Confederate veteran who expresses many of the ideas of Dew and Fitzhugh.

> Those waste-weirs [says Rolfe] which the New World yields
> To inland freshets — the free vents
> Supplied to turbid elements;
> The vast reserves — the untried fields;
> These long shall keep off and delay
> The class-war, rich-and-poor-man fray
> Of history. From that alone
> Can serious trouble spring.

But Ungar, in the manner of the *Southern Literary Messenger*, refuses to accept this flattering unction. History moves faster in modern times; the slumberous combustibles are sure to explode, and before very long.

> 'Twill come, 'twill come!
> One demagogue can trouble much:
> How of a hundred thousand such?
> And universal suffrage lent
> To back them with brute element
> Overwhelming?

A Thirty Years' War between the classes is fated; its probable sequel will be a dead level of rank commonplace, an Anglo-Saxon China which for Ungar (if indeed not for Melville himself) is significantly located in the West, on the vast plains where the garden of the world had been expected to materialize. There, in an almost explicit contrast with the confident earlier prophecies of a Western flowering of the arts and of civic virtue, the American society of the future will "shame the race / In the Dark Ages of Democracy." Even Clarel's companions are jolted into half-agreement with him:

> Nor dull they were in honest tone
> To some misgivings of their own:
> They felt how far beyond the scope
> Of elder Europe's saddest thought

Might be the New World sudden brought
In youth to share old age's pains —
To feel the arrest of hope's advance,
And squandered last inheritance;
And cry — "To Terminus build fanes!
Columbus ended earth's romance:
No New World to mankind remains!" [27]

CHAPTER XXI

The Agricultural West in Literature

I. COOPER AND THE STAGES OF SOCIETY

The Wild West beyond the frontier lent itself readily to interpretation in a literature developing the themes of natural nobility and physical adventure, but the agricultural West, as we have already remarked, proved quite intractable as literary material. The myth of the garden and the ideal figure of the Western yeoman were poetic ideas, as Tocqueville rightly called them, but they could not be brought to fictional expression. The difficulty lay in the class status of the Western farmer. The Declaration of Independence had proclaimed that all men were created equal, and American political institutions had reflected a general acceptance of the proposition in the widespread removal of property qualifications for the franchise as early as the 1820's and 1830's. But there was a lag of half a century between the triumph of the idea of equality in politics and its embodiment in imaginative literature.

The early literary characters in the pattern of Leatherstocking did not really bear upon the problem because they were outside society. In his capacity as Indian fighter and hunter the Western hero could be celebrated without regard to class lines. But we have noted how slowly the Western hunter gained sufficient social standing to be allowed to marry the heroine. This fictional emancipation of the Wild Westerner was not clearly worked out before the late 1870's.

The yeoman had an even harder struggle to achieve full status in literature. Cooper, for all his delight in Leatherstocking and his theoretical approval of political equality, stoutly resisted the tendency to break down distinctions between social classes. Indeed, as he became aroused over the "Anti-Rent War" in upstate New York he concluded that even in the political sphere the cult of the yeoman had been carried too far. He declared in 1848 that politicians eager for votes had made the small farmer into an idol before which they fell down in worship. "We can see citizens in these yeomen," continued the crusty novelist, "but not princes, who are to be especially favored by laws made to take from others to bestow on them." [1] The cult seemed to him a phase of the "bastard democracy" that was coming into favor, a movement to seek for the sovereign people in the gutters, "forgetting that the landlord has just as much right to protection as the tenant, the master as the servant, the rich as the poor, the gentleman as the blackguard." [2] In his Littlepage trilogy, Cooper had roundly denounced the tenants in the Hudson Valley who had resorted to violence in protest against a system of tenures that made it difficult for small farmers to acquire title to land. The ideal of the yeoman society was obviously incompatible with Cooper's aristocratic ideal of a society dominated by great landed proprietors.

Few writers of Cooper's generation were as frank as he in stating their conservative social bias. Perhaps they were not even conscious of it. But it was evidently at work as a force inhibiting the use of the small farmer as a character in fiction. James K. Paulding is a case in point. More than a decade after he had celebrated the career of Basil in *The Backwoodsman* he turned again to the agricultural West in his novel *Westward Ho!* published in 1832. Although the novelist acknowledges Flint's *Recollections of the Last Ten Years* as his source of information about the Mississippi Valley,[3] he builds his plot around a group of plantation gentry who migrate from Virginia to Kentucky; the only character really belonging to the West is the old hunter Ambrose Bushfield, a composite of Leatherstocking and Daniel Boone.[4] The story contains no characters representing the yeoman class.

The expatriate sculptor Thomas Buchanan Read's determined

effort to depict an Arcadian West in his long blank verse narrative *The New Pastoral* (1855) shows even more clearly how difficult it was to devise a literary interpretation of the movement of
the agricultural frontier into the Mississippi Valley. Read has an
ample store of the clichés of agrarian theory. With his oaten pipe,
he announces, he plans to celebrate the sweetly contented middle
state between the hut and the palace, "The simple life of nature,
fresh from God!" He will write of the great mass of Western
farmers who labor that the structure of society may be sustained,
for these folk are morally superior to the idle rich in their purple
and fine linen.[5] But how can this claim be made good? Read
follows a group of emigrants from rural Pennsylvania overland
to Pittsburgh, down the Ohio to Cincinnati, and on into the
Indiana forest. As they carve their homes from the wilderness
civilization sweeps onward, and soon a golden harvest waves
where once dark forests stood. But the poet is hard pressed for
incident. He turns in desperation to a wilder West by describing
a buffalo hunt and the lassoing of wild horses, and presents an
elaborate metrical version of the standard vision of the Mississippi
Valley in the future with its cheerful farms, quiet herds, cities,
steamboats, a Pacific railway, and a great metropolis on the Lakes.

> Onward still
> The giant movement goes with rapid pace,
> And civilization spreads its arms abroad;
> While the cleared forest-lands look gladly up,
> And nod their harvest plumes.[6]

Of the actual process of agricultural settlement we have little
except an account of the malaria among the farmers. Two of the
patriarchs of the colony at last give up and make their way back
to Pennsylvania — "Too stern the battle for such souls as theirs." [7]
The whole performance is remarkably tame, despite Read's in-
gratiating fluency. As in the case of Paulding's *The Backwoodsman*, the trouble lies not in the poet so much as in an unfortunate
lack of congruence between the materials and the literary mode
he has chosen. His conventionally bland manner can not convey
the coarse and salty reality of his subject, and he is evidently
convinced only in theory of the dignity of his characters.

Mrs. Caroline A. Soule's *Little Alice*, to mention only one further effort at a mild and cheerful interpretation of agricultural settlement in the West, is likewise a failure. The author states in her preface that the novel is the fruit of "four years of actual pioneer life in the valley of the Upper Des Moines, of emigrant life in a cabin on the prairie." [8] She is perfectly convinced that frontier farmers are noble and that the process of advancing the agricultural frontier yields vast consequences for the good of mankind. The guests at a wedding, for example, are bathed in an aura of primitive sentiment:

Fifty sturdy pioneers, clad in clean homespun, stood about in various attitudes, their frank open faces radiant with light from their honest hearts. Upon the mossy logs, sat as many noble women, their coarse garments betokening thrift and neatness, while their pleasant faces told of their sympathy with the fair girl whose bridal they had come to witness. [9]

Mrs. Soule asserts that in the earliest period of settlement, hardship and danger promote the spirit of mutual aid to such an extent that "the brotherhood of men is recognized as an actual as well as an ideal thing." [10] Fifteen years later the community shows many evidences of change,

but thank heaven, only a bright, beautiful change, which has brought hundreds of struggling, debt-ridden, homeless and hungry men and women from the crowded cities of older States, and given them peace and plenty, houses and lands, while they in grateful return have "made the wilderness and the solitary place glad for them; and the desert to rejoice, and blossom as the rose." [11]

Yet the story that is intended to exhibit the process is as unconvincing as Read's poem. The hero and heroine are recent arrivals from New England, formerly wealthy and very genteel. Uncle Billy, an "old and experienced hunter" speaking a strong dialect, is a benign Leatherstocking whose frontier skills are employed in the fashion prescribed by Wild Western convention. [12] Mrs. Soule also provides a female counterpart of Uncle Billy in the charitable but uneducated Grandma Symmes. [13] These characters represent the Western flavor of the book; but they are distinctly subordinate, just as Leatherstocking was subordinate to Cooper's gentry. The scheme of values in the novel is organized about the superiority of the hero and heroine, whose merits have nothing to do with the West or with agriculture. For all her four years on the prairie, Mrs. Soule can not find the literary means to embody the affirmation of the agrarian ideal that her theory calls for.

These early efforts to deal with the agricultural West in literature prove that the frontier farmer could not be made into an acceptable hero. His sedentary and laborious calling stripped him of the exotic glamor that could be exploited in hunters and scouts of the Wild West. At the same time his low social status made it impossible to elaborate his gentility. Whatever the orators might say in glittering abstractions about the virtues of the yeoman, the novelists found themselves unable to control the emotions aroused by the Western farmer's degraded rank in the class system. Since class feeling about the yeoman is the crux of the literary problem presented by the agricultural West, we are obliged to look as closely as possible into prevalent notions concerning the place of the West and its people in American society.

Such an inquiry leads back once again to the contrast between civilization and savagery that lay at the root of the distinction between the Wild West and the domesticated or agricultural West. The frontier of agricultural settlement was universally recognized as the line separating civilization from savagery; but the structure of civilized society within the frontier was conceived according to two contrasting schools of thought. The agrarian tradition that stemmed from Jefferson held up as its ideal simple agricultural communities in which an approximate equality of wealth prevailed, and in which social stratification was accordingly kept to a minimum. But the equalitarian overtones of this ideal were by no means acceptable to the country as a whole. The concept of a classless society appealed only to a radical minority, and was constantly in danger of being obliterated by the much older and deeper belief in social stratification. The situation could hardly have been otherwise. Equalitarianism, especially social and economic equalitarianism, was a recent and perhaps transient notion deriving in large part from French radical thought of the eighteenth century. The ideal of social subordination, of a hierarchy of classes, of a status system, had the weight of centuries behind it. Still more important for the imaginative interpretation of American life was the fact that the assumptions underlying the class structure of English society permeated the genre of the sentimental novel, which was built about the genteel hero and heroine. There was no coherent literary tradition embodying equalitarian assumptions.

The belief in the Western farmer's social inferiority was further strengthened by certain ideas derived from the New England theocratic tradition. From this standpoint, all emigrants were actually or potentially criminal because of their flight from an orderly municipal life into frontier areas that were remote from centers of control. The attitude had developed naturally out of the Puritan devotion to social order maintained by church and state as coöperating agencies. A sermon preached before a Boston congregation by the Reverend Thomas Barnard in 1758 states the theocratic case against the backwoodsman quite clearly. Religion, he said, will flourish most where the arts of peace are cultivated, "especially Industry, among those born for Labour." For a quiet steady life in an orderly community keeps alive a regard for whatever is virtuous and pious, facilitates attendance upon public worship, tends to implant clear notions of justice and a regard for property, and leads men toward a proper submission to their civil rulers. On the other hand, when people wander into the wilderness and settle far apart from one another, the result is "Savageness of Temper, Ignorance, Want of the Means of Religion; (which will attend a solitary State and distant Neighborhood)." Worse still, when a plenty of free land allows men to support themselves "by the spontaneous Products of Nature with Little Labour; Experience has shewn, that Habits of Idleness and Intemperance have been contracted, much to the public Damage." [14]

This general view is so familiar it hardly needs elaborate illustration, but a few later comments may be mentioned to indicate the persistence of the Eastern belief in frontier depravity. The most famous among such statements is that of the Reverend Timothy Dwight, President of Yale, who wrote a characterization of the "*foresters*, or *Pioneers*" of Vermont on the basis of his travels in the state in 1798 and 1806. Such men, in the opinion of the noted divine, had proved too idle, talkative, passionate, and shiftless to acquire either property or reputation in stable communities, and therefore wished to escape the restraints of law, religion, morality, and government. Unable to adjust themselves to the social state, "they become at length discouraged: and under the pressure of poverty, the fear of a gaol, and the consciousness of public contempt, leave their native places, and betake themselves to the wilderness." [15] Dwight distinguishes between such dissolute foresters and the virtuous farmers who establish orderly communities after the first pioneers have moved on, but he implies that most settlers in the farther West are of the depraved class which he has described in Vermont.

The class of men, who have been the principal subject of these remarks [he asserts], have already straggled onward from New-England, as well as from other parts of the Union, to Louisiana. In a political view, their emigration is of very serious utility to the ancient inhabitants. . . . The institutions, and habits, of New-England, more I suspect than those of any other country, have prevented, or kept down, this noxious disposition; but they cannot entirely prevent either its existence, or its effects. In mercy, therefore, to the sober, industrious, and well-disposed, inhabitants, Providence has opened in the vast Western wilderness a retreat, sufficiently alluring to draw them away from the land of their nativity. We have many troubles even now: but we should have many more, if this body of foresters had remained at home.[16]

These characteristics of life in new settlements continued to be especially clear to New Englanders who had enjoyed the advantages of theological training. The tradition was so explicit that even the young and relatively radical Unitarian minister James Freeman Clarke, who had been exposed to Transcendentalism and had gone out to Louisville with vaguely evangelistic aims, struggled in vain against it. In a review of Mann Butler's *History of the Commonwealth of Kentucky* and James Hall's *Sketches of History, Life, and Manners, in the West*, Clarke allowed the West a "genius deep, rich, strong, various, and full of promise," but he was alarmed at the fact that this genius was unbridled, undirected, and ungoverned. Western mothers encouraged their children to fight, women favored duelling, grave judges gambled, and vice ate into the heart of social virtue. The West needed religious restraint, it needed moral principle, it needed greater respect for law and a disposition to follow duty as pointed out to it by wise guidance — presumably from New England.[17]

The covert class bias characteristic of this attitude appears even more clearly in a review of Caroline M. Kirkland's *Forest Life* by Cornelius C. Felton, of Harvard, in 1842. A population was growing up in the West, according to the reviewer, "with none of the restraints which fetter the characters of the working classes in other countries." No feudal feeling of loyalty tempered the natural overflow of passion or restrained the full growth of individual humors. Each man in the West considered himself a sovereign by indefeasible right, and had no idea anyone else was his better in any respect.[18]

To the theocratic suspicion of the Western farmer as a rebellious fugitive from society must be added the unfavorable view of him derived from the idea of civilization and progress. The conception of civilization, like the word itself, had first gained currency in the middle decades of the eighteenth century in the writings of Turgot and Rousseau.[19] Its most persuasive formulation came in the 1790's with Condorcet's *Esquisse d'un tableau historique des progrès de l'esprit humain*, which was immediately translated into English and had two editions in the United States before 1825.[20] The most influential aspect of Condorcet's theory of civilization was the notion that all human societies pass through the same series of social stages in the course of their evolution upward from barbarism toward the goal of universal enlightenment. He divided the history of the human race into ten epochs, the first nine stretching from the dawn of existence to the foundation of the French Republic, the tenth embracing the glorious future opened up for mankind by the triumph of Reason. The most important of these epochs for social theory were the earliest, which comprised the union of autonomous families who subsisted mainly by hunting, into "hordes"; the domestication of animals, inaugurating the pastoral stage of society; and the transition from a pastoral to an agricultural stage. Other writers developed the idea that civilization actually began when a given society adopted an agricultural way of life.[21]

Although in Europe the successive stages of society were naturally thought of as succeeding one another in time, so that primitive conditions could be studied only through historical and archeological research, the situation in America was quite different. When the theory of civilization became current in this country many observers were struck by its applicability to the actual state of affairs in the West. The comment was frequently made that in America one could examine side by side the social stages that were believed to have followed one another in time in the long history of the Old World. William Darby, for example, wrote in his *Emigrant's Guide* in 1818 that a journey from New Orleans westward to the Sabine showed man in every stage of his progress, from the most civilized to the most savage. New Orleans represented the summit of cultivation, refinement, and luxury. The plantations of the lower Mississippi likewise offered "all that art, aided by wealth, can produce." In Attacapas and Opelousas parishes the glare of luxury vanished, and in its stead the traveler encountered substantial, independent farmers living in rough though comfortable houses. In the western parts of Opelousas parish could be found pastoral hunters who recalled to the imagination the primitive ages of history. Still farther west, along the Sabine, the way of life of the scattered inhabitants suggested "the utmost verge of inhabited earth, and the earliest dawn of human improvement." [22]

In 1824 the *Port Folio* of Philadelphia quoted a remark to this same effect made by the British traveler Adam Hodgson after a journey from west to east across the United States. "I have seen the roving hunter acquiring the habit of the herdsman," said Hodgson; "the pastoral state merging into the agricultural, and the agricultural into the manufacturing and commercial." [23] Jefferson himself, whom Hodgson had visited at Monticello,[24] a short time later expounded the theory at length.

Let a philosophic observer [he wrote] commence a journey from the savages of the Rocky Mountains, eastwardly towards our sea-coast. These he would observe in the earliest stage of association living under no law but that of nature, [subsisting] and covering themselves with the flesh and skins of wild beasts. He would next find those on our frontiers in the pastoral state, raising domestic animals, to supply the defects of hunting. Then succeed our own semi-barbarous citizens, the pioneers of the advance of civilization, and so in his progress he would meet the gradual shades of improving man until he would reach his, as yet, most improved state in our seaport towns. This, in fact, is equivalent to a survey, in time, of the progress of man from the infancy of creation to the present day.[25]

One or two examples from imaginative literature will be enough to indicate how widespread the theory was. In his *Francis Berrian*, published serially in 1825–1826, Timothy Flint causes the hero to remark that when he traveled westward from Natchitoches into Texas he "had occasion to experiment the truth of the remark, that in travelling towards the frontier, the decreasing scale of civilization and improvement exhibits an accurate illustration of inverted history." Berrian felt that he had traveled down six centuries in as many days. The half-savage settlers on the remote frontier, who lived as much by hunting as by agriculture, were "the intermediate race between savage and civilized man." [26] A final illustration may be taken from Cooper's *The Prairie* (1827):

The gradations of society, from that state which is called refined to that which approaches as near barbarity as connexion with an intelligent people will readily allow, are to be traced from the bosom of the states, where wealth, luxury and the arts are beginning to seat themselves, to those distant and ever-receding borders which mark the skirts and announce the approach of the nation, as moving mists precede the signs of the day. [27]

This theoretical statement introduces the character of Ishmael Bush, a Kentucky backwoodsman who represents Cooper's deepest penetration into the problem of the agricultural frontier, and well deserves to stand as the counterpart of Leatherstocking, the Child of the Forest. Whereas Leatherstocking has a natural virtue and an exotic splendor derived from his communion with untouched nature, Bush and his sons are at war with nature. They are the very axemen from whom Leatherstocking has fled halfway across the continent. Cooper is so eager to make this symbolic point that he has Bush's sons chop down a grove of trees conjured up for the purpose in the midst of the treeless great plains.[28] Although Leatherstocking and Bush figure in the same novel, they belong to entirely distinct conceptual systems. The line that divides them is the agricultural frontier. Leatherstocking, living beyond the frontier and following the vocation of a hunter and trapper, is not a member of society at all. Bush, the husbandman, belongs to society; his "connexion with an intelligent people" is his participation in the Social Compact to which Leatherstocking is not a party.

But if Bush has a place in the scheme of civilization that flowers at the top into Cooper's gentry, he represents the lowest of its stages, at a great remove from the level of refinement.[29] He is a wanderer — Cooper's readers would not have missed the biblical allusion in his name; and he also arouses suspicion as a property-less member of the lowest social class. He is just such a back-woodsman as Barnard and Dwight had described. He is clad in "the coarsest vestments of a husbandman," but wears "a singular and wild display of prodigal and ill-judged ornaments" that be-speak a half-barbaric taste. The lower part of his face is "coarse, extended, and vacant," while the upper part is "low, receding, and mean." His manner is characterized by apathy and indolence, although it is evident that he has great muscular strength. He is, in short, half animal, as Cooper insists in a simile: ". . . he suf-fered his huge frame, to descend the gentle declivity, in the same sluggish manner that an over fatted beast would have yielded to the downward pressure."[30] The novelist makes Bush the accom-plice of his brother-in-law Abiram White, slave-stealer by trade, who has abducted the heroine Inez de Certavallos and is keeping her prisoner in one of the wagons of Bush's train. And we learn that Bush has shot a deputy sheriff who tried to evict him and fifty other squatters from a tract of land back in Kentucky.[31] This act of rebellion seems somehow vastly more sinister than Leather-stocking's defiance of the law in *The Pioneers*, which was moti-vated by feudal loyalty to his patron Major Effingham.

All these traits of Bush are in perfect accord with conservative theory. Yet the character has an interest for Cooper that defies theory. The idea of Bush's barbarism, along with its connotations of mere criminality, carries a suggestion of moral sublimity. It is related to the moral beauty of Leatherstocking as the somber and tormented landscapes of Salvator Rosa seemed to Cooper and his contemporaries to be related to the mild and smiling landscapes of their other favorite Claude Lorrain. In exploring this esthetic aspect of Bush, Cooper was able to view him for the moment, so to speak, purely, without judging him by the criterion of refine-ment or the theory of social stages, and in consequence was led to write one of the best sequences in all the Leatherstocking series. Near the end of the story, Ishmael as patriarch of his tribe sets

about administering justice for the murder of his son Asa. A dim
acquaintance with the Scriptures has left in his mind the barbaric
notion that an eye for an eye is the law of God. When the mur-
derer is revealed to be his wife's brother Abiram, the law of God
comes into conflict with primitive clan loyalty, but Ishmael and
his wife consult the Scriptures and come to the conclusion that
Abiram must die. If Leatherstocking is notable for his intuitive
ability to distinguish right from wrong, Ishmael too has his terri-
fying sense of justice. Abiram's craven pleas for one more hour of
life suggest the grim expedient of binding his arms, tying a noose
about his neck, and leaving him upon a narrow ledge from which
as his strength fails he must in the end cast himself. That night, in
a setting of wind and drifting clouds intended to suggest Salvator's
style, Ishmael and his wife return to the place of execution, cut
down the swinging body, and bury it.[32] The same sense of justice
had earlier led Bush, after ponderous meditation, to release Inez
of his own volition.[33]

Cooper's perception of values in Ishmael Bush's character that
sprang from the conditions of life in a primitively agricultural
West, yet could not be accounted for by reference to the ideas of
civilization and refinement, pointed the way toward a more adequate literary treatment of the agricultural frontier. But the idea
of civilization was so deeply rooted in American thought that it
could not be cast aside overnight. Writers who sought to deal with
the agricultural West therefore continued for decades to waver
between a direct response to their materials and the attitude of
reserve or disapproval of Western coarseness dictated by the prevalent social theory. Cooper himself found the problem persistently
challenging, although he did not advance very far toward solving
it. In *Home as Found*, published in 1838, he returned to the
Cooperstown whose early history he had chronicled in *The
Pioneers* fifteen years before. He did not try again to draw a
Western character on the scale of Ishmael Bush, but he did undertake an elaborate theoretical analysis of what happens in the wake
of agricultural settlement in the wilderness.

The goal toward which all such communities evolve is in his
opinion clear enough: it is the establishment of a secure class of
gentry whose ownership of land confers on them the wealth and

the leisure that are indispensable to the flowering of the higher graces of human nature. This social ideal obviously depends upon what Cooper calls a "division into castes," and can not be realized under the conditions of rough equality that prevail in the earliest stages of settlement. It is true that he has a rather unexpected Arcadian dream of the adventurous first years, when for a time "life has much of the reckless gaiety, careless association, and buoyant merriment of childhood." But this is a transient phase. Only when gradations of social station, based on differences in inherited wealth, have become clearly marked, does the society reach its final and ordered stability.[34]

Cooper, a consistent and explicit conservative in social theory despite his carefully limited endorsement of political democracy, was quite willing to acknowledge that refinement and gentility were conceivable only in members of an upper class with enough wealth to guarantee its leisure, and a sufficiently secure social status to give it poise and assurance. The form of the sentimental novel suggested exactly these assumptions. But other novelists who tried to deal with the agricultural West felt themselves under some compulsion to extend the application of the sounding platitudes of democracy and equality from politics to social and economic life. They therefore faced a continual struggle to reconcile their almost instinctive regard for refinement with their democratic theories and their desire to find some values in the unrefined West.

The conflict would not be resolved so long as they clung to the theory of civilization with its fixed series of social stages. For the West could have only one place in such a scheme: it was primitive and therefore unrefined. This was indeed its defining characteristic. In proportion as the West lost its primitive character it became indistinguishable from the East and there was no basis for a characteristic Western literature. Writers who were attracted by Western materials had an obscure awareness that the unprecedented adventure of agricultural settlement in the Mississippi Valley was somehow worthy of imaginative interpretation. The theory of progress and civilization, on the other hand, could take no account of novelty except as an increase of enlightenment in the most advanced societies. Abstract and rationalistic as it was, it implied that only the most advanced stage of social development produced characters worthy of admiration. The theory offered little ground for finding a value in America as contrasted with Europe, or in the American West as contrasted with the American East. From Cooper's day to that of Hamlin Garland, writers about the West had to struggle against the notion that their characters had no claim upon the attention of sophisticated readers, except through their alarming or at best their picturesque lack of refinement.

II. FROM CAROLINE KIRKLAND TO HAMLIN GARLAND

Literary historians have long been accustomed to find Joseph Kirkland and Hamlin Garland important because they contributed "the bitterness of the frontier" to the development of realism in fiction.[1] It is more relevant here to ask a different question about these men. What were their origins? From what literary background did they proceed? Since there are no absolute beginnings or endings in the history of literature, Kirkland and Garland can be considered the culmination of one development just as profitably as they can be considered the pioneers of another. To see in them nothing except a prophetic mood of disillusionment is to oversimplify a rich and suggestive chapter in the history of American thought. Whatever their shortcomings as artists, they signalize a slow but far-reaching change in literary attitudes toward the Western farmer. In the early nineteenth century, as we have seen, the farmer could be depicted in fiction only as a member of a low social class. By 1890 he could be presented as a human being, unfortunate perhaps, but possessed of dignity even in his tribulations. The purpose of the present chapter is to trace this process through the work of representative writers who dealt with the agricultural West during the half century between the last of the Leatherstocking novels and *Main Travelled Roads*.[2]

The earliest of these was Mrs. Caroline M. Kirkland. A native of New York, she spent five years in southern Michigan during the late 1830's and early 1840's while her husband took a fling at land speculation and town building. On the basis of this exposure to the West Mrs. Kirkland wrote three books: *A New Home — Who'll Follow?* (1839), *Forest Life* (1842), and *Western Clearings*

(1845), besides minor sketches and stories dealing with the same materials. Her books were widely read, and deserved to be, for they have the merits of clear observation and lively reporting. They are also a valuable repository of upper-class Eastern attitudes toward the raw West.

As a grand-daughter of Samuel Stansbury, the Loyalist poet of the Revolutionary period, Mrs. Kirkland had an assured social standing that made it impossible for her to identify herself with the free-and-easy outlook and customs of the Michigan frontier.[3] Instead, she conceived of herself as a traveler who happened to have made an unusually long sojourn in the wilderness "beyond the confines of civilization." [4] Her first book is cast in the form of letters to cultivated friends back home. She realizes these sophisticated readers will hardly be able to believe that Western backwoodsmen "are partakers with themselves of a common nature." [5] The Western indifference to class lines arouses in her by turns a lively amusement and something not far from indignation. She is greatly annoyed with people who pretend to believe in the principle of social equality. To carry out such doctrines in practice would, she assures us, "imply nothing short of a lingering mental martyrdom to the cultivated and the refined." [6]

Yet she responds almost in spite of herself to the generosity and kindness of the pioneer farmers. She says she always returns from her little excursions about the countryside with an increased liking for the people.

There is after all [she explains] so much kindness, simplicity and trustfulness — one catches so many glimpses of the lovelier aspect of our common nature — that much that is uncouth is forgotten, and much that is offensive is pardoned. One sees the rougher sort of people in their best light, and learns to own the "tie of brotherhood." [7]

To her second volume of sketches she prefixed six Spenserian stanzas in praise of Sympathy, "Nature's blest decree," which she had learned from the Wizard of the North. The master had taught her that the backwoodsman was human after all:

> The power that stirred the universal heart
> Dwells in the forest, in the common air —
> In cottage lone, as in th' o'er burdened mart —
> For Nature's painter learned from Nature all his art.[8]

If the reader will compare this sentimental theory of the nobility of humble Western farmers — reminiscent of Timothy Flint's preface to *George Mason* — with the kittenish remark which opens Mrs. Kirkland's first volume ("I intend to be 'decidedly low'")[9] he will recognize how instructive a confusion of attitudes her writing exhibits.

The contradictions between her high-flown theory and her instinctive revulsion from the crudities of backwoods Michigan are reflected in her vain struggle to find a satisfactory literary form. The structure of her books is extremely simple. She writes as if she were keeping a travel diary in which, as a cultivated outsider, she makes notes concerning the natives of a strange land. The form is that which comes naturally to the first explorers of a new area. Hundreds of such narratives had been written about the West by travelers with no literary pretensions. But Mrs. Kirkland uses the strategy of writing in the first person to keep her sensibility constantly before the reader and to emphasize her detachment from her surroundings. She takes it for granted that her readers share with her a higher social status than that of the natives and underlines the assumption by plentiful literary allusions and quotations, plus a sprinkling of French and Italian phrases that authenticate her implied claim to rank as a bluestocking cast among unlettered country folk.

But she can not be permanently content with so simple a literary form and tries valiantly to devise something more complicated. In her three volumes are interpolated perhaps a dozen pieces of fiction that she tries to endow with a plot. The experiments range from the brief autobiography put into the mouth of the admirable Mrs. Danforth in *A New Home*[10] to the more ambitious efforts which Mrs. Kirkland was encouraged to make by the success of her first book. *Forest Life* contains, for example, the tale of how the worthy young backwoodsman Seymour won the hand of Caroline Hay, daughter of the greatest landowner in the country,[11] and an account of an English couple named Sibthorpe which ends up in the epistolary mode of the previous century.[12] Several of the sketches in *Western Clearings* threaten to become plotted narratives, such as the story of the shiftless Silas

Ashburn who is still not base enough to resort to illegal violence against a man he considers an enemy,[13] or "Ambuscades," which relates how the enthusiastic huntsman Tom Oliver forgot to hunt and became a hard-working farmer through love of Emma Levering.[14]

Despite the variety of these experiments in fiction, it cannot be said that Mrs. Kirkland succeeded in finding an adequate form for her Western materials. She could not discover any dependable plot structure except a love story, and her lovers develop toward the stereotypes of the sentimental tradition. In proportion as they are worked into a plot they lose any Western characteristics they may have had at the outset. There is no progress toward overcoming the lack of coherence between materials and form that constituted her literary problem. She demonstrated that the agricultural West offered interesting and even challenging themes for fiction but she could not find a satisfactory method for dealing with them.

During the next two decades the obvious strategy of writing a conventional love story against a Western background was adopted by a number of women novelists, including Mrs. Metta V. Victor, her sister Mrs. Frances Fuller Barritt, and Mrs. Caroline A. Soule, who has been mentioned before. Mrs. Victor's *Alice Wilde, the Raftsman's Daughter. A Forest Romance*, issued in 1860 as Number 4 of Beadle's Dime Novels, conducts the elegant and cultivated Philip More of New York to a remote region of the West. Although the sophisticated Virginia, likewise of New York, cannot understand why he wishes to throw himself away upon "a rude and uncultivated community," [15] Philip falls in love with Alice, daughter of the raftsman David Wilde. The father speaks a strong dialect but the daughter's speech is correct; her rusticity is indicated mainly by the fact that she dresses in the style of twenty years before.[16] After the hero has declared his love, Alice is sent to a seminary at Centre City for a little polishing. Mrs. Victor's conception of the problem she is dealing with is indicated in Alice's exclamation to her fiancé: ". . . you had pride, prejudice, rank, fashion, every thing to struggle against in choosing me." [17] That the triumph of love over these obstacles was widely approved is indicated by the enormous sale of the novel — 250,000 copies in the United States, besides an immense run in England.[18]

In *The Backwoods Bride. A Romance of Squatter Life* [19] Mrs. Victor seized upon a conflict growing more directly out of agricultural settlement on the frontier. The elegant and cultivated Harry Gardiner has bought a large tract of government land in Michigan in the 1840's. When he comes out to take possession he finds that numerous squatters have settled on it, including Enos Carter, father of the beautiful seventeen-year-old Susan.[20] Although Mr. Gardiner has bought the land as a speculation, his noble nature leads him to offer to sell to the squatters at the price he gave for it. But the squatters, perhaps under the influence of George Henry Evans, are convinced that "in the new country men are entitled to all they could cultivate. . . ." [21] Enos Carter states their position eloquently:

> God made this earth to be free to all; and whoever takes wild land, and clears it, and cultivates it, makes it his own — he's a right to it. What right have these men that never did a day's work in their lives, coming along and takin' the bread out of our mouths? [22]

Mrs. Victor allows this very real conflict to develop to the point where a mob, including Enos, tries to break into Gardiner's hotel room to lynch him, whereupon the young hero kills one of the mob with a pistol.[23] But the author is not willing to follow through the issue she has stated, and takes refuge in a reconciliation which leaves Gardiner the squatters' candidate for Congress.[24] He can marry Susan without too great violation of the proprieties because her father was once better off and she retains some gentility from her childhood in rural New York.

Mrs. Victor returns to the problem of the social status of Western farmers in *Uncle Ezekiel and his Exploits on Two Continents*, but this time the roles of hero and heroine are reversed. Edith Lancaster, daughter of an upper-class Englishman, is brought through great exertions of the author to an Illinois prairie. Amos Potter, son of a squatter, does not have his father's backwoods dialect but is still too humble in status to satisfy Edith's father, who takes her to his London mansion.[25] There she pines for her Western lover until the eccentric Uncle Ezekiel, a character in the humorous Down East tradition, manages to reunite the young people and reconcile the father to the match.[26]

Mrs. Barritt, in her *East and West; or, The Beauty of Willard's Mill*, simplifies the problem at the expense of probability by creating an Iowa heroine of impeccable gentility. Although Minnie Willard, the miller's daughter, is unsophisticated in comparison with the urbane Constance, her highbred visiting cousin from New York, the country girl has the elegant accomplishments of writing verses and sketching in charcoal.[27] Fletcher Harris, an artist sent on tour by an Eastern magazine, falls in love with Minnie and draws a picture entitled "The Fawn of the Prairie" that celebrates a lyric moment described in one of Minnie's poems.[28] Yet before this marriage can take place Minnie must be sent to New York to become cultivated by looking at pictures and hearing music.[29] The heroine of Mrs. Barritt's *The Land Claim. A Tale of the Upper Missouri* is established as genteel by being made the daughter of an Englishwoman of noble family who eloped with the gardener and came to America; in the end the heroine is restored to her grandfather, Sir Deming.[30] It will be recalled that Margaret Belden, heroine of Mrs. Soule's *Little Alice*, could be presented as refined despite her backwoods setting because she had been reared in an affluent New England home.

Each of these authors cleaves to the theory of social stages which places the West below the East in a sequence to which both belong. The West has no meaning in itself because the only value recognized by the theory of civilization is the refinement which is believed to increase steadily as one moves from primitive simplicity and coarseness toward the complexity and polish of urban life. The values that are occasionally found in the West are anomalous instances of conformity to a standard that is actually foreign to the region. This principle is exemplified in the Western heroines, who seem to be worthy of admiration only in proportion as they have escaped from the crudity and vulgarity of their surroundings, either by virtue of birth elsewhere, or through the possession of an implausible innate refinement. The occasional half-hearted tendency to contrast Western freshness with Eastern oversophistication will be recognized as a remnant of the dying theory of cultural primitivism. It is quite inconsistent with the cult of refinement that furnished the intellectual framework for sentimental fiction.

The first step toward solving the literary problem of the agricultural West was to find some means of escape from the assumption that the East was the standard of value and that Westerners were of inferior social status. If novelists were to deal with the West on its own terms, they would have to adopt some criterion besides that of refinement and would have to rid themselves of their unconscious devotion to class distinctions. In practice this meant getting rid of the theory of social stages.

The stories and sketches of Alice Cary of Ohio, published during the 1850's, are the earliest body of writing in which the relation of the West to the East has ceased to be the major problem. It is significant that Miss Cary was the first native of the Ohio Valley who attempted to interpret the region in fiction. With all its shortcomings, her work supports Edward Eggleston's statement that she was the founder of the tradition of honest interpretation of the West.[31] Transmitted through Eggleston to Hamlin Garland, her repudiation of the conventional way of looking at sectional relationships was destined to have important literary consequences. Her indifference toward the East appears to have sharpened her eye for detail and to have helped her achieve moments of direct reporting that still seem sharp and fresh. But her writing suffers from defects that fully account for the neglect into which it has fallen. She is seldom free of conventional sentiment and often verges toward a familiar kind of religiosity. The schoolmaster in the sketch "Two Visits," [32] whose hands evince his gentle origin if indeed his glossy black curls, pale complexion, great melancholy eyes, and fondness for Coleridge were not more than sufficient indications, is pure claptrap. Like Emmeline Grangerford in *Huckleberry Finn*, he shows his gentility by sketching; and like her, he prefers funerary subjects. His masterpiece is a drawing of the grave of his first love, with himself kneeling by it.[33]

Furthermore, Miss Cary's literary method impedes the full development of her characters. She takes over Mrs. Kirkland's habit of writing in the first person and is seldom able to get her-

self out of the picture. She cannot refrain from occasional re-
minders that she too is a lady who knows her Spenser and Milton,
and is qualified to make judgments concerning refinement or the
lack of it in people and houses. In abandoning the intellectual
framework offered by the theory of social stages, she was not able
to construct any coherent theory to take its place. She asserts
that "the independent yeoman, with his simple rusticity and
healthful habits, is the happiest man in the world," but this
judgment is supported by the condescending line from Gray
which she quotes immediately afterward: "When ignorance is
bliss, 'tis folly to be wise." [34] She believes that her Western farm
and village characters are the "humbler classes" and that she is
writing the simple annals of the poor, in contrast with other lady
authors who "have apparently been familiar only with wealth and
splendor, and such joys or sorrows as come gracefully to mingle
with the refinements of luxury and art. . . "

> In our country [she continues], though all men are not "created
> equal," such is the influence of the sentiment of liberty and political
> equality, that
>> "All thoughts, all passions, all delights,
>> Whatever stirs this mortal frame,"
> may with as much probability be supposed to affect conduct and ex-
> pectation in the log cabin as in the marble mansion; and to illustrate
> this truth, to dispel that erroneous belief of the necessary baseness of
> the "common people" which the great masters in literature have in all
> ages labored to create, is a purpose and an object in our nationality to
> which the finest and highest genius may wisely be devoted; but which
> may be effected in a degree by writings as unpretending as these remi-
> niscences of what occurred in and about the little village where I from
> childhood watched the pulsations of the surrounding hearts.[35]

This is perhaps a little more explicit than Flint's and Mrs.
Kirkland's statements of similar ideas, and Miss Cary came
nearer than they did to realizing her program in fiction. But her
sketches are still not consistently organized about her thesis.
They reveal an interesting but in the end annoying instability of
attitude in the author.

The sketch which contains the touching portrait of the school-
master, for example, begins as a contrast between the over-
austere household of the prosperous Knights and the charming

household of the poorer Lytles. But before she is done, Miss Cary
manages to insert the death and funeral of little Henry Hathaway,
the courtship and marriage of Hetty Knight, and the death of
Kitty Lytle, presumably from heartbreak. The author is not sure
where her interest lies or what she is trying to do. To mention
only one other example, the sketch "Charlotte Ryan" deals with
the daughter of the "last" family in the neighborhood who,
brought up in poverty, goes for a visit with relatives near Cincinnati, encounters true elegance for the first time, suffers for her
rusticity in the presence of the splendid Mr. Sully Dinsmore, is
taken to some vague but glittering greater city by other friends,
becomes herself the cynosure of all eyes at the ball, and snubs
Mr. Dinsmore in return for his cruelty to her back in Ohio. But
Charlotte is no happier in her silks than she had been in her
homespun.[36]

Miss Cary's most ambitious effort to deal with the countryside about Cincinnati in fiction is *Married, Not Mated*, published
in 1856. This confused work seems to have grown out of an
autobiographical reminiscence; one of the young ladies introduced in Part II carries the remainder of the narrative in the first
person. The nearest approach to a thread of plot is the story of
how the headstrong Annette Furniss of Cincinnati determines to
escape from domestic monotony by marrying Henry Graham, a
young farmer who supplies the family with butter. Annette is a
selfish creature and is really in love with Henry's unpleasant
brother Stafford. The marriage therefore fails and Henry dies.
By calling her hero a farmer Miss Cary seems to promise a study
of rural Western character. There is a faint suggestion that Henry
Graham's language and dress need to be refined by the power
of love, but he is never made to speak dialect and his character
is so profoundly genteel that one cannot take him seriously as a
Westerner. He reads poetry, for example, in a secluded grove,
and leaves a strip of willows standing along a brook because they
improve the landscape. The actual work of the farm is carried
on offstage by hired hands. The only labor Henry performs is the
sentimental task of tending the grave of Annette's sister Nellie.[37]

The latter half of the novel wanders off into a tedious character sketch of the pompous Mr. Peter Throckmorton and a desper-

ately comic study of the cures undertaken in his behalf by a
series of amateur and professional physicians. And there are other
grotesque things in the book. It is nevertheless oddly interesting,
in part because Miss Cary stumbles almost accidentally into a
remarkable technical experiment by telling the story of Henry and
Annette from several points of view, in part because she manages
to render directly observed depths of squalor and neurosis, but
most of all because of the character of Raphe Muggins. Raphe
appears first as an adolescent backwoods waif serving the Graham
household as maid of all work; later she is married and rearing
a vigorous family. She and her husband are of the folk and there
is no doubt in the author's mind that they belong to a social
class distinct from that of the Grahams. Yet Raphe is made much
more real than any other character in the story. Miss Cary not
only reproduces her robust speech at length, but admires her
shrewd and healthy insight into the tortured lives of the Grahams,
and uses Raphe's successful marriage as a foil for the introspective complications of the principal characters. The author's un-
patronizing affection for this very ungenteel Western woman all
but breaks down the literary convention that consigns the character to an inferior status.[38]

Despite Miss Cary's occasional triumphs, Edward Eggleston's
work marks a distinct advance toward the discovery of literary
values in the agricultural West. It is true that he was no more
able than Miss Cary to get beyond the accepted dogma that a
novel is a love story; all his heroes and heroines exhibit a stereotyped variety of sentimental virtue. It is also true that his novels
contain traces of the old *a priori* doctrine of Western inferiority.
One of the principal themes of *The Hoosier School-Master*, for
example, is the desire of Bud Means to "git out of this low-lived
Flat Crick way of livin'" by putting in "his best licks for Jesus
Christ." [39] Eggleston remarks with approval that Patty Lumsden,
heroine of *The Circuit-Rider*, was saved by her pride "from possible assimilation with the vulgarity about her." [40] The character
Nancy Kirtley in *Roxy*, studied in considerable detail, is intended
as a representation of "that curious poor-whitey race which is
called 'tarheel' in the northern Carolina, 'sand-hiller' in the
southern, 'corn-cracker' in Kentucky, 'yahoo' in Mississippi and in

California 'pike.'" These backwoodsmen, like most of the Means family in *The Hoosier School-Master*, resemble Ishmael Bush in *The Prairie*. They are coarse, illiterate, lawless — in a word, "half-barbarous." Eggleston, like Cooper, is interested in the type, and his conclusions deserve quotation:

They never continue in one stay, but are the half gypsies of America, seeking by shiftless removals from one region to another to better their wretched fortunes, or, more likely to gratify a restless love of change and adventure. They are the Hoosiers of the dark regions of Indiana and the Egyptians of southern Illinois. Always in a half-barbarous state, it is among them that lynchings most prevail. Their love of excitement drives them into a daring life and often into crime. From them came the Kentucky frontiersmen, the Texan rangers, the Murrell highway-men, the Arkansas regulators and anti-regulators, the ancient keel-boatmen, the more modern flat-boatmen and raftsmen and roustabouts, and this race furnishes, perhaps, more than its share of the "road agents" that infest the territories. Brave men and generous men are often found among them; but they are never able to rise above Daniel Boones and Simon Kentons.[41]

After Mark Bonamy has been led into sin by Nancy, he has a momentary impulse to give up all his past life and go with her to Texas, where he may live out his degradation with no reproach from any moral censor. Among the fugitive criminals and bank-rupts there he may hope to become a leader and thus make some sort of a life for himself.

This Nance was a lawless creature — a splendid savage, full of ferocity. Something of the sentiment of Tennyson's "Locksley Hall" was in him. He would commit moral suicide instead of physical, — release the ani-mal part of his nature from allegiance to what was better; and, since he had failed in civilized life, he might try his desperate luck as a savage. It was easier to sink the present Bonamy in the wild elements of the South-western frontier, than to blow out his brains or drown himself.[42]

Evidently, Eggleston is willing to go as far as any New Eng-land clergyman in painting the lawless savagery of the remote frontier. And though he considers Indiana more civilized than Texas, vestiges of a dark earlier barbarism linger even there. After all, Nancy belongs to Indiana as much as Mark does. In the West of his fiction Eggleston finds petty political corruption, dis-honest manipulation of the preëmption law, and a sordid devotion to profit at any cost.[43] He notes that the greatest wealth of postfrontier communities has come not from hard work but from land speculation.[44] Whiskey Jim, the sympathetic Minnesota stage driver in *The Mystery of Metropolisville*, remarks that the West isn't the country of ideas, but of corner lots. "I tell you," he exclaims, "here it's nothin' but per-cent." [45]

It is rather odd that, holding such conventional views of Western depravity and "materialism," Eggleston should nevertheless have been so thoroughly convinced that the region deserved literary treatment. In the preface to *The Hoosier School-Master* he remarks:

It used to be a matter of no little jealousy with us, I remember, that the manners, customs, thoughts, and feelings of New England country people filled so large a place in books, while our life, not less interesting, not less romantic, and certainly not less filled with humorous and grotesque material, had no place in literature. It was as though we were shut out of good society. And, with the single exception of Alice Cary, perhaps, our Western writers did not dare speak of the West otherwise than as the unreal world to which Cooper's lively imagination had given birth.[46]

But this does not take us very far, and it is certainly not an adequate analysis of Eggleston's attitude toward his Hoosiers. A year later he prefaced *The End of the World* with a quotation from Principal John C. Sharp's lecture on Wordsworth that relates how the poet found "pith of sense and solidity of judgment," as well as the essential feelings and passions of mankind, in greater simplicity and strength among humble country folk.[47] But this too fails to get at Eggleston's own attitude. For one thing, Wordsworth's theory would imply that the Kirtleys (and with them, Western poor whites as a class), as primitive children of nature, are even more admirable than the Mark Bonamys and the Ralph Hartsooks who have acquired a certain degree of literacy and cultivation. Eggleston's acceptance of the theory of progressive refinement through successively higher social stages prevented him from accepting the implications of Wordsworth's attitude. The conception of nature as a source of spiritual value could have little meaning for him. If his intense although undogmatic piety had allowed him to entertain the idea, he would still have found it in conflict with the deterministic notions he had taken over from Taine and Darwin.⁴⁸

Since Eggleston's statement of his intentions is so meager we must make our own inferences from his work. It has been often remarked that before he began *The Hoosier School-Master* he had written a brief notice of a translation of Taine's *Philosophy of Art in the Netherlands* for *The Independent*.⁴⁹ The debt cannot have been great, but there are a few indications in the novels that Taine had given him at least an inkling of a pure pictorial feeling for common and familiar scenes, without overtones of moral or social evaluation. Chapter VI of *Roxy* is entitled "A Genre Piece." It relates how the young minister Whittaker spent an evening with Roxy and her father the shoemaker, and began to fall in love with her. Eggleston apparently wishes to call attention to the visual image of these figures grouped in a kitchen. A clearer example of the novelist's exploitation of pure visual interest is a passage in *The Circuit Rider* which describes Patty Lumsden spinning. Our sculptors, Eggleston remarks, ought to realize that in "mythology and heroics" Americans can never be anything but copyists. If they would turn to our own primitive life they would find admirable subjects like the girl spinning — an activity that reveals as no other can the grace of the female figure. Eggleston adds that the kitchen of the Lumsden home would make a genre subject good enough for the old Dutch masters.⁵⁰

It is refreshing to find even so slight a hint that crude Western materials could be viewed disinterestedly, without the apparatus of theory that had so often beclouded the vision of observers like Mrs. Kirkland. But so long as the achievement was limited to the plane of visual perception, it could not have very far-reaching consequences for literary attitude and method. The borrowing of effects from painting had long been an established convention in writing about the West. Many authors, for example, had invoked the paintings of wild Salvator Rosa to convey their response to Western landscapes felt to be picturesque and sublime.⁵¹ Merely to turn from Salvator to Dutch masters of "realism" was not a startling advance in literary practice. What was requisite was an extension of the technique of disinterested observation to the sphere of ethics, to the psychological interior of the characters as contrasted with their outer appearance or the houses they lived in.[52]

Taine did not help Eggleston very far along this road. The novelist's religiosity and recurrent retreats into sentimentalism lend a strongly archaic air to his work. Yet he did make a beginning. The aspect of his fiction that proved most valuable to the writers who came after him and is most interesting nowadays is his sincere feeling for the "folk" — for the characteristic traits of human beings in a specific geographical and social setting. This is the germ at once of what has been called his "realism" and of the interest in social history that eventually led him to abandon fiction altogether.

The notion that the lore and the mores of the backwoodsman might be interesting without reference to his function as a standard-bearer of progress and civilization, or his alarming and exciting barbarism, or his embodiment of a natural goodness, was quite late in appearing. Although travelers had reported a few snatches of the songs of French Canadian *voyageurs* and an occasional tall tale from the Far West, especially from the 1830's onward, apparently the first indications of an interest in the folklore of the agricultural West are contained in Alice Cary's work. Since her attitude toward these materials is at once complicated and highly suggestive for the future, it deserves more than a passing glance.

In describing her visit to the household of the grim Mrs. Knight, Miss Cary tells how Sally and Jane Ann, left alone for a few moments with their guest, entertain her by reciting riddles: "Four stiff-standers, four down-hangers, two crook-abouts, two look-abouts, and a whisk-about"; "Through a riddle and through a reel, Through an ancient spinning wheel . . ."; "Long legs, short thighs, Little head, and no eyes"; and "Round as an apple, deep as a cup, And all the king's oxen can't draw it up." They have begun a counting-out rime ("Oneary, oreary, kittery Kay . . .") when their mother comes in and angrily sends them away as if they had been misbehaving. The problem here is of course to define Miss Cary's own attitude toward the charming bits of folklore she has recorded. "Mrs. Knight," she remarks, "had been mortified when she found her daughters indulging in the jargon I have reported, and so imprisoned them, as I have described; but if she had accustomed herself to spend some portion of the day devoted to scolding the children, in their cultivation, few punishments of any kind would have been required. If they had known anything sensible, they would probably not have been repeating the nonsense which seemed to please them so." Miss Cary offered to bring over "some prettily illustrated stories . . . which might please her little girls. . . ." [53]

The riddles and counting-out rime are, then, jargon and nonsense, which should be replaced in the children's minds by systematic cultivation through proper children's books — perhaps the Peter Parley series. Yet Miss Cary is interested enough in the rimes to set them down, as apparently no one before her had done. Furthermore, she considers it deplorable that Mrs. Knight refuses to allow her older girls to attend play-parties where the games depend on folk songs:

Many a time [she writes] had the young women gone to bed with aching hearts to hear in dreams the music of —

> "We are marching forward to Quebec
> And the drums are loudly beating,
> America has gained the day
> And the British are retreating.
>
> The wars are o'er and we'll turn back
> And never more be parted;
> So open the ring and choose another in
> That you think will prove true-hearted." [54]

Despite her lapse into a conventionally obtuse attitude concerning the children's rimes, Miss Cary was at least vaguely aware that the nonliterary culture of the Western folk embodied some value. [55]

Eggleston likewise describes a game involving choice of a true-love to the accompaniment of chanted verses ("Oats, peas, beans, and barley grow . . .") of which he reports three stanzas. [56] He perceives that this material raises a literary issue of some consequence, although he does not succeed very well in stating the case for the use of it. People who enjoy society novels, he declares, will consider "these boisterous, unrefined sports" a far from promising beginning for a story. Readers find it easy to imagine heroism, generosity, and courage in people who dance on velvet carpets, but difficult to ascribe similar merits to crude backwoodsmen. This hardly seems a satisfactory statement of the issue. What he is feeling for is a value in the mores of the folk comparable to the pictorial values he could perceive in his backwoods interiors. But he argues instead somewhat irrelevantly that people crude enough to play rowdy kissing games may nevertheless be quite heroic: "the great heroes, the world's demigods, grew in just such rough social states as that of Ohio in the early part of this century." And this leads to a little homily for the benefit of sophisticated readers:

There is nothing more important for an over-refined generation than to understand that it has not a monopoly of the great qualities of humanity, and that it must not only tolerate rude folk, but sometimes admire in them traits that have grown scarce as refinement has increased. So that I may not shrink from telling that one kissing-play took the place of another until the excitement and merriment reached a pitch which would be thought not consonant with propriety by the society that loves round-dances with *roués*, and "the German" untranslated — though, for that matter, there are people old-fashioned enough to think that refined deviltry is not much better than rude freedom, after all.[57]

Although it seems a little stuffy even for the 1870's to call round-dances and the german "refined deviltry," we must remember that Eggleston was a clergyman. Furthermore, he is justified in attacking the snobbery of the genteel East toward the rural West. At least he has realized that folk rhymes and games are more than jargon and nonsense, since they represent a tradition "that has existed in England from immemorial time." [58] If the culture of the folk attested a continuity of social evolution reaching far back into the past, it acquired a new dignity. It had a historical dimension that could never be accounted for by the abstract and schematic and even antihistorical theory of uniform progress through fixed social stages. This way of looking at illiteracy and barbarism offered a valid means of escape from the theory of civilization and refinement, and suggested how Western farmers could be rescued from their degraded social status.

The gradual emergence of a new conception of the Western folk in Eggleston and his successors can be traced clearly in the changing attitudes toward language, which after all was the most intimate, the most flexible, the most characteristic and suggestive of all the aspects of folk culture. What were literary interpreters of the agricultural West to do with vernacular speech?

We are familiar with the role of dialect in the tradition of Cooper, and indeed in sentimental fiction generally, as a simple and unambiguous badge of status. No "straight" character could be allowed to speak dialect, and every character who used dialect was instantly recognizable as having a low social rank. In books of more or less direct reporting, like Mrs. Kirkland's, the upper-class observer regales his presumably upper-class readers by rendering the outlandish speech of the natives as a foil for his own elegant rhetoric. Similarly, the heroes and heroines of fiction who come into the West from outside are distinguished from the natives by their correct and elevated diction. If a Westerner is to be made into a hero, like Cooper's Ben Boden the bee hunter in *The Oak Openings*, the author must take pains to tidy up the character's speech. The first notable departure from this simple set of literary conventions is in the work of Miss Cary, where indifference to the contrast between East and West lessens her interest in speech as a badge of social and sectional status. Although she makes a few experiments in transcribing the Western vernacular, she is capable of reporting the speech of characters living in abject poverty, in a remote rural area, without self-conscious attention to dialect at all, using an easy, colloquial style for people of quite various classes.[59]

But if it was a necessary first step to cease exploiting dialect as a badge of status, the achievement was merely negative. The effort to discover positive values in the culture of the folk would obviously suggest some affirmative use of the vernacular. The analogy of Dutch genre painting would imply a pure esthetic concern with dialect, an ability to enjoy it for its own sake without insisting on its meaning as a badge of status or (what amounted to the same thing) as an index of refinement or the lack of it. There is evidence that the germ of Eggleston's first novel, *The Hoosier School-Master*, was precisely such an interest in the folk speech of southern Indiana. The novelist's biographer has found a list of "Hoosierisms" jotted down by Eggleston in

February, 1863, eight years before the novel was published.[60] Eggleston was corresponding with James Russell Lowell about this list of dialect terms in January, 1870, and the Harvard professor's enthusiasm doubtless did much to convince him that his linguistic interest was reputable from a scholarly and literary standpoint.[61] Years later, in an issue of *The Critic* honoring Lowell's seventieth birthday, Eggleston wrote that Lowell had been his master more than anyone else. "His magnanimous appreciation of the first lines I ever printed on the subject of American dialect and his cordial encouragement and wise advice gave me heart to go on. . . ." [62] The indebtedness had been acknowledged long before in the preface to *The Hoosier School-Master* by a reference to the "admirable and erudite preface to the Biglow Papers."

To Mr. Lowell [Eggleston asserted] belongs the distinction of being the only one of our most eminent authors and the only one of our most eminent scholars who has given careful attention to American dialects. But while I have not ventured to discuss the provincialisms of the Indiana backwoods, I have been careful to preserve the true *usus loquendi* of each locution, and I trust my little story may afford material for some one better qualified than I to criticise the dialect.[63]

The attitude of a linguist is not identical with that of a genre painter, but they have in common the fact that neither is primarily concerned with implications about social status.

If *The Hoosier School-Master* was indeed the leader of the procession of American dialect novels, as Eggleston later asserted,[64] the fact may arouse mixed emotions in modern readers. For much of the dialect writing produced by the local color school in the two decades following the appearance of Eggleston's novel is both unskilful and patronizing. "In all use of dialect," remarked George Philip Krapp, "there is probably present some sense of amused superiority on the part of the conventional speaker as he views the forms of the dialect speech. . . ." [65] The generalization certainly applies to run-of-the-mill local color writing, which depends for too many of its effects upon the supposed quaintness of the illiterate natives of various American regions. But despite this danger in the literary use of dialect, it opened up pathways of advance in two directions. On the one hand, the perception that the speech of Western backwoodsmen exemplified the historian's principle that "all which is partakes of that which was" [66] saved it from being considered merely crude, coarse, and unrefined. The discovery added a dignity to the uneducated folk which they could never have acquired within the framework of the theory of progress and civilization. In *Roxy* Eggleston causes the Swiss-American girl Twonnet (Antoinette) to defend the use of "right" for "very" by pointing out to the young minister Whittaker, a graduate of Yale, that "right" occurs in this sense in the Bible; indeed, she even goes on to make the revolutionary suggestion that Yale itself, students and faculty, has its own local dialect.[67] This was a novel way of conceiving the differences between Eastern and Western speech.

The other line of literary development opened up by the growing respect for Western dialect is merely hinted at in Eggleston's work. This is the creation of an American literary prose formed on the vernacular. Whitman had been a pioneer in this respect, but Eggleston found Whitman merely "coarse." [68] And he had little more respect for Mark Twain, whose *Huckleberry Finn* was the first masterpiece of vernacular prose.[69] Yet Eggleston was moving with the current. His style has far fewer literary flourishes than that of Mrs. Kirkland, and on at least one occasion, when his own use of a provincialism (the word "hover" as a transitive verb to describe the action of a hen brooding her chicks) was pointed out to him by a proofreader, he let it stand, merely adding a note to the effect that the word was so used "at least in half the country." [70] Later in his career he became even more fully aware of the potential richness of folk speech as a literary medium. In 1888, commenting on James Whitcomb Riley's language, he wrote very shrewdly: "As dialect it is perfectly sound Hoosier but a little thin. He has known it more among villagers than among rustics. He has known it at a later period than I did, and the tremendous — almost unequalled vigor of the public school system in Indiana must have washed the color out of the dialect a good deal." [71]

Eggleston's scientific interest in the speech of Western farmers was carried even farther by Joseph Kirkland in *Zury, the Meanest Man in Spring County* (1887) and *The McVeys* (1888).[72] The plots of these novels are dominated by Anne Sparrow, a New England school teacher who brings an unexampled cultivation and refinement to rural Illinois, but the character of the avaricious Zury Prouder is well observed in the period before he is regenerated by Anne's virtue, and the speech of the countryside is reported with care and skill. Kirkland's ear for what people actually said was keener than that of any other writer who has dealt with the agricultural West, except Sinclair Lewis. In addition to accurate phonetic notations, he made the discovery that in conversation people often use an elliptical syntax and altogether omit various kinds of unemphatic words.

But Zury is more than a dialect. He gives the impression of having been created through the accumulation of tall tales about stinginess just as the legendary Davy Crockett was created through accumulation of tales about coon-hunting, fighting, and drinking whiskey. Kirkland says he is repeating stories told by a man who once worked for Zury and later delighted his comrades in the Union army with them; some of the yarns, he adds, have already found their way into print.[73] The political speech which Zury makes with the assistance of Anne is a masterpiece of vernacular prose filled with shrewd anecdotes, like those of Lincoln, which Kirkland greatly admired.[74] If the novelist's simultaneous devotion to folklore and to female gentility led him to consummate one of the strangest matings in all literature by marrying Zury to Anne Sparrow — a transaction as odd as would have been the marriage of Davy Crockett to Miss Alcott's Jo March — he was nevertheless aware that the folk elements in Zury held a new and vital kind of literary interest. Kirkland makes the point explicitly. Anne's daughter Margaret edits the "Third Page" of the *Springville Bugle*, a section given over to book reviews, anecdotes, pointed paragraphs, and editorials. She and her cultivated friend Dr. Strafford notice that whenever Zury has spent an evening with them her writing is much improved. "How is it, Margaret?" asks Strafford. "How does he help us so much?"

"Well [she replies, evidently speaking for the author], as nearly as I can make out, it is the *tone* he gives our thoughts. If I read too much, the T. P. grows eastern and literary. If I leave it to you, it is scientific and political; but when Mr. Prouder is the inspiration, it is frontierish, quaint, common-sensical, shrewd, strong, gay, and — I don't know what all." [75]

Despite the soft spot in the vicinity of the word "quaint," this is not a bad statement of the qualities that Eggleston and Kirkland were beginning to discover in their Western folk.

But neither the rendering of dialect nor the use of folklore proved after all to be the decisive factor in the complex literary evolution preceding the appearance of Hamlin Garland's *Main Travelled Roads* in 1891. It is true that when Garland was writing his memoirs toward the end of his long life he began his account of this movement by discussing the earliest uses of the "New World's vernacular" — in a few of Leatherstocking's speeches, in the *Biglow Papers*, and in Whittier, Bret Harte, and John Hay.[76] But he passes at once to a discussion of E. W. Howe. This transition is remarkable because Howe was not interested in reporting dialect. The Western farm people of his stories have a colorless diction that tends toward conventional rhetoric, rather than the carefully constructed dialect of Eggleston's or Kirkland's characters. Garland refers to Howe's "strong, idiomatic Western prose," [77] but this is not the same thing as dialect and Garland does not probe further into the interesting problem of an American vernacular literary prose as contrasted with the reported speech of characters held distinct from the narrator.

The letter to Howe which Garland wrote in July, 1886, congratulating him on his novel *Moonlight Boy*, is a valuable document for the study of the various trends and currents that were at work in this important decade. It touches upon a number of attitudes and literary procedures that Garland endorsed, and develops a literary credo of some dimensions. Howe is for Garland one of the representative names standing for "local scene and character painting," the only one who represents the prairie West. He has depicted "homely, prosaic people in their restricted lives," not viewing them from a distance as picturesque, but writing "as from among them." [78] The pattern of the travel narrative, as in Mrs. Kirkland's sketches, has disappeared along with the status system that elevated Easterners above Westerners. In Howe's first and best book, *The Story of a Country Town* (1883), the narrator who speaks in the first person is a young man looking back upon his own bleak childhood in the prairie West.

But the most important trait of Howe's work is the constant note of sadness and disillusionment that bespeaks the fading of the dream of an agrarian utopia. *The Story of a Country Town* is a sardonic commentary on the theme of going West to grow up with the country. Through an eccentric character named Lytle Biggs, who sometimes speaks for the author, Howe attacks the cult of the yeoman as explicity as Cooper had attacked it, although from a somewhat different standpoint. The notions that there is a peculiar merit in agricultural labor and that farmers are more virtuous than other men, Biggs declares to be falsehoods circulated by politicians for their own advantage.[79] Howe's West offers neither color to the observer from without nor consolations to the people themselves. It is a world of grim, savage religion, of silent endurance, of families held together by no tenderness, of communities whose only amusement is malicious gossip. Howe's farmers seem on the whole to be prosperous enough, but some not easily analyzed bitterness has poisoned the springs of human feeling. The Reverend John Westlock, father of the narrator, a stern minister and a successful farmer, runs away with a woman he does not love after years of a strange silent battle with himself. Jo Erring, the narrator's closest friend, is destroyed by insane jealousy. The symbol that dominates the opening and the close of the novel is a great bell in the steeple of Fairview church which is used to announce deaths in the community, and is also tolled by the winds "as if the ghosts from the grave lot had crawled up there, and were counting the number to be buried the coming year. . . ."[80]

Garland described this book as "a singularly gloomy, real yet unreal, narrative written in the tone of weary and hopeless age."[81] It is at this point that Howe differs most clearly from Joseph Kirkland, who considered the novel too melodramatic and told Garland that Howe's country town "never had any existence outside of his tired brain."[82] Yet the description of Zury's childhood in Kirkland's own novel is dark and bitter, as is the characterization of the half-insane Hobbs in *The McVeys*, with

its end in the ghastly lynching scene; and both Mrs. Kirkland (in
her shocked description of the death of a girl from an attempted
abortion) [83] and Miss Cary (in her sketch of the newsboy Ward
Henderson) [84] had included ominous shadows in their pictures
of the West. These shadows had no doubt been somewhat blurred,
but in devoting himself to a prolonged exploration of the dark
recesses of his own childhood, Howe was merely developing
hints in the works of his predecessors. The self-castigating Westlock is only a degree more neurotic than Mrs. Knight in Miss
Cary's sketch, and both characters are thwarted by a grim and
colorless environment.

Although Howe's extreme conservatism made him unsympathetic with the efforts of Western farmers to organize themselves for political action in the Farmers' Alliance,[85] the stories
collected in *Main Travelled Roads* owe more to Howe's melancholy than to Kirkland's rather cold fidelity to linguistic fact or
his use of a tall-tale tradition. Garland did practice faithfully the
lesson of exact description, and despite his lack of a good ear for
language he worked hard at transcribing the actual speech of his
characters. But the method was with him only a means of bringing home to his readers the farmers' sufferings. Many years later
he wrote that his point of view when he came back in 1887 to
his old homes in Iowa and South Dakota "was plainly that of
one who, having escaped from this sad life, was now a pitying
onlooker." "That my old neighbors were in a mood of depression,"
he continued, "was evident. Things were going badly with them.
Wheat was very low in price and dairying had brought new problems and new drudgery into their lives. Six years had made little
improvement in farm conditions." [86] The visit coincided with the
collapse of the great Western boom. Garland's success as a por-
trayer of hardship and suffering on Northwestern farms was due
in part to the fact that his personal experience happened to
parallel the shock which the entire West received in the later
1880's from the combined effects of low prices in the international
wheat market, grasshoppers, drought, the terrible blizzards of the
winter of 1886–1887, and the juggling of freight rates that led
to the Interstate Commerce Act in 1887.

In Garland, Howe's undefined sadness, which had no acknowledged connection with economic distress, came into focus about the creed of Henry George's Single Taxers. "There was nothing humorous about the lives of these toilers," he wrote of his trip West in 1887. "On the contrary, I regarded them as victims of an unjust land system. An immense pity took possession of me. I perceived their helplessness. They were like flies in a pool of tar." [87] In the Preface to *Jason Edwards,* a novel written for Benjamin Flower's *Arena* in 1891 and dedicated to the Farmers' Alliance, Garland states his interpretation of what had happened in the agricultural West:

For more than a half century the outlet toward the free lands of the West has been the escape-valve of social discontent in the great cities of America. Whenever the conditions of his native place pressed too hard upon him, the artisan or the farmer has turned his face toward the prairies and forests of the West. . . . Thus long before the days of '49, the West had become the Golden West, the land of wealth and freedom and happiness. All of the associations called up by the spoken word, the West, were fabulous, mythic, hopeful.[88]

But the hopeful myth had been destroyed. With an element of exaggeration that can certainly be forgiven a novelist if it appeared also in the historian Frederick Jackson Turner, Garland declared, "Free land is gone. The last acre of available farmland has now passed into private or corporate hands." [89] His story is an apologue on the closing of the safety valve. Jason Edwards, a Boston mechanic, takes his family to the Western prairies in search of the free land promised by advertising circulars, only to find that all land within thirty miles of a railroad has been taken up by speculators. After five years of desperate struggle to pay interest and get title to his farm, Edwards is prostrated by a hailstorm that destroys his wheat just before harvest. The family return to Massachusetts in defeat under the protection of Alice Edwards's fiancé, a Boston newspaperman. The evil forces oppressing the farmer are represented by Judge S. H. Balser, land agent, who falsifies the evidences of a boom in order to market his lands, and sits back collecting his interest while Edwards and other farmers grind themselves to illness and despair in their fields.[90] Reeves, the fiancé, points the moral of the tale: "So this is the reality of the dream! This is the 'homestead in the Golden

West, embowered in trees, beside the purling brook!' A shanty on
a barren plain, hot and lone as a desert. My God!"[91]

In view of actual conditions in the West, the ideal of the
yeoman society could be considered nothing but a device of
propaganda manipulated by cynical speculators. Yet Garland
continued to hope that the ideal might be realized. He endorsed
the single-tax program because he saw in it a means to this end.
Ida Wilbur, the radical lecturer who voices many of Garland's
ideas in A Spoil of Office, announces to the hero Bradley Talcott:

I believe in thickly settled farming communities, communities where
every man has a small, highly cultivated farm. That's what I've been
advocating and prophesying, but I now begin to see that our system of
ownership in land is directly against this security, and directly against
thickly-settled farming communities. The big land owners are swallowing up the small farmers, and turning them into renters or laborers.[92]

The social theories which shaped Garland's early stories are
evident enough. Land monopolists had blighted the promise of
the West; the single tax would eliminate the speculator and allow
the yeoman ideal to be realized. But Garland was seldom able to
integrate his theories with the materials he had gathered by
personal experience and observation. The radical ideas occur as
concepts. They are seldom realized imaginatively — perhaps
never fully except in "Under the Lion's Paw," which exhibits a
shrewd landowner exploiting a tenant.[93] Garland's strength lay
rather in a simple humanitarian sympathy that was entirely
congruous with the sentimental tradition. His description of an
imaginary painting on the wall of Howard McLane's apartment in
"Up the Coulé" expresses an emotion deeper than his conscious
doctrines. The picture is "a sombre landscape by a master greater
than Millet, a melancholy subject, treated with pitiless fidelity."
It evidently has a portentous meaning for him:

A farm in the valley! Over the mountain swept jagged, gray, angry,
sprawling clouds, sending a freezing, thin drizzle of rain, as they passed,
upon a man following a plough. The horses had a sullen and weary
look, and their manes and tails streamed sidewise in the blast. The
ploughman clad in a ragged gray coat, with uncouth, muddy boots
upon his feet, walked with his head inclined toward the sleet, to shield
his face from the cold and sting of it. The soil rolled away black and

sticky and with a dull sheen upon it. Near by, a boy with tears on his cheeks was watching cattle, a dog seated near, his back to the gale.⁵⁴

This plowman is neither the yeoman of agrarian tradition, nor a picturesque rural swain, nor a half-barbarian like Ishmael Bush, nor an amusingly unrefined backwoodsman, nor even a victim of a perverted land system. His most direct relation is to nature, and even though this relation is one of conflict, it confers on him a certain dignity and tends to enlarge his stature by making him a representative of suffering humanity, of man in general. Garland's early stories are not a literary achievement of the first or even of the second rank, but they mark the end of a long evolution in attitudes. It had at last become possible to deal with the Western farmer in literature as a human being instead of seeing him through a veil of literary convention, class prejudice, or social theory.

CHAPTER XXII

The Myth of the Garden
and Turner's Frontier Hypothesis

By far the most influential piece of writing about the West produced during the nineteenth century was the essay on "The Significance of the Frontier in American History" read by Frederick Jackson Turner before the American Historical Association at Chicago in 1893. The "frontier hypothesis" which he advanced on that occasion revolutionized American historiography and eventually made itself felt in economics and sociology, in literary criticism, and even in politics.[1]

Turner's central contention was that "the existence of an area of free land, its continuous recession, and the advance of American settlement westward explain American development."[2] This proposition does not sound novel now because it has been worked into the very fabric of our conception of our history, but in 1893 it was a polemic directed against the two dominant schools of historians: the group interpreting American history in terms of the slavery controversy, led by Hermann Edouard von Holst, and the group headed by Turner's former teacher, Herbert B. Adams of Johns Hopkins, who explained American institutions as the outgrowth of English, or rather ancient Teutonic germs planted in the New World. Turner maintained that the West, not the proslavery South or the antislavery North, was the most important among American sections, and that the novel attitudes and institutions produced by the frontier, especially through its encouragement of democracy, had been more significant than the imported European heritage in shaping American society.

To determine whether Turner's hypothesis is or is not a valid interpretation of American history forms no part of the intention of this book.[3] The problem here is to place his main ideas in the intellectual tradition that has been examined in earlier chapters. Whatever the merits or demerits of the frontier hypothesis in explaining actual events, the hypothesis itself developed out of the myth of the garden. Its insistence on the importance of the West, its affirmation of democracy, and its doctrine of geographical determinism derive from a still broader tradition of Western thought that would include Benton and Gilpin as well, but its emphasis on agricultural settlement places it clearly within the stream of agrarian theory that flows from eighteenth-century England and France through Jefferson to the men who elaborated the ideal of a society of yeoman farmers in the Northwest from which Turner sprang. Turner's immersion in this stream of intellectual influence had an unfortunate effect in committing him to certain archaic assumptions which hampered his approach to twentieth-century social problems. But one must not forget that the tradition was richer than these assumptions, and that it conferred on him the authority of one who speaks from the distilled experience of his people.[4] If the myth of the garden embodied certain erroneous judgments made by these people concerning the economic forces that had come to dominate American life, it was still true to their experience in the large, because it expressed beliefs and aspirations as well as statistics. This is not the only kind of historical truth, but it is a kind historians need never find contemptible.

Turner's most important debt to his intellectual tradition is the ideas of savagery and civilization that he uses to define his central factor, the frontier. His frontier is explicitly "the meeting point between savagery and civilization."[5] For him as for his predecessors, the outer limit of agricultural settlement is the boundary of civilization, and in his thought as in that of so many earlier interpreters we must therefore begin by distinguishing two Wests, one beyond and one within this all-important line.

From the standpoint of economic theory the wilderness beyond the frontier, the realm of savagery, is a constantly receding area of free land. Mr. Fulmer Mood has demonstrated that Turner derived this technical expression from a treatise on economics by Francis A. Walker used as a text by one of his teachers at Johns Hopkins, Richard T. Ely. In Walker's analysis Turner found warrant for his belief that free land had operated as a safety valve for the East and even for Europe by offering every man an opportunity to acquire a farm and become an independent member of society. Free land thus tended to relieve poverty outside the West, and on the frontier itself it fostered economic equality. Both these tendencies made for an increase of democracy.[6] Earlier writers from the time of Franklin had noted that the West offered freedom and subsistence to all,[7] but Turner restated the idea in a more positive form suggested by his conviction that democracy, the rise of the common man, was one of the great movements of modern history.

In an oration delivered in 1883 when he was still an undergraduate he had declared: "Over all the world we hear mankind proclaiming its existence, demanding its rights. Kings begin to be but names, and the sons of genius, springing from the people, grasp the real sceptres. The reign of aristocracy is passing; that of humanity begins." [8] Although "humanity" is a broad term, for Turner it referred specifically to farmers. He conceived of democracy as a trait of agricultural communities. About this time, for example, he wrote in his Commonplace Book that historians had long occupied themselves with "noble warriors, & all the pomp and glory of the higher class — But of the other phase, of the common people, the lowly tillers of the soil, the great mass of humanity . . . history has hitherto said but little." And he fully accepted the theory of small landholdings that underlay the cult of the yeoman. He planned to develop the idea in an "Oration on Peasant Proprietors in U. S." (by which he meant small farmers tilling their own land).

. . . the work of the Cobden Club on Land Tenure [he wrote] giving the systems of the various countries the paper on America — opens by showing how uninteresting is the subject being as it is purely peasant proprietorship — In this simplicity of our land system lies one of the greatest factors in our progress. Enlarge on the various systems & show the value of it here — point out the fact that if our lands in the west had not been opened to & filled with foreign emigrant it is not unlikely that they would have fallen into the hands of capitalists & hav been made great estates — e. g. Dalyrymple farm — Show effects of great estates in Italy — in Eng.[9]

In systems of land tenure, he felt, lay the key to the democratic upsurge that had reached a climax in the nineteenth century:

> It is not by Contrat Socials that a nation wins freedom & prosperity for its people — ; it is by attention to minor details — like this — it is by evolution —
> Show place of F. R. [French Revolution] — ring in Shelleys Prometheus this was an awakening but now — in our own age is the real revolution going on which is to raise *man* from his low estate to his proper *dignity* (enlarge from previous oration) — in this grand conception it is not an anticlimax to urge the value — the essential necessity of such institutions as the peasant proprietors — a moving force, all the stronger that it works quietly in the great movement.[10]

This is the theoretical background of the proposition in the 1893 essay that "democracy [is] born of free land," [11] as well as of the celebrated pronouncement made twenty years later: "American democracy was born of no theorist's dream; it was not carried in the Susan Constant to Virginia, nor in the Mayflower to Plymouth. It came stark and strong and full of life out of the American forest, and it gained new strength each time it touched a new frontier." [12]

But while economic theory still underlies this later statement, the change of terminology has introduced new and rich overtones. We have been transferred from the plane of the economist's abstractions to a plane of metaphor, and even of myth — for the American forest has become almost an enchanted wood, and the image of Antaeus has been invoked to suggest the power of the Western earth. Such intimations reach beyond logical theory. They remind us that the wilderness beyond the limits of civilization was not only an area of free land; it was also nature. The idea of nature suggested to Turner a poetic account of the influence of free land as a rebirth, a regeneration, a rejuvenation of man and society constantly recurring where civilization came into contact with the wilderness along the frontier.[13]

Rebirth and regeneration are categories of myth rather than of economic analysis, but ordinarily Turner kept his metaphors under control and used them to illustrate and vivify his logical propositions rather than as a structural principle or a means of cognition: that is, he used them rhetorically not poetically. The

nonpoetic use of a vivid metaphor is illustrated in a speech he
delivered in 1896:

Americans had a safety valve for social danger, a bank account on
which they might continually draw to meet losses. This was the vast
unoccupied domain that stretched from the borders of the settled area
to the Pacific Ocean. . . . No grave social problem could exist while
the wilderness at the edge of civilizations [sic] opened wide its portals
to all who were oppressed, to all who with strong arms and stout heart
desired to hew out a home and a career for themselves. Here was an
opportunity for social development continually to begin over again,
wherever society gave signs of breaking into classes. Here was a magic
fountain of youth in which America continually bathed and was rejuve-
nated.[14]

The figure of the magic fountain is merely a rhetorical ornament
at the end of a paragraph having a rational structure and subject
to criticism according to recognized canons. But sometimes, especially when the conception of nature as the source of occult
powers is most vividly present, Turner's metaphors threaten to
become themselves a means of cognition and to supplant discur-
sive reasoning. This seems to happen, for example, in an essay
he wrote for the *Atlantic* in 1903. After quoting a clearly animistic
passage from Lowell's Harvard Commemoration Ode on how
Nature had shaped Lincoln of untainted clay from the unexhausted West, "New birth of our new soil, the first American,"
Turner builds an elaborate figurative structure:

Into this vast shaggy continent of ours poured the first feeble tide of
European settlement. European men, institutions, and ideas were lodged
in the American wilderness, and this great American West took them
to her bosom, taught them a new way of looking upon the destiny of
the common man, trained them in adaptation to the conditions of the
New World, to the creation of new institutions to meet new needs; and
ever as society on her eastern border grew to resemble the Old World
in its social forms and its industry, ever, as it began to lose faith in the
ideal of democracy, she opened new provinces, and dowered new
democracies in her most distant domains with her material treasures
and with the ennobling influence that the fierce love of freedom, the
strength that came from hewing out a home, making a school and a
church, and creating a higher future for his family, furnished to the
pioneer.[15]

It would be difficult to maintain that all these metaphors are merely ornamental. Is it wholly meaningless, for example, that the West, the region close to nature, is feminine, while the East, with its remoteness from nature and its propensity for aping Europe, is neuter?

In the passage just quoted, a beneficent power emanating from nature is shown creating an agrarian utopia in the West. The myth of the garden is constructed before our eyes. Turner is asserting as fact a state of affairs that on other occasions he recognized as merely an ideal to be striven for. Earlier in the same essay, for example, he had summarized Jefferson's "platform of political principles" and his "conception that democracy should have an agricultural basis." [16] The "should" easily becomes "did": Jefferson's agrarian ideal proves to be virtually identical with the frontier democracy that Turner believed he had discovered in the West. To imagine an ideal so vividly that it comes to seem actual is to follow the specific procedure of poetry.

The other member of the pair of ideas which defined the frontier for Turner was that of civilization. If the idea of nature in the West provided him with a rich and not always manageable store of metaphorical coloring, his use of the idea of civilization had the equally important consequence of committing him to the theory that all societies, including those of successive Wests, develop through the same series of progressively higher stages. Mr. Mood has traced this conception also to Ely and to Walker, and back of them to the German economic theorist Friedrich List.[17] But, as we have had occasion to notice earlier in this study, the idea had been imported into the United States from France soon after 1800 and by the 1820's had become one of the principal instruments for interpreting the agricultural West.

Turner's acceptance of this theory involved him in the difficulties that it had created for earlier observers of frontier society, such as Timothy Flint. For the theory of social stages was basically at odds with the conception of the Western farmer as a yeoman surrounded by utopian splendor. Instead, it implied that the Western farmer was a coarse and unrefined representative of a primitive stage of social evolution. Turner's adoption of these two contradictory theories makes it difficult for him to manage the question of whether frontier character and society, and frontier influence on the rest of the country, have been good or bad. As long as he is dealing with the origins of democracy in the West he evidently considers frontier influence good. A man who refers to "the familiar struggle of West against East, of democracy against privileged classes" [18] leaves no doubt concerning his own allegiance. This attitude was in fact inevitable as long as one maintained the doctrine that frontier society was shaped by the influence of free land, for free land was nature, and nature in this system of ideas is unqualifiedly benign. Indeed, it is itself the norm of value. There is no way to conceive possible bad effects flowing from the impact of nature on man and society.

But when Turner invokes the concept of civilization, the situation becomes more complex. His basic conviction was that the highest social values were to be found in the relatively primitive society just within the agricultural frontier. But the theory of social stages placed the highest values at the other end of the process, in urban industrial society, amid the manufacturing development and city life which Jefferson and later agrarian theorists had considered dangerous to social purity. Turner wavered between the two views. In the 1893 essay, to take a minute but perhaps significant bit of evidence, he referred to the evolution of each successive region of the West "into a higher stage" — in accord with the orthodox theory of civilization and progress. When he revised the essay for republication in 1899, he realized that such an assumption might lead him into inconsistency and substituted "a different industrial stage." [19]

But he could not always maintain the neutrality implied in this revision. For one thing, he strongly disapproved of the Western love of currency inflation, which he considered a consequence of the primitive state of frontier society. "The colonial and Revolutionary frontier," he asserted in the 1893 essay, "was the region whence emanated many of the worst forms of an evil currency," and he pointed out that each of the periods of lax financial integrity in American history had coincided with the rise of a new set of frontier communities. The Populist agitation for free coinage of silver was a case in point.

Many a state that now declines any connection with the tenets of the Populists [he wrote] itself adhered to such ideas in an earlier stage of the development of the state. A primitive society can hardly be expected to show the intelligent appreciation of the complexity of business interests in a developed society.[20]

In his revision of the essay in 1899 Turner noted with satisfaction that Wisconsin had borne out his principles:

Wisconsin, to take an illustration, in the days when it lacked varied agriculture and complex industrial life, was a stronghold of the granger and greenback movements; but it has undergone an industrial transformation, and in the last presidential contest Mr. Bryan carried but one county in the state.[21]

Here the evolution of society from agrarian simplicity toward greater complexity is assumed to bring about improvement.

Yet if Turner could affirm progress and civilization in this one respect, the general course of social evolution in the United States created a grave theoretical dilemma for him. He had based his highest value, democracy, on free land. But the westward advance of civilization across the continent had caused free land to disappear. What then was to become of democracy? The difficulty was the greater because in associating democracy with free land he had inevitably linked it also with the idea of nature as a source of spiritual values. All the overtones of his conception of democracy were therefore tinged with cultural primitivism, and tended to clash with the idea of civilization. In itself this was not necessarily a disadvantage; the conception of civilization had been invoked to justify a number of dubious undertakings in the course of the nineteenth century, including European exploitation of native peoples all over the world. Furthermore, as we have had occasion to observe in studying the literary interpretation of the agricultural West, the theory of social progress through a uniform series of stages was poor equipment for any observer who wished to understand Western farmers. But Turner had accepted the idea of civilization as a general description of the society that had been expanding across the continent, and with the final disappearance of free land this idea was the only remaining principle with which he could undertake the analysis of contemporary American society.

Since democracy for him was related to the idea of nature and seemed to have no logical relation to civilization, the conclusion implied by his system was that postfrontier American society contained no force tending toward democracy. Fourierists earlier in the century, reaching a conclusion comparable to this, had maintained that civilization was but a transitory social stage, and that humanity must transcend it by advancing into the higher stage of "association." Henry George in Turner's own day had announced that progress brought poverty, that civilization embodied a radical contradiction and could be redeemed only by a revolutionary measure, the confiscation of the unearned increment in the value of natural resources. But Turner did not share the more or less revolutionary attitude that lay back of these proposals.[22] On the contrary, he conceived of social progress as taking place within the existing framework of society, that is, within civilization. Whatever solution might be found for social problems would have to be developed according to the basic principles already accepted by society. This meant that his problem was to find a basis for democracy in some aspect of civilization as he observed it about him in the United States. His determined effort in this direction showed that his mind and his standards of social ethics were subtler and broader than the conceptual system within which the frontier hypothesis had been developed, but he was the prisoner of the assumptions he had taken over from the agrarian tradition.[23] He turned to the rather unconvincing idea that the Midwestern state universities might be able to save democracy by producing trained leaders,[24] and later he placed science beside education as another force to which men might turn for aid in their modern perplexity. But these suggestions were not really satisfying to him, and he fell back at last on the faith he had confided to his Commonplace Book as an undergraduate — a faith neither in nature nor in civilization but simply in man, in the common people. In 1924, after reviewing the most urgent of the world's problems, Turner declared with eloquence and dignity:

I prefer to believe that man is greater than the dangers that menace him; that education and science are powerful forces to change these tendencies and to produce a rational solution of the problems of life on the shrinking planet. I place my trust in the mind of man seeking solutions by intellectual toil rather than by drift and by habit, bold to find new ways of adjustment, and strong in the leadership that spreads new ideas among the common people of the world; committed to peace on earth, and ready to use the means of preserving it.[25]

This statement is an admission that the notion of democracy born of free land, colored as it is by primitivism, is not an adequate instrument for dealing with a world dominated by industry, urbanization, and international conflicts. The first World War had shaken Turner's agrarian code of values as it destroyed so many other intellectual constructions of the nineteenth century. He continued to struggle with the grievous problems of the modern world, but his original theoretical weapons were no longer useful.

Turner's predicament illustrates what has happened to the tradition within which he worked. From the time of Franklin down to the end of the frontier period almost a century and a half later, the West had been a constant reminder of the importance of agriculture in American society. It had nourished an agrarian philosophy and an agrarian myth that purported to set forth the character and destinies of the nation. The philosophy and the myth affirmed an admirable set of values, but they ceased very early to be useful in interpreting American society as a whole because they offered no intellectual apparatus for taking account of the industrial revolution. A system which revolved about a half-mystical conception of nature and held up as an ideal a rudimentary type of agriculture was powerless to confront issues arising from the advance of technology. Agrarian theory encouraged men to ignore the industrial revolution altogether, or to regard it as an unfortunate and anomalous violation of the natural order of things. In the restricted but important sphere of historical scholarship, for example, the agrarian emphasis of the frontier hypothesis has tended to divert attention from the problems created by industrialization for a half century during which the United States has become the most powerful industrial nation in the world.[26] An even more significant consequence of the agrarian tradition has been its effect on politics. The covert distrust of the city and of everything connected with industry that is implicit in the myth of the garden has impeded coöperation between farmers and factory workers in more than one crisis of our history, from the time of Jefferson to the present.

The agrarian tradition has also made it difficult for Americans to think of themselves as members of a world community because it has affirmed that the destiny of this country leads her away from Europe toward the agricultural interior of the continent. This tendency is quite evident in Turner.[27] Although he devoted much attention to the diplomatic issues arising out of westward expansion, the frontier hypothesis implied that it would be a last misfortune for American society to maintain close connections with Europe. The frontier which produced Andrew Jackson, wrote Turner with approval in 1903, was "free from the influence of European ideas and institutions. The men of the 'Western World' turned their backs upon the Atlantic Ocean, and with a grim energy and self-reliance began to build up a society free from the dominance of ancient forms." [28] It was only later, when he was trying to find a theoretical basis for democracy outside the frontier, that Turner criticized the American attitude of "contemptuous indifference" to the social legislation of European countries.[29]

But if interpretation of the West in terms of the idea of nature tended to cut the region off from the urban East and from Europe, the opposed idea of civilization had even greater disadvantages. It not only imposed on Westerners the stigma of social, ethical, and cultural inferiority, but prevented any recognition that the American adventure of settling the continent had brought about an irruption of novelty into history. For the theory of civilization implied that America in general, and the West *a fortiori*, were meaningless except in so far as they managed to reproduce the achievements of Europe. The capital difficulty of the American agrarian tradition is that it accepted the paired but contradictory ideas of nature and civilization as a general principle of historical and social interpretation. A new intellectual system was requisite before the West could be adequately dealt with in literature or its social development fully understood.

NOTES

NOTES

PROLOGUE: EIGHTEENTH-CENTURY ORIGINS

1. "God's Controversy with New England," *Proceedings of the Massachusetts Historical Society*, XII (1871–1873), 83, 84.

2. *Calendar of State Papers. Colonial Series. America and West Indies. March, 1720, to December, 1721*, ed. Cecil Headlam (London, 1933), pp. 443–444.

3. Quoted by Thomas P. Abernethy, *Western Lands and the American Revolution* (New York, 1937), pp. 20–21.

4. Clarence W. Alvord, *The Mississippi Valley in British Politics*, 2 vols. (Cleveland, 1917), I, 52.

5. "Observations Concerning the Increase of Mankind, Peopling of Countries, Etc.," *The Writings of Benjamin Franklin*, ed. Albert H. Smyth, 10 vols. (New York, 1905–1907), III, 63, 71. The pamphlet was written in 1751 and published in 1755.

6. *Ibid.*, IV, 55 (1760).

7. *Ibid.*, III, 71.

8. *Ibid.*, IV, 4.

9. "Verses on the Prospect of Planting Arts and Learning in America," *The Works of George Berkeley, D. D.*, ed. Alexander C. Fraser, 4 vols. (Oxford, 1901), IV, 364.

10. Quoted by Fred J. Hinkhouse, *The Preliminaries of the American Revolution as Seen in the English Press, 1763–1775* (New York, 1926), pp. 106–107.

11. *The Poems of Philip Freneau, Poet of the American Revolution*, ed. Fred L. Pattee, 3 vols. (Princeton, 1902), I, 73n. When Freneau revised the text for republication in 1809 he changed "Britain's sons" to "we" and added that American ships would "people half the convex of the main" (*ibid.*, I, 75).

12. Thomas Hutchins, *An Historical Narrative and Topographical Description of Louisiana, and West-Florida* (Philadelphia, 1784), pp. 93–94.

13. Timothy Dwight, *Greenfield Hill: A Poem* (New York, 1794), pp. 52–53.

14. "Observations on the Article Etats-Unis Prepared for the Encyclopedie," June 22, 1786, *The Writings of Thomas Jefferson*, ed. Paul L. Ford, 10 vols. (New York, 1892–1899), IV, 180–181.

15. *The Freeman's Journal: or, The North American Intelligencer* (Philadelphia), January 9, 1782, p. [1].

CHAPTER I. A HIGHWAY TO THE PACIFIC

1. *The Writings of Thomas Jefferson*, ed. H. A. Washington, 9 vols. (Philadelphia, 1868–1871), IV, 509 (letter to Du Pont de Nemours, Washington, November 1, 1803).

2. *The Writings of Thomas Jefferson*, ed. Andrew A. Lipscomb, 20 vols. (Washington, D. C., 1904–1905), XI, 20 (letter to William Dunbar, March 13, 1804).

3. *Original Journals of the Lewis and Clark Expedition*, ed. Reuben G. Thwaites, 8 vols. (New York, 1904–1905), VII, 195–197, 202–205.

4. Jefferson's "Secret Message to Congress," January 18, 1803, *ibid.*, VII, 206–209.

5. *Ibid.*, VII, 208.

6. *Ibid.*, VII, 334.

7. Harrison C. Dale, *The Ashley-Smith Explorations and the Discovery of a Central Route to the Pacific 1822–1829* (Cleveland, 1918), pp. 36–40, 89–112.

8. James C. Bell, *Opening a Highway to the Pacific, 1838–1846* (New York, 1921), pp. 183–190.

CHAPTER II. PASSAGE TO INDIA

1. Clarence W. Alvord and Lee Bidgood, *The First Explorations of the Trans-Allegheny Region by the Virginians 1650–1674* (Cleveland, 1912), p. 61.

2. *The Poems of Philip Freneau*, ed. Pattee, I, 76n., 77n.

3. *An Historical Narrative and Topographical Description of Louisiana, and West-Florida*, p. 94.

4. *Original Journals of the Lewis and Clark Expedition*, ed. Thwaites, VII, 204.

5. *Kentucky Gazette* (Lexington), February 28, 1795, p. 2.

6. *Original Journals*, ed. Thwaites, VII, 248.

7. *Ibid.*, VII, 335. In a letter to Lewis dated July 15, 1803, Jefferson had quoted without comment a communication from "Mr. La Cepede at Paris" containing the following statement: "If your nation can establish an easy communication by rivers, canals, & short portages between N. York for example & . . . the mouth of the Columbia, what a route for the commerce of Europe, Asia, & America" (*Writings*, ed. Ford, VIII, 200n.).

8. *Original Journals*, VII, 334.

9. Philip A. Rollins, ed., *The Discovery of the Oregon Trail. Robert Stuart's Narratives of his Overland Trip Eastward from Astoria in 1812–13* (New York, 1935), pp. lxv–lxxi.

10. "Remarks Made on a Tour to Prairie du Chien; Thence to Washington City, in 1829," in *The Writings of Caleb Atwater* (Columbus, Ohio, 1833), p. 202.

11. *Hunt's Merchants' Magazine*, XIX, 530 (November, 1848).

12. John Charles Frémont, *Memoirs of My Life . . . . Together with a Sketch of the Life of Senator Benton, in Connection with Western Expansion*, Volume I (all published) (Chicago and New York, 1887), p. 10; Thomas Hart Benton, *Thirty Years' View; or, A History of the Working of the American Government for Thirty Years, from 1820 to 1850*, 2 vols. (New York, 1854), I, 43.

13. *Thirty Years' View*, I, 14.

14. Frémont, *Memoirs*, p. 12.

15. *Ibid.*, pp. [1]–2.

16. *Ibid.*, p. 8.

17. *Ibid.*, p. 17.

18. *Selections of Editorial Articles from the St. Louis Enquirer, on the Subject of Oregon and Texas, as Originally Published in That Paper in the Years 1818–19; and Written by the Hon. Thomas H. Benton* (St. Louis, 1844), p. [5].

19. *Ibid.,* p. 7.

20. *Ibid.,* p. 17.

21. *Ibid.,* p. 23.

22. 18 Cong., 2 Sess., *Register of Debates in Congress,* Senate, I, cols. 712–713 (March 1, 1825).

23. *Ibid.,* cols. 711–712.

24. 30 Cong., 2 Sess., *Congressional Globe,* Senate, p. 473 (February 7, 1849).

25. *Idem.*

26. *Idem.*

27. 29 Cong., 1 Sess., *Congressional Globe,* Senate, p. 916 (May 28, 1846).

28. *Idem.*

29. *Letter from Col. Benton to the People of Missouri. Central National Highway from the Mississippi River to the Pacific* (1854), n. p., n. d.

30. 30 Cong., 1 Sess., *Congressional Globe,* Senate, p. 1011 (July 29, 1848).

31. *Discourse of Mr. Benton, of Missouri, before the Boston Mercantile Library Association, on the Physical Geography of the Country between the States of Missouri and California . . . Delivered in the Tremont Temple, at Boston . . . December 20, 1854* (Washington, 1854), p. 4.

32. *Ibid.,* p. 17.

33. *Ibid.,* p. 21.

34. *Address of Mr. A. Whitney, before the Legislature of Pennsylvania, on His Project for a Railroad from Lake Michigan to the Pacific* (Harrisburg, 1848), pp. 16–17.

35. *Atlantic and Pacific Railroad. A Letter, from the Hon. S. A. Douglass* [sic], *to A. Whitney, Esq., N. Y.* (dated Quincy, Illinois, October 15, 1845), n. p., n. d., pp. 5–6.

36. Asa Whitney, *A Project for a Railroad to the Pacific* (New York, 1849), p. 12.

37. *Hunt's Merchants' Magazine,* XXI, 75 (July, 1849).

38. *Address of Mr. A. Whitney before the Legislature of Pennsylvania,* p. 14.

CHAPTER III. THE UNTRANSACTED DESTINY

1. Hubert H. Bancroft, *History of the Life of William Gilpin. A Character Study* (San Francisco, 1889), pp. 6–9, 14–23, 28–32. Mr. Bernard DeVoto has called attention to Gilpin in an article in *Harper's Magazine* (CLXXXVIII, 313–323, March, 1944) entitled "Geopolitics with the Dew On It." Gilpin's activities in Oregon are discussed by Maurice O. Georges, "A Suggested Revision of the Role of a Pioneer Political Scientist," *Reed College Bulletin,* XXV, 67–84 (April, 1947).

2. Bancroft, *Life,* p. 43.

3. *The Central Gold Region. The Grain, Pastoral and Gold Regions of North America* (Philadelphia and St. Louis, 1860), pp. 132–133.

4. *Mission of the North American People, Geographical, Social, and Political* (Philadelphia, 1874), p. 130 (quoting a letter of 1846).

5. "Settlement of Oregon — Emigrants of 1843," 29 Cong., 1 Sess., Senate Document No. 306. Report of the Committee on the Post Office and Post Roads (April 20, 1846), pp. 39–40.

6. *Central Gold Region*, pp. 178–179.

7. *Ibid.*, p. 55.

8. *Ibid.*, p. 133.

9. *Ibid.*, p. 103.

10. *Ibid.*, pp. 20–21.

11. *An Essay on Criticism* (London, 1711), p. 7.

12. Leonard C. Jones, *Arnold Guyot et Princeton* (Neuchâtel, 1929).

13. Arnold H. Guyot, *The Earth and Man: Lectures on Comparative Physical Geography, in its Relation to the History of Man*, trans. Cornelius C. Felton (New York, 1887), p. 33.

14. *Ibid.*, pp. 176–177.

15. *Ibid.*, pp. 236–237.

16. *Ibid.*, pp. 183–185.

CHAPTER IV. WALT WHITMAN AND MANIFEST DESTINY

1. The substance of this chapter, under the same title, appeared in the *Huntington Library Quarterly*, X, 373–389 (August, 1947). I wish to thank the editor of that journal for permission to reprint portions of the text.

2. "Poem of the Sayers of the Words of the Earth," *Leaves of Grass* (New York, 1856); (hereafter "*Leaves of Grass* [1856]"), p. 329.

3. *Ibid.*, p. iv.

4. In "Calamus," Section 30 (later revised and given the title, "A Promise to California"), *Leaves of Grass* (Boston, 1860); (hereafter "*Leaves of Grass* [1860]"), p. 371.

5. In "Chants Democratic," Section 14, *ibid.*, p. 187.

6. *Leaves of Grass by Walt Whitman. Reproduced from the First Edition (1855)*, ed. Clifton J. Furness (New York, 1939); (hereafter "*Leaves of Grass* [1855]"), p. iii; *Leaves of Grass* (1860), p. 368 ("Calamus," Section 25).

7. *Leaves of Grass* (1860), p. 183.

8. *Ibid.*, p. 312.

9. *Drum-Taps* (New York, 1865); (hereafter "*Drum-Taps* [1865]"), pp. 25–30. The central idea and many details of "Pioneers!" closely parallel Gilpin's accounts of his Western experiences and discussions of the westward movement. I am strongly disposed to believe that Whitman was borrowing directly from Gilpin, although the exact circumstances are not easy to make out. The most relevant documents are a letter describing the emigration of 1843 to Oregon (29 Cong., 1 Sess., Senate Report No. 306. Committee on the Post Office and Post Roads . . . Submitted April 20, 1846, pp. 19–47); an address on the Doniphan Expedition delivered by Gilpin in 1847 (reprinted in Gilpin's *The Mission of the North American People* [Philadelphia, 1874],

pp. 131–140); and Gilpin's speech on the Pacific Railway delivered in 1849 (reprinted in *The Central Gold Region*, pp. 145–180).

10. 29 Cong., 1 Sess., Senate Report No. 306, p. 46.

11. *Drum-Taps* (1865), pp. 53–54.

12. *Ibid.*, pp. 64–65.

13. *Two Rivulets* (Camden, New Jersey, 1876), p. 5n.

14. *Passage to India* (Washington, D. C., 1871), pp. 8–9.

15. *Ibid.*, pp. 6–7.

16. *Ibid.*, pp. 9–10.

CHAPTER V. DANIEL BOONE: EMPIRE BUILDER OR PHILOSOPHER OF PRIMITIVISM?

1. *The Journals of Francis Parkman*, ed. Mason Wade, 2 vols. (paged continuously); (New York, 1947), p. 53.

2. *Ibid.*, p. 77.

3. *The Oregon Trail*, rev. ed. (New York, 1872), pp. 12–13.

4. *Journals*, p. 3.

5. *The Oregon Trail*, pp. [vii]–viii.

6. The work is described in *Ballou's Pictorial Drawing-Room Companion*, IX (1855), 284.

7. The painting is in the possession of Washington University, St. Louis. It was reproduced in *The Magazine of Art*, XXXII, 330 (June, 1939).

8. John E. Bakeless, *Daniel Boone, Master of the Wilderness* (New York, 1939), pp. 85, 89, 144–145. The *Port Folio* mentioned Boone in 1814 as an example of American "enterprize" (Third [Fourth] Series, IV, 337).

9. *The Discovery, Settlement and Present State of Kentucke* (Wilmington, Delaware, 1784), pp. 81–82.

10. Daniel Bryan, *The Mountain Muse: Comprising The Adventures of Daniel Boone; and The Power of Virtuous and Refined Beauty* (Harrisonburg, Virginia, 1813), pp. 42–43.

11. *Ibid.*, p. 54.

12. *Ibid.*, p. 59.

13. *Ibid.*, pp. 184–185.

14. *Niles' Register*, X, 361 (June 15, 1816).

15. *Niles' Register*, XXIV, 166 (May 17, 1823); *American Monthly Magazine and Critical Review*, III, 152 (New York, June, 1818). *Niles' Register* picked up a similar remark from the St. Louis *Enquirer*, XV, 328 (December 26, 1818).

16. Edwin James, ed., *Account of an Expedition from Pittsburgh to the Rocky Mountains, Performed in the Years 1819 and '20 . . . under the Command of Major Stephen H. Long*, 2 vols. and atlas (Philadelphia, 1823), I, 105.

17. *Ibid.*, I, 106.

18. They were reprinted, for example, in *Life and Adventures of Colonel Daniel Boone, the First White Settler of the State of Kentucky . . . Written by Himself . . . Annexed Is a Eulogy on Col. Boone and Choice of Life, by Lord Byron* (Brooklyn, 1823), reprinted in *The Magazine of History*, Extra No. 180 (Tarrytown, New York, 1932), pp. 226–227.

19. *Ibid.*, pp. 217–221.

20. *The Life and Adventures of Daniel Boone, the First Settler of Kentucky, Interspersed with Incidents in the Early Annals of the Country* (first published 1833); (Cincinnati, 1868), pp. 226–227. According to the *Dictionary of American Biography,* this work went through fourteen editions.

21. *Ibid.,* pp. 229–230.

22. *Ibid.,* p. 246.

23. *Ibid.,* p. 41.

24. *Lives of Daniel Boone and Benjamin Lincoln,* The Library of American Biography, ed. Jared Sparks, Second Series, XIII (Boston, 1847), pp. 186–189. Peck's characterization of Boone exhibits a number of parallels with the character of Leatherstocking. He was one of Nature's noblemen — benevolent, rigidly honest, reluctant to shed blood. Although he never joined any church, he had received religious instruction in his youth, and "was a believer in Christianity as a revelation from God in the sacred scriptures." The character of Boone in James Hall's "The Backwoodsman" also strongly suggests Leatherstocking, although Hall develops the functions of the hunter in rescuing a heroine rather than his ethical nobility (*Legends of the West,* "second edition," Philadelphia, 1833, pp. [1]–40).

25. *North American Review,* LXII, 97, 86–87 (January, 1846).

26. Notes of a Military Reconnoissance from Fort Leavenworth . . . to San Diego (1848), 30 Cong., 1 Sess. House Executive Document No. 41, in Vol. IV, p. 25.

27. *Wild Western Scenes: A Narrative of Adventures in the Western Wilderness, the Nearest and Best California. Wherein the Exploits of Daniel Boone, the Great American Pioneer, Are Particularly Described,* by Luke Shortfield (pseud.); (Philadelphia, 1849), p. 22. Since Boone plays but a negligible part in the story, the exploitation of his name in the title suggests the currency of the Boone legend.

CHAPTER VI. LEATHERSTOCKING AND
THE PROBLEM OF SOCIAL ORDER

1. Bakeless, *Daniel Boone,* p. 139. The reviewer of *The Pioneers* in the *Port Folio* (Fourth [Fifth] Series, XV, 232, March, 1823) remarked that Leatherstocking had been "modelled from the effigies of old Daniel Boone."

2. *The Last of the Mohicans: A Narrative of 1757,* 2 vols. (Philadelphia, 1826), I, 146.

3. Bakeless, *Daniel Boone,* pp. 133–139; *Mohicans,* I, 166–174.

4. *The Prairie: A Tale,* 2 vols. (Philadelphia, 1827), I, 14–15.

5. *The Prairie,* Red Rover ed. (New York, n. d.), p. 3n. Cooper has adopted Jefferson's estimate of the point at which density of population makes Americans "uneasy" (above, p. 10).

6. *The Prairie,* I, x.

7. *Niles' Register,* XXIX, 217 (December 3, 1825). The roving propensities of Leatherstocking had impressed an anonymous writer for *Niles' Register* within a few months after the publication of *The Pioneers:* "A settlement at the mouth of the *Columbia* has been seriously advocated in Congress, and will soon be made under the sanction of government; and, in a few years, we may expect that some persons *there,* feeling themselves too much crowded, like 'Leather Stocking' in the 'Pioneers,' will seek a country more *west* —

Japan, perhaps, if good hunting could be expected therein!" (XXIV, 71, April 5, 1823).

8. *Prose Sketches and Poems, Written in the Western Country* (Boston, 1834), p. 60. Bushfield was a Kentucky hunter in James K. Paulding's novel *Westward Ho!* (1832).

9. Although critics often objected to the Indians of the Leatherstocking tales, they were enthusiastic about the old hunter from his first appearance. A reviewer in the generally unsympathetic *North American Review* called Leatherstocking "a bold and original conception . . . . upon the whole, the best piece of invention our author has ever produced; one, we may say, which deserves to be ranked in the first class of the creations of genius" (XXIII, 172, July, 1826). A later reviewer in this periodical, on the other hand, was cool toward the character (XXXII, 517, April, 1831). The *United States Review and Literary Gazette* said in 1827 that Cooper must mainly depend on Leatherstocking for his future fame (II, 307, July). Four years after Cooper had described the death of the hunter in *The Prairie*, the *American Monthly Magazine* of Boston declared, "in the whole range of fictitious writing, you will not find anything finer than Long Tom and Natty Bumpo [*sic*]" (II, 696, January, 1831). — The suggestion that the Leatherstocking series should be read in terms of "a tension between civilization and noncivilization" is interestingly set forth in Roy Harvey Pearce's article, "The Leatherstocking Tales Re-examined" (*South Atlantic Quarterly*, XLVI, 524–536, October, 1947). I have profited greatly in my discussion of Cooper from Mr. Pearce's observations.

10. *The Pioneers, or The Sources of the Susquehanna; A Descriptive Tale*, 2 vols. (New York, 1823), I, viii.

11. *Ibid.*, I, 21, 27.

12. *Ibid.*, I, 8–20; II, 206–215.

13. *Ibid.*, I, 269.

14. *Ibid.*, II, 228.

15. *Ibid.*, I, 254–255.

16. Susan Fenimore Cooper, *Pages and Pictures, from the Writings of James Fenimore Cooper, with Notes* (New York, 1861), p. 157.

17. *The Pathfinder; or, The Inland Sea*, 2 vols. (Philadelphia, 1840), I, 14.

18. *Ibid.*, I, 114.

19. *Ibid.*, I, 135–136.

20. *Ibid.*, II, 34–40.

21. *Ibid.*, II, 214–225.

22. *The Prairie*, Red Rover ed., p. 3n.

23. *The Oak Openings; or, The Bee-Hunter*, 2 vols. (New York, 1848), I, 14, 18, 30–31.

24. *Ibid.*, II, 227.

CHAPTER VII. THE INNOCENCE AND WILDNESS OF NATURE

1. *The Prairie* (1827), II, 92.

2. Thomas J. Farnham, *Travels in the Great Western Prairies, the Anahuac and Rocky Mountains, and in the Oregon Territory* (Poughkeepsie, N. Y., 1841), p. 72.

3. *Ibid.*, pp. 72–73.

4. *Old Hicks, the Guide; or, Adventures in the Camanche Country in Search of a Gold Mine,* first published 1848, 2 vols. (paged continuously); (New York, 1855), p. 46.

5. *Ibid.*, pp. 311–313.

6. *Ibid.*, pp. 304–305.

7. *Ibid.*, p. 311.

8. *Idem.*

9. *Ibid.*, p. 121.

10. *Idem.*

11. Evart A. Duyckinck and George L. Duyckinck, *Cyclopaedia of American Literature,* 2 vols. (New York, 1855), II, 665–669.

12. *Graham's Magazine,* XXXIV, 386 (June, 1849).

13. *Ibid.*, XXXII, 356 (June, 1848).

14. *United States Magazine and Democratic Review,* New Series, XXII, 332 [properly 432], 328 [properly 428] (May, 1848).

15. "Experience," *Complete Works,* ed. Edward Waldo Emerson, 12 vols. (Boston, 1903–1904), III, 63–64.

16. *Walden,* Chapter I, *Writings,* Riverside edition, 11 vols. (Boston, 1893–1894), II, 21–23, 25–28.

17. *Ibid.*, IX, 266–267.

18. *Ibid.*, IX, 272–273.

19. *Ibid.*, IX, 275–276.

20. *Ibid.*, II, [327].

21. *Ibid.*, IX, 276.

22. *Mardi, and a Voyage Thither* (London, 1922), II, 264–267, [225]–231, 238–245.

23. *Moby-Dick or The Whale,* ed. Willard Thorp (New York, 1947), pp. 178–179. The widely current legend of the White Steed of the Prairies is discussed in *Mustangs and Cow Horses,* edd. J. Frank Dobie, Mody C. Boatright, and Harry F. Ransom (Austin, Texas, 1940), pp. 171–183. Melville's use of this legend is noted at p. 245.

24. *Ibid.*, p. 183.

CHAPTER VIII. THE MOUNTAIN MAN AS WESTERN HERO

1. *The Shoshonee Valley; A Romance,* 2 vols. (Cincinnati, 1830), I, 21. — The substance of Chapters VIII, IX, and X appeared in the *Southwest Review* (XXVIII, 164–189, Winter, 1943; XXXIII, 276–284, 378–384, Summer, Autumn, 1948; XXXIV, 182–188, Spring, 1949). I wish to thank the editor of that magazine for permission to reprint the material here.

2. *Ibid.*, I, 20.

3. *Ibid.*, I, 21–22.

4. Charles Sealsfield (pseud. of Karl Anton Postl), *Life in the New World; or, Sketches of American Society,* first published in 1835–1837, in German; Eng. trans. Gustavus C. Hebbe and James Mackay (New York, 1844), p. 42.

5. *Ibid.*, p. 43.

6. David H. Coyner, *The Lost Trappers; A Collection of Interesting Scenes and Events in the Rocky Mountains* (New York, 1847), pp. xii–xiii.

7. *The Prairie Flower; or, Adventures in the Far West* (Cincinnati, 1849), p. 31. Harold A. Blaine has noted extensive plagiarism from George F. Ruxton's *Adventures in Mexico* and *Life in the Far West* in *The Prairie Flower* ("The Frontiersman in American Prose Fiction: 1800–1860," unpublished doctor's thesis, Western Reserve University, 1936, pp. 239–240).

8. *Ibid.*, p. 29; *Leni-Leoti; or, Adventures in the Far West* (Cincinnati, 1849), p. 38.

9. *The Prairie Flower*, p. 29.

10. *Idem.*

11. Lewis H. Garrard, *Wah-To-Yah, and the Taos Trail; or, Prairie Travel and Scalp Dances, with a Look at Los Rancheros from Muleback and the Rocky Mountain Campfire* (Cincinnati, 1850), pp. 270–271.

12. The publicizing of Carson through Frémont's reports is pointed out by James Madison Cutts, *The Conquest of California and New Mexico* (Philadelphia, 1847), pp. 166–167; and by Charles E. Averill, *Kit Carson, The Prince of the Gold Hunters; or, The Adventurers of the Sacramento* (Boston, 1849), p. 58.

13. Cutts, *Conquest of California*, pp. 165–167. This anonymous account of Carson was also reprinted in *The Rough and Ready Annual; or Military Souvenir* (New York, 1848), pp. 153–168.

14. Edwin L. Sabin, *Kit Carson Days: 1809–1868* (Chicago, 1914), p. 506.

15. DeWitt C. Peters, *The Life and Adventures of Kit Carson, the Nestor of the Rocky Mountains, from Facts Narrated by Himself* (New York, 1858), p. 50.

16. Charles Burdett, *Life of Kit Carson: The Great Western Hunter and Guide* (Philadelphia, 1862), pp. 83–84, 367, 369.

17. John S. C. Abbott, *Christopher Carson. Familiarly Known as Kit Carson* (New York, 1873), p. 70.

18. *Ibid.*, pp. 183–184.

19. *The Prairie Flower*, pp. 58–60.

20. *Kit Carson's Autobiography*, ed. Milo M. Quaife (Chicago, 1935), p. 135. Later Wild Western heroes sometimes took it for granted that they would be described in the newspapers and books down in the clearings (Oregon Sol in Edward S. Ellis, *Nathan Todd; or, the Fate of the Sioux' Captive*. Beadle's Dime Novels, No. 18, 1860, p. 64).

21. Frederic Hudson, *Journalism in the United States, from 1690 to 1872* (New York, 1873), pp. 587–589.

22. Ralph Admari, "Ballou, the Father of the Dime Novel," *American Book Collector*, IV, 121–122 (September–October, 1933).

23. Ralph Admari, "Bonner and 'The Ledger,'" *ibid.*, VI, 176–181 (May–June, 1935).

24. *Ibid.*, IV, 123; Hudson, *Journalism in the United States*, p. 647.

25. Admari, "Ballou," *American Book Collector*, IV, 124.

26. Bennett's early novels were published by various firms in Cincinnati (including J. A. & U. P. James) and subsequently by T. B. Peterson of Philadelphia: these publishing centers were feeling the same impulses that were motivating Ballou and Gleason in Boston, and Bonner in New York. In 1856 Bonner hired Bennett to write for the *New York Ledger*, and in 1867 Bennett became a contributor to Street & Smith's *New York Weekly*

(with "Sol Slocum; or, The Maid of the Juniata. A Tale of the Frontier," beginning on December 26 in Vol. XXIII, No. 6, p. 4).

27. *Kit Carson, The Prince of the Gold Hunters,* pp. 57–58.

28. Carson appears occasionally in the Beadle stories, as for example in James F. C. Adams's *The Fighting Trapper; or Kit Carson to the Rescue.* Beadle's New York Dime Library, No. 1045 (1901, reprint of original ed. 1879). The story contains an old trapper, Vic Vannoven, "rough but generous," toward whom the heroine feels as she would toward her father, so that we recognize him as a legitimate descendant of Leatherstocking. Kit Carson, young and agile, "the most renowned Indian fighter the world ever produced," appears briefly toward the end of the story to rescue the heroine and her party. He preserves the elusive, almost elfish quality he had had in Emerson Bennett's *The Prairie Flower.* Adams, incidentally, was not so violent a prohibitionist as the genteel biographers were. After the fight Kit offers brandy to the party, and he consumes "quiet draughts" during his turn on guard during the night (p. 26).

CHAPTER IX. THE WESTERN HERO IN THE DIME NOVEL I: FROM SETH JONES TO DEADWOOD DICK

1. Ralph Admari, "The House That Beadle Built 1859 to 1869," *American Book Collector,* IV, 223–225 (November, 1933).

2. *Ibid.,* IV, 288 (December, 1933).

3. *The Beadle Collection of Dime Novels Given to the New York Public Library by Dr. Frank P. O'Brien* (New York, 1922), p. 8; Edmund Pearson, *Dime Novels; or, Following an Old Trail in Popular Literature* (Boston, 1929), pp. 46, 83.

4. Admari, "The House That Beadle Built," *American Book Collector,* IV, 225.

5. Obituary note in "Chronicle and Comment," *Bookman,* XX, 92 (October, 1904).

6. Pearson, *Dime Novels,* pp. 106–107; George C. Jenks, "Dime Novel Makers," *Bookman,* XX, 112 (October, 1904).

7. Pearson, *Dime Novels,* p. 99.

8. In Edward L. Wheeler, *Corduroy Charlie, the Boy Bravo; or, Deadwood Dick's Last Act.* Beadle's Half Dime Library, No. 77 (1879).

9. Pearson, *Dime Novels,* p. 99. The editors of the *New York Weekly* felt they were making a strong claim when they said that Dr. John H. Robinson's *Nick Whiffles* was "the greatest story since the days of Fennimore [*sic*] Cooper, and . . . not inferior to that great author's best work" (XXII, No. 41, August 29, 1867, p. 4).

10. *Seth Jones* was published in 1860 as Beadle's Dime Novels, No. 8. Victor's comment is quoted by Henry Morton Robinson, "Mr. Beadle's Books," *Bookman,* LXIX, 22 (March, 1929). We are told that Seward once entered a cabinet meeting "waving a copy of *Seth Jones* in unconcealed delight" (LXIX, 20).

11. Boy's Library of Sport, Story and Adventure, No. 144.

12. *Ibid.,* pp. 6, 26.

13. *Ibid.,* p. 31.

14. Reprinted in 1875 as Beadle's New Dime Novels, New Series, No. 45.

15. *Ibid.*, p. 16.

16. Beadle's Dime Novels, No. 18 (1861), p. 44.

17. Beadle's New Dime Novels, New Series, No. 133 (1879), p. 52 (first published in 1871).

18. *Mustang Sam; or, The Mad Rider of the Plains. A Romance of Apache Land.* Beadle's Pocket Novels, No. 184 (1881), p. 19 (first published in 1877).

19. Albert Bigelow Paine, *Mark Twain, A Biography,* 3 vols. (paged continuously); (New York, 1912), I, 203.

20. *Old Avalanche, the Great Annihilator; or, Wild Edna, the Girl Brigand.* Beadle's Half Dime Library, No. 45 (1878), p. 4 (first published in 1877).

21. He is, for example, in Wheeler's *Corduroy Charlie, the Boy Bravo,* and also in his *Blonde Bill; or, Deadwood Dick's Home Base. A Romance of the "Silent Tongues."* Beadle's Half Dime Library, No. 138 (1880).

22. *Apollo Bill, the Trail Tornado; or, Rowdy Kate from Right Bower.* Beadle's Half Dime Library, No. 236 (1882), p. 6.

23. Beadle's Dime Novels, No. 18 (1861).

24. *Ibid.*, pp. 119, 122.

25. *Ibid.*, pp. 75, 87, 118.

26. Beadle's Dime Novels, No. 36 (1862), p. 50.

27. Beadle's Dime Novels, No. 41 (1862), p. 10.

28. *Ibid.*, p. 35.

29. *Ibid.*, p. 65.

30. Beadle's New Dime Novels, New Series, No. 462 (1880), p. 14 (first published in 1867).

31. *Ibid.*, pp. 18, 36.

32. Beadle's New Dime Novels, New Series, No. 133 (1879), p. 12 (first published in 1871).

33. Beadle's Pocket Novels, No. 140 (1879; first published in 1872).

34. Beadle's Dime Novels, No. 257 (1872), p. 28. "W. J. Hamilton" was the pseudonym of Charles Dunning Clark, a member of the staff of the Oswego (New York) *Times* and a local historian of the Cooper country.

35. *Ibid.*, p. 45.

36. *Ibid.*, p. 100.

37. Beadle's Half Dime Library, No. 30 (1878), pp. 4, 10, 12.

38. "Dime Novels and the American Tradition," *Yale Review,* XXVI, 765 (Summer, 1937).

39. W. H. Bishop, "Story-Paper Literature," *Atlantic,* XLIV, 387 (September, 1879).

40. Edward L. Wheeler, *Deadwood Dick's Dream; or, The Rivals of the Road. A Mining Tale of "Tombstone."* Beadle's Half Dime Library, No. 195 (1881), p. 8.

41. *Deadwood Dick's Protégée; or, Baby Bess, the Girl Gold Miner. A Tale of Pistol Pocket.* Beadle's Half Dime Library, No. 515 (1887), pp. 6, 14.

42. Edward L. Wheeler, *Deadwood Dick, Jr., in Chicago; or, The Anarchist's Daughter.* Beadle's Half Dime Library, No. 572 (1888), p. 2.

43. The change of tone in this period is noted by W. H. Bishop in *Atlantic,* XLIV, 384–386 (September, 1879). Ralph Admari remarks that writers of dime novels began to shape their stories consciously for a juvenile audience during the 1870's (*American Book Collector,* V, 24, January, 1934).

II: BUFFALO BILL AND BUCK TAYLOR

1. Richard J. Walsh in collaboration with Milton S. Salsbury, *The Making of Buffalo Bill. A Study in Heroics* (Indianapolis, 1928), p. 368. The *New Buffalo Bill Weekly*, in which every story dealt with Buffalo Bill, was still running in 1918 (John A. Hayes, *A Catalog of Dime Novel Material, Including a Section on Buffalo Bill* [Red Bank, New Jersey, 1936], p. 21).

2. Pearson, *Dime Novels*, pp. 202–203.

3. The *New York Weekly*, for example, printed a dispatch from the North Platte (Nebraska) *Democrat* dated May 2, 1872, quoting William F. Cody on the subject of his recent participation in an Indian fight with B Troop of the Third Cavalry. "Ned Buntline takes his characters from life," exclaimed the editors of the *Weekly*, and they promised that Buntline would soon add to his Buffalo Bill stories a tale about Buffalo Bill's companion, Texas Jack (XXVII, No. 31 [June 10, 1872], p. 8).

4. Walter Blair, "Six Davy Crocketts," *Southwest Review*, XXV, [443]– 462 (July, 1940).

5. Frederick E. Pond, *Life and Adventures of "Ned Buntline" with Ned Buntline's Anecdote of "Frank Forester" and Chapter of Angling Sketches* (New York, 1919), pp. 23, 48–51, 138.

6. *New York Weekly*, XXV, No. 2 (November 25, 1869), p. 4; Pond, *Life and Adventures*, p. 93.

7. *New York Weekly*, XXV, No. 2 (November 25, 1869), p. 4. Buntline's biographer states that he made a tour in California and along the Pacific Coast in 1867 and 1868 delivering temperance lectures. He probably took advantage of this tour to collect Western materials (Pond, *Life and Adventures*, p. 86).

8. Walsh, *Making of Buffalo Bill*, pp. 155, 156.

9. *New York Weekly*, XXV, No. 2 (November 25, 1869), p. 4. The serial began in the issue of December 23, 1869 (XXV, No. 6) and ran until March 10, 1870 (XXV, No. 17). Buffalo Bill's first appearance in fiction, however, had been in a short anecdote Buntline contributed to the *Weekly* on December 2, 1869 (XXV, No. 3, p. 8) as a part of the advance publicity for the serial. In this sketch Buntline refers to a letter he had received from Cody in November. An illustration for the first installment of *Buffalo Bill, the King of Border Men* depicts the hero in an authentic Leatherstocking costume with Indian leggings and moccasins. He carries a long flintlock rifle and is on foot. He wears a full beard (in contrast with the neat imperial and moustache of his later career). *Buffalo Bill's Best Shot; or, The Heart of Spotted Tail. A Sequel to "Buffalo Bill"* began in the *Weekly* March 25, 1872 (XXVII, No. 20). The illustration for the first installment shows the hero wearing a moustache but no beard. The standard goatee and moustache appear with the second installment (XXVII, No. 21 [April 1, 1872], p. [1]).

10. Walsh, *Making of Buffalo Bill*, p. 367.

11. Ned Buntline, *Buffalo Bill* (New York: International Publishers, n. d.), pp. 3, 11, 16, 142, 145, 202.

12. *Ibid.*, p. 183.

13. George D. C. Odell, *Annals of the New York Stage*, 14 vols. (New York, 1927–1945), IX, 168 (February 19, 1872).

14. Walsh, *Making of Buffalo Bill*, pp. 168–172. Maeder's play began something like a craze for border drama (Odell, *Annals*, IX, 218, 501). Within a month it was being burlesqued in *Bill Buffalo, with His Great Buffalo Bull* at Hooley's Opera House in Brooklyn (*ibid.*, IX, 226). The original play held the boards, however, for several years, with various actors in the title role (*ibid.*, IX, 278, 290, 328, 349, 431, 570, 633).

15. Walsh, *Making of Buffalo Bill*, pp. 178–180. *The Scouts of the Plains* reached New York March 31, 1873 (Odell, *Annals*, IX, 276) and became a competitor of Maeder's *Buffalo Bill* (*ibid.*, IX, 353, 414, 568).

16. Walsh, *Making of Buffalo Bill*, p. 182.

17. XXV, No. 2 (November 25, 1869), p. 4.

18. Walsh, *Making of Buffalo Bill*, p. 18.

19. *Buffalo Bill, from Boyhood to Manhood. Deeds of Daring, Scenes of Thrilling Peril, and Romantic Incidents in the Early Life of W. F. Cody, the Monarch of Bordermen.* Beadle's Boy's Library of Sport, Story and Adventure, No. 2 (1884), p. 2 (first published in 1881).

20. *The Life of Hon. William F. Cody, Known as Buffalo Bill, the Famous Hunter, Scout and Guide. An Autobiography* (Hartford, Conn., 1879), p. 365.

21. Walsh, *Making of Buffalo Bill*, p. 368; William C. Miller, *Dime Novel Authors 1860–1900* (Grafton, Mass., 1933), p. 7.

22. Beadle's Half Dime Library, No. 204 (1881), p. 3.

23. *Life of Hon. William F. Cody*, p. 282.

24. Walsh, *Making of Buffalo Bill*, p. 191.

25. First published in 1875.

26. *Ibid.*, pp. 60, 66.

27. Beadle's Dime New York Library, No. 83 (1879), pp. 2–3.

28. *Ibid.*, pp. 22–23.

29. *Bison Bill, the Prince of the Plains; or, Buffalo Bill's Pluck.* Beadle's Half Dime Library, No. 216 ("Twelfth Edition," 1881), p. 14; *Buffalo Bill's Secret Service Trail; or, The Mysterious Foe. A Romance of Red-Skins, Renegades and Army Rencounters.* Beadle's Dime New York Library, No. 682 (1891; first published in 1887).

30. Edward King, "Glimpses of Texas," *Scribner's*, VII, 303 (January, 1874).

31. "Eight Hundred Miles in an Ambulance," *Lippincott's*, XV, 695 (June, 1875).

32. "Picturesque Features of Kansas Farming," *Scribner's*, XIX, 139–140 (November, 1879).

33. "Over Sunday in New Sharon," *ibid.*, XIX, 771 (March, 1880).

34. James D. Richardson, ed., *A Compilation of the Messages and Papers of the Presidents, 1789–1897*, 11 vols. (Washington, 1909), VIII, 53–54.

35. Walsh, *Making of Buffalo Bill*, pp. 217–225.

36. *Buck Taylor, King of the Cowboys; or, The Raiders and the Rangers. A Story of the Wild and Thrilling Life of William L. Taylor.* Beadle's Half Dime Library, No. 497 (1887), pp. 2–3, 5, 12–13.

37. *Buck Taylor, The Saddle King; or, The Lasso Rangers' League. A Romance of the Border Heroes of To-Day.* Beadle's New York Dime Library, No. 649 (1891), p. 2.

38. Beadle's New York Dime Library, No. 658 (1891), p. 7. On p. 24 of this story Valerie Tracey, the Tigress of Texas, plays the guitar and sings

a song of which four lines are reported. They may well be of folk origin. If so, this is the first appearance of a cowboy ballad in print with which I am familiar.

39. *Buck Taylor, The Saddle King*, p. 21.

40. Beadle's Half Dime Library, No. 556 (1888).

CHAPTER X. THE DIME NOVEL HEROINE

1. *A Fable for Critics* (New York, 1848), p. 47.

2. Ralph Admari, "Ballou, the Father of the Dime Novel," *American Book Collector*, IV, 128 (September–October, 1933).

3. *Life in California; or, The Treasure Seekers' Expedition. A Sequel to Kit Carson, the Prince of the Gold Hunters* (Boston, 1850), pp. 12, 26.

4. Beadle's Pocket Novels, No. 222 (1882), p. 87. The copyright date of this story reads "1862," but it refers to events of the Civil War and to the collapse of the Confederacy; the date must be an error.

5. *Ibid.*, p. 48.

6. *Ibid.*, p. 61.

7. Beadle's Pocket Novels, No. 127 (1879), p. 23 (first published in 1870).

8. *Ibid.*, pp. 78–79, 92.

9. *Ibid.*, p. 97.

10. Joseph E. Badger, *The Forest Princess; or, The Kickapoo Captives. A Romance of the Illinois*. Beadle's New Dime Novels, New Series, No. 133 (1879), p. 102 (first published in 1871).

11. *Mountain Kate; or, Love in the Trapping Grounds. A Tale of the Powder River Country*. Beadle's Pocket Novels, No. 143 (1879), pp. 94, 102 (first published in 1872).

12. Beadle's New Dime Novels, No. 389 (1877; first published in 1872).

13. *Ibid.*, pp. 51, 92, 102.

14. Beadle's Dime Library, No. 1 (1878), p. 2.

15. *Ibid.*, p. 14.

16. *Ibid.*, p. 4.

17. *Ibid.*, p. 16.

18. *Bob Woolf, the Border Ruffian; or, The Girl Dead-Shot*. Beadle's Half Dime Library, No. 32 (1878), p. 3 (first published in 1877).

19. *Ibid.*, p. 8.

20. *Ibid.*, p. 11.

21. *Ibid.*, pp. 6, 16.

22. *Old Avalanche, the Great Annihilator; or, Wild Edna, the Girl Brigand*. Beadle's Half Dime Library, No. 45 (1878), p. 17 (first published in 1877).

23. Beadle's Half Dime Library, No. 138 (1880), pp. 2, 6.

24. *Ibid.*, p. 12.

25. Beadle's Half Dime Library, No. 156 (1880), pp. 13, 15.

26. *Deadwood Dick's Dream; or, The Rivals of the Road. A Mining Tale of "Tombstone."* Beadle's Half Dime Library, No. 195 (1881), pp. 5, 6, 10.

27. *Ibid.*, pp. 4–5.

28. *Ibid.*, pp. 6, 8.

29. Beadle's Pocket Library, No. 57 (1885), p. 2 (first published in 1878).

30. *Ibid.*, p. 16.
31. *Ibid.*, p. 4.
32. *Ibid.*, p. 13.
33. *Ibid.*, p. 31.
34. *The Pathfinder; or, The Inland Sea*, 2 vols. (Philadelphia, 1840), I, 139.
35. Literary depiction of the cowboy in the twentieth century is traced in Douglas Branch, *The Cowboy and His Interpreters* (New York, 1926), pp. 185–191, 210–235.

CHAPTER XI. THE GARDEN OF THE WORLD AND AMERICAN AGRARIANISM

1. Alexis de Tocqueville, *Democracy in America*. The Henry Reeve text as revised by Francis Bowen, ed. Phillips Bradley, 2 vols. (New York, 1945), II, 74.
2. *The Uncollected Poetry and Prose of Walt Whitman*, ed. Emory Holloway, 2 vols. (Garden City, New York, 1921), II, 35.
3. Lewis Evans, *Geographical, Historical, Political, Philosophical Essays. The First, Containing An Analysis of a General Map of the Middle British Colonies in America*, 2nd ed. (Philadelphia, 1775), p. 31.
4. Jonathan Carver, *Travels through the Interior Parts of North-America, in the Years 1766, 1767, and 1768* (London, 1778), p. viii.
5. Nathaniel Ames, *An Astronomical Diary: or, an Almanack for the Year of Our Lord Christ 1758* (Boston, n. d.), p. [16].
6. Philip Freneau and Hugh Henry Brackenridge, "The Rising Glory of America," *The Poems of Philip Freneau*, ed. Fred L. Pattee, I, 76n., 77n.–78n.
7. *The Writings of Benjamin Franklin*, ed. Albert H. Smyth, IX, 245–248 (from a letter to Benjamin Vaughan, Passy, July 26, 1784).
8. "The Internal State of America; Being a True Description of the Interest and Policy of That Vast Continent," *ibid.*, X, 117–118.
9. *Ibid.*, X, 121.
10. "The Freehold Concept in Eighteenth-Century American Letters," *William and Mary Quarterly*, Third Series, IV, 42–59 (January, 1947); "The Influence of Natural Rights and Physiocratic Doctrines on American Agrarian Thought during the Revolutionary Period," *Agricultural History*, XXI, 12–23 (January, 1947).
11. These doctrines are set forth, for example, in George Logan's *Letters, Addressed to the Yeomanry of the United States: Shewing the Necessity of Confining the Public Revenue to a Fixed Proportion of the Net Produce of the Land; and the Bad Policy and Injustice of Every Species of Indirect Taxation and Commercial Regulations*, "by a Farmer" (Philadelphia, 1791). As the title suggests, Logan is a dogmatic Physiocrat, and to this extent not entirely representative of the vaguer and more eclectic ideas that were generally current. But his praise of "an independent yeomanry," virtuously aloof from the dissipations, effeminacy, indolence, and vice of cities, is thoroughly typical (pp. 34–35).
12. Howard C. Rice, *Le cultivateur américain, étude sur l'œuvre de Saint John de Crèvecœur* (Paris, 1933), pp. [7]–18.

13. Bernard Faÿ, *The Revolutionary Spirit in France and America* (London, 1928), pp. 233, 235, 532; Rice, *Le cultivateur*, pp. 73–75. Julia P. Mitchell (*St. Jean de Crèvecœur*, New York, 1916, pp. 346–350) lists more than fifty reprintings of passages from Crèvecœur's works in American periodicals between 1782 and 1805. Crèvecœur's description of the Ohio country, added to the 1787 French translation of the *Letters* (Rice, *Le cultivateur*, p. 95) and translated into English for use in promotional literature of the Ohio Company (Mitchell, *Crèvecœur*, pp. 347–348), was a favorite item with American editors, being reprinted eight times between July and December, 1787.

14. *Letters from an American Farmer* (London, 1782), p. 48.

15. Faÿ, *Revolutionary Spirit*, p. 23; Anatole Feugère, *Un précurseur de la révolution. L'Abbé Raynal (1713–1796). Documents inédits* (Angoulème, 1922), p. iii.

16. *Letters*, p. x.

17. Guillaume-Thomas-François Raynal, *A Philosophical and Political History of the Settlements and Trade of the Europeans in the East and West Indies*, trans. J. Justamond, 4 vols. (Edinburgh, 1776), IV, 310.

18. *Letters*, pp. 46–48.

19. *Writings*, ed. Paul L. Ford, VII, 36 (to the Rev. James Madison, October 28, 1785). An often-quoted passage to similar effect from the *Notes on Virginia* is at III, 268.

20. *Ibid.*, IV, 479–480.

21. *Ibid.*, II, 25. Jefferson's views are ably summarized in A. Whitney Griswold, "The Agrarian Democracy of Thomas Jefferson," *American Political Science Review*, XL, 657–681 (August, 1946), and "The Jeffersonian Ideal," in *Farming and Democracy* (New York, 1948), pp. 18–46.

22. The long agrarian tradition in Europe is discussed in two extremely suggestive articles by Paul H. Johnstone, "In Praise of Husbandry," *Agricultural History*, XI, 80–95 (April, 1937); "Turnips and Romanticism," *ibid.*, XII, 224–255 (July, 1938). English imitators of Virgil's *Georgics* are dealt with in detail in Dwight L. Durling, *Georgic Tradition in English Poetry*, Columbia University Studies in English and Comparative Literature, No. 121 (New York, 1935), especially pp. 43–107. Jefferson's relations with the Physiocrats are discussed by Professor Griswold in the article cited in note 21 above; by Gilbert Chinard, *Thomas Jefferson, The Apostle of Americanism* (Boston, 1929), pp. 493–495; and by Chester E. Eisinger in *Agricultural History*, XXI, 20–22.

23. Translation by an unknown hand of a passage first published in the French version of the *Letters of an American Farmer* (*Lettres d'un cultivateur américain*, Paris, 1787), included in [Manasseh Cutler], *An Explanation of the Map Which Delineates That Part of the Federal Lands, Comprehended between Pennsylvania West Line, the Rivers Ohio and Sioto* [sic], *and Lake Erie* (Salem, Massachusetts, 1787), p. 23. This pamphlet was intended as advertising for the Ohio Company, a notorious scheme of land speculation.

24. John Filson, *The Discovery, Settlement, and Present State of Kentucke*, pp. 107–109.

25. Ralph L. Rusk, "The Adventures of Gilbert Imlay," *Indiana University Studies*, X, No. 57 (March, 1923).

26. *A Topographical Description of the Western Territory of North America* (London, 1792), pp. [1]–2.

27. *Ibid.*, pp. 39–40.
28. *Ibid.*, pp. 138–139.
29. *American Museum*, IV, 212 (September, 1788).
30. *Ibid.*, III, 280 (March, 1788).
31. (August 19, 1797), p. [4].
32. *Kentucky Gazette* (April 1, 1797), p. 3.
33. Josiah Morrow, ed., "Tours into Kentucky and the Northwest Territory. Three Journals by the Rev. James Smith of Powhatan County, Va., 1783–1795–1797," *Ohio Archeological and Historical Quarterly*, XVI (1907), 396.

CHAPTER XII. THE YEOMAN AND THE FEE-SIMPLE EMPIRE

1. *The Speech of Charles Jas. Faulkner, (of Berkeley) in the House of Delegates of Virginia, on the Policy of the State with Respect to Her Slave Population. Delivered January 20, 1832* (Richmond, 1832), p. 9.
2. The triumph of the plantation ideal in Southern thought was so complete that the large and important yeoman class of the Old South almost dropped from sight and has had to be rediscovered by historical research. "Little was written of them [the yeomen of the Plantation South], and when generalizations were made, this group was often ignored" (Blanche H. Clark, *The Tennessee Yeomen 1840–1860* [Nashville, Tennessee, 1942], p. 3). The fact that contemporary observers so completely ignored the Southern yeoman is striking testimony to the way in which preconceptions like the pastoral ideal of the plantation can become actual categories of perception.
3. Edmund Dana, *Geographical Sketches on the Western Country: Designed for Emigrants and Settlers* (Cincinnati, 1819), p. 26.
4. Thomas Cooper wrote in 1794: "Nor is the term 'farmer' synonimous [*sic*] with the same word in England. With you it means a tenant, holding of some lord, paying much in rent, and much in tythes, and much in taxes: an inferior rank in life, occupied by persons of inferior manners and education. In America a farmer is a land-owner, paying no rent, no tythes, and few taxes, equal in rank to any other rank in the state, having a voice in the appointment of his legislators, and a fair chance, if he deserve it, of becoming one himself" (*Some Information Respecting America*, Dublin, pp. 72–73). This passage and other early comments on the status of the farmer in America are quoted and discussed by Chester E. Eisinger, "Land and Loyalty: Literary Expressions of Agrarian Nationalism in the Seventeenth and Eighteenth Centuries," *American Literature*, XXI, [160]–178 (May, 1949).
5. The important adjective "independent" had also changed its meaning. In England it was applied to a tenant who owed no feudal obligations to his landlord (Adam Smith, *Wealth of Nations*, London, 1899, I, 420). In this country it had come to imply fee-simple ownership of land.
6. *The Backwoodsman. A Poem* (Philadelphia, 1818), p. 11.
7. *Ibid.*, pp. 80–81.
8. *Ibid.*, pp. 149–150.
9. *Ibid.*, p. 155. At p. 162 they are "our brave yeomen."
10. *Ibid.*, p. [7].
11. *Ibid.*, pp. 173–174. Cooper, more than twenty years later, was to

follow the same procedure with his worthy Ben Boden, the bee hunter (above, p. 69).

12. *Recollections of the Last Ten Years, Passed in Occasional Residences and Journeyings in the Valley of the Mississippi* (Boston, 1826), p. 290.

13. *Western Monthly Review*, I, 169–170 (July, 1827).

14. From Flint's *Oration before the Washington Benevolent Society of Lancaster and Sterling and of Leominster and Fitchburg. Delivered at Leominster [Massachusetts], July 4, 1815*, quoted in John E. Kirkpatrick, *Timothy Flint Pioneer, Missionary, Author, Editor, 1780–1840* (Cleveland, 1911), p. 52.

15. Timothy Flint, *The History and Geography of the Mississippi Valley*, 3rd ed., 2 vols. (Cincinnati, 1833), I, 396.

16. *Ibid.*, II, 15–16.

17. *George Mason, the Young Backwoodsman; or 'Don't Give Up the Ship.' A Story of the Mississippi* (Boston, 1829), pp. 4, 5.

18. *Ibid.*, pp. 7, 18.

19. *Ibid.*, p. 154.

20. *Hunt's Merchants' Magazine*, III, 38–39 (July, 1840).

21. *Ibid.*, V, 219–220 (September, 1841). An anonymous article published in the same periodical a few months later developed similar themes in discussing Michigan (VI, 348, April, 1842). But the most striking fictional account of life in Michigan at this period, Mrs. Caroline Kirkland's *A New Home — Who'll Follow?* (New York, 1839), while written with more humor and a much sharper eye for character than Flint could command, shows an upper-class condescension toward the backwoods settlers fully equal to Flint's and bears no trace of the cult of the yeoman.

22. "Greeley on Reforms," *Southern Literary Messenger*, XVII, 271–272 (May, 1851).

23. "L. C. B.," "The Country in 1950, or the Conservatism of Slavery," *ibid.*, XXII, 432 (June, 1856).

24. (Richmond, 1857), p. 335.

CHAPTER XIII. THE SOUTH AND THE MYTH OF THE GARDEN

1. 29 Cong., 1 Sess. Senate Report No. 306. Committee on the Post Office and Post Roads (April 20, 1846), pp. 28–29.

2. *Leaves of Grass*, inclusive edition, ed. Emory Holloway (Garden City, New York, 1931), pp. 248–249.

3. *The Writings of James Monroe*, ed. Stanislaus M. Hamilton, 7 vols. (New York, 1898–1903), I, 150.

4. Max Farrand, ed., *The Records of the Federal Convention of 1787*, 4 vols. (New Haven, 1911–1937), I, 533.

5. *Ibid.*, II, 2.

6. *Speech of Mr. Benton, of Missouri, in Reply to Mr. Webster: The Resolution Offered by Mr. Foot, Relative to the Public Lands, Being under Consideration. Delivered in the Senate, Session 1829–1830* (Washington, 1830), pp. 53–54.

7. *Ibid.*, p. 65.

8. James Gadsden, urging Calhoun to accept the invitation, wrote: "Now is the time to meet our Western friends at Memphis – to set the ball in motion which must bring the Valley to the South: and make them feel as allies of the Great Commercial and Agricultural interests – instead of the Tax gathering and Monopolizing interests of the North" (J. Franklin Jameson, ed., *Correspondence of John C. Calhoun* [Washington, 1900], p. 1062). Calhoun's attitude is discussed in Herbert Wender, *Southern Commercial Conventions 1837–1859*, Johns Hopkins University Studies in Historical and Political Science, Series XLVIII, No. 4 (Baltimore, 1930), p. 54.

9. *Reports and Public Papers of John C. Calhoun*, being Volume VI of *Works*, ed. Richard K. Crallé (New York, 1856), pp. 273–274.

10. *Ibid.*, p. 280. Benton had called the Mississippi and its tributaries *"mare nostrum"* in his speech during the Webster-Hayne debate fifteen years before (*Speech of Mr. Benton . . . in Reply to Mr. Webster*, p. 66). An anonymous contributor to the *Southern Quarterly Review* of Charleston, more orthodox than the Pope, greeted Calhoun's "inland sea" doctrine with the cry, *"Et tu, quoque, Brute?"* (IX, 267, January, 1846).

11. *Works*, VI, 284.

12. Buckner H. Payne, "New Orleans – Her Commerce and Her Duties," *DeBow's Review*, III, 39–48 (January, 1847).

13. Thomas B. Hewson, "Thoughts on a Rail-Road System for New Orleans," *ibid.*, X, 175–188 (February, 1851).

14. "Progress of the Great West in Population, Agriculture, Arts and Commerce," *ibid.*, IV, 31–85 (September, 1847).

15. "Hemp-Growing Region of the United States," *ibid.*, XXIV, 56–58 (January, 1858); "The Great Basin of the Mississippi," *ibid.*, XXIV, 159–165 (February, 1858).

16. "The North American Plain," *ibid.*, XXVI, 564 (May, 1859). Scott also contributed "Westward the Star of Empire," *ibid.*, XXVII, [125]–136 (August, 1859).

17. "The Cause of the South," *ibid.*, X, 107 (January, 1851).

18. 36 Cong., 1 Sess., *Congressional Globe*. Senate (March 22, 1860), pp. 1303–1304.

19. Francis P. Gaines, *The Southern Plantation. A Study in the Development and Accuracy of a Tradition* (New York, 1925).

20. Lewis C. Gray, *A History of Agriculture in the Southern United States to 1860*, 2 vols. (Washington, 1933), II, 906–907.

21. *Letter of Mr. Walker, of Mississippi, Relative to the Annexation of Texas: In Reply to the Call of the People of Carroll County, Kentucky, to Communicate his Views on That Subject* (Washington, 1844), p. 5.

22. *Ibid.*, pp. 8–9. The prevalence of this argument is indicated by Albert K. Weinberg, *Manifest Destiny. A Study of Nationalist Expansionism in American History* (Baltimore, 1935), pp. 52–56. It should be pointed out that many proslavery Southerners were opposed to the annexation of Texas (Chauncey S. Boucher, "In Re That Aggressive Slaveocracy," *Mississippi Valley Historical Review*, VIII, 27, June–September, 1921).

23. *Letter of Mr. Walker*, p. 9.

24. *Ibid.*, p. 11.

25. *Ibid.*, p. 14.

26. *Ibid.*, p. 15.

282 NOTES

27. Mathew F. Maury, "Gulf of Mexico," in James D. B. DeBow, ed., *The Industrial Resources, Etc., of the Southern and Western States,* 3 vols., (New Orleans, 1852), I, 365–373.

28. Reprinted in *DeBow's Review,* XVII, 280–281 (September, 1854). The Democratic platform in 1856 demanded that the United States maintain its ascendency in the Gulf of Mexico to protect the mouth of the Mississippi, and that American "preponderance" in the Interoceanic Isthmus be guaranteed also.

29. "J. C.," "The Destinies of the South," *Southern Quarterly Review,* N. S. XXIII, 201 (January, 1853).

30. *John Brown's Body* (Garden City, New York, 1928), p. 374.

31. Albert Bigelow Paine, ed., *Mark Twain's Letters,* 2 vols. (New York, 1917), I, 34–35. Mark Twain mentions the report by Lieutenants William L. Herndon and Lardner Gibbon (*Exploration of the Valley of the Amazon, Made under Direction of the Navy Department,* 2 vols. and volume of maps, [Washington, 1853–1854], 32 Cong., 2 Sess. Senate Executive Document No. 36). Herndon was a Virginian and the brother-in-law of Maury, whose views about the development of the Amazon valley as a slave empire he shared (I, 193, 281). The expedition was ordered by John Pendleton Kennedy, Secretary of the Navy, and bore an obvious relation to Southern policy. Coca, in which Mark Twain was interested, is mentioned at I, 88–89, 249; II, 46–47.

CHAPTER XIV. THE NEW CALCULUS OF WESTERN ENERGIES

1. "Present Population and Future Prospects of the Western Country," *Western Monthly Review,* I, 331 (October, 1827).

2. *Sketches, Historical and Descriptive, of Louisiana* (Philadelphia, 1812), p. 387.

3. *Natural and Statistical View, or Picture of Cincinnati and the Miami Country* (Cincinnati, 1815), p. 227.

4. *Western Monthly Review,* I, 332 (October, 1827).

5. Filson, *The Discovery . . . of Kentucke* (1784), pp. 44–45; Imlay, *Topographical Description* (1792), pp. 99–100.

6. *Western Souvenir* (Cincinnati, n. d.), pp. 107–108.

7. "Progress of the West," *Western Monthly Review,* I, 25–26 (May, 1827).

8. 2nd ed. (Philadelphia, 1834), p. 60. This anonymous work is sometimes ascribed to Robert Baird.

9. "Remarks Made on a Tour to Prairie du Chien; Thence to Washington City, in 1829," in *The Writings of Caleb Atwater* (Columbus, Ohio, 1833), pp. 203–204.

10. *Statistics of the West, at the Close of the Year 1836* (Cincinnati, 1836), p. 217.

11. "The Progress of Navigation and Commerce on the Waters of the Mississippi River and the Great Lakes. A. D. 1700 to 1846," *Publications of the Mississippi Historical Society,* VII (1903), 493–494.

12. Quoted in Henry C. Hubbart, *The Older Middle West, 1840–1880* (New York, 1936), p. 20.

13. For example, Alice Freeman Palmer, "Some Lasting Results of the World's Fair," *Forum*, XVI, [517]–523 (December, 1893); Henry Van Brunt, "The Columbian Exposition and American Civilization," *Atlantic*, LXXI, [577]–588 (May, 1893).

14. *The Education of Henry Adams* (Washington, 1907), pp. 296–297.

15. "Internal Trade of the United States," *Hunt's Merchants' Magazine*, VIII, 325 (April, 1843).

16. "The Progress of the West; Considered with Reference to Great Commercial Cities in the United States," *Hunt's Merchants' Magazine*, XIV, 164 (February, 1846).

17. *Ibid.*, VIII, 329.

18. "Internal Trade in the United States," *ibid.*, IX, 31 (July, 1843).

19. *Ibid.*, IX, 42.

20. "The Great West," *DeBow's Review*, XV, 52 (July, 1853).

21. "Westward Movement of the Center of Population, and of Industrial Power in North America," *Hunt's Merchants' Magazine*, XXXVI, 198–199 (February, 1857).

22. "Westward the Star of Empire," *DeBow's Review*, XXVII, 125 (August, 1859).

23. "Railroads in the Great Valley," *Hunt's Merchants' Magazine*, XXVII, 50–51 (July, 1852).

24. *DeBow's Review*, XV, 51.

25. "The North American Plain — Valley of the Mississippi, Etc.," *ibid.*, XXVI, 561 (May, 1859).

26. Allen Johnson, *Stephen A. Douglas: A Study in American Politics* (New York, 1908), p. 481.

27. *Ibid.*, pp. 483–484. Douglas's position is discussed in Carl R. Fish, "The Decision of the Ohio Valley," *American Historical Association Report* (1910), p. 161.

28. *The Writings of Abraham Lincoln*, ed. Arthur B. Lapsley, 8 vols., (New York, 1905–1906), VI, 194 (Annual Message to Congress, December 1, 1862).

29. *Ibid.*, VI, 196–197.

30. *Ibid.*, VI, 197.

31. *Ibid.*, VI, 198.

CHAPTER XV. THE AGRARIAN UTOPIA IN POLITICS: THE HOMESTEAD ACT

1. William E. Dodd, "The Fight for the Northwest," *American Historical Review*, XVI, 785 (July, 1911); Roy M. Robbins, "Horace Greeley: Land Reform and Unemployment, 1837–1862," *Agricultural History*, VII, 40 (January, 1933); Henry C. Hubbart, *The Older Middle West*, p. 20. — This chapter, in slightly revised and condensed form, appeared in the *Pacific Spectator* under the title "Soil of Freedom" (II, 151–158, Spring, 1948).

2. Reinhard H. Luthin, *The First Lincoln Campaign* (Cambridge, Massachusetts, 1944), p. 150.

3. *Ibid.*, p. 151.

4. *The Nebraska Question Comprising Speeches in the United States Senate by Mr. Douglas, Mr. Chase, Mr. Smith, Mr. Everett, Mr. Wade, Mr. Badger, Mr. Seward, and Mr. Sumner* (New York, 1854), p. 21 (March 11, 1850).

5. *Ibid.*, p. 70 (February 8, 1854).

6. *Ibid.*, p. 105 (February 17, 1854).

7. *Ibid.*, p. 99 (February 17, 1854).

8. *Ibid.*, pp. 65, 66 (February 6, 1854).

9. *Ibid.*, p. 66.

10. "Horace Greeley and the Working Class Origins of the Republican Party," *Political Science Quarterly*, XXIV, 488 (September, 1909).

11. Fred A. Shannon, "The Homestead Act and the Labor Surplus," *American Historical Review*, XLI, 643 (July, 1936).

12. Joseph G. Rayback, "Land for the Landless. The Contemporary View," Unpublished Master's Thesis, Western Reserve University, 1936, pp. 58–59; Table III and Map III in Appendix, pp. 97–98.

13. Helene S. Zahler, *Eastern Workingmen and National Land Policy, 1829–1862* (New York, 1941), p. 33, quoted from *Working Man's Advocate* (March 3, 1834).

14. *Ibid.*, pp. 33–35, 45–46. Grow's speech in 1852 favoring a homestead system was "merely an oratorical transcript" of articles in Evans's *Working Man's Advocate* (John R. Commons in *Political Science Quarterly*, XXIV, 484, September, 1909).

15. A. Whitney Griswold, "The Agrarian Democracy of Thomas Jefferson," *American Political Science Review*, XL, 672–680 (August, 1946).

16. James T. DuBois and Gertrude S. Mathews, *Galusha A. Grow, Father of the Homestead Law* (Boston, 1917), p. 84.

17. Zahler, *Eastern Workingmen*, pp. 29, 34, 194. John Locke's labor theory of property implied that no man had a right to more land than he himself could cultivate (Griswold, *American Political Science Review*, XL, 675–676).

18. Zahler, *Eastern Workingmen*, pp. 194–197; Paul W. Gates, "The Homestead Law in an Incongruous Land System," *American Historical Review*, XLI, 652–681 (July, 1936).

19. DuBois and Mathews, *Galusha A. Grow*, pp. 99–101.

20. 31 Cong., 2 Sess. *Congressional Globe*, Appendix, p. 137 (January 29, 1851). The description of agriculture as the nursing father of the State is from Vattel (Emerich de Vattel, *The Law of Nations; or, Principles of the Law of Nature*, anonymous trans. [London, 1793], p. 31). Chapter VII of Vattel's treatise, "Of the Cultivation of the Earth" (pp. 31–33), from which Julian's phrase was quoted, is a tissue of the stereotypes of eighteenth-century agrarian theory. Andrew Johnson quoted the same dictum from Vattel, adding his warning against allowing large tracts of land to lie uncultivated and against holding the husbandman in contempt (35 Cong., 1 Sess. *Congressional Globe*, Senate, p. 2265, May 20, 1858).

21. 32 Cong., 1 Sess. *Congressional Globe*, Appendix, p. 410 (April 6, 1852).

22. *Idem.*

23. Quoted in Horace Greeley, *The American Conflict: A History of the*

Great Rebellion in the United States of America, 1860–'65, 2 vols. (Hartford, Conn., 1866), I, 200n.

24. 31 Cong., 2 Sess. *Congressional Globe*, Appendix, p. 136 (January 29, 1851).

25. 36 Cong., 1 Sess. *Congressional Globe*, Senate, p. 1650 (April 11, 1860).

26. 36 Cong., 1 Sess. *Congressional Globe*, Senate, p. 1635 (April 10, 1860).

27. 31 Cong., 2 Sess. *Congressional Globe*, Appendix, p. 136 (January 29, 1851). During the fifty years that had elapsed since the end of the eighteenth century, the word "freeman" had acquired an additional overtone of meaning. It now meant not only "a man possessing the franchise" and "a freeholder," but also, more emphatically, "a man not a slave."

CHAPTER XVI. THE GARDEN AND THE DESERT

1. The subject of this chapter is dealt with at greater length in my article, "Rain Follows the Plow: The Notion of Increased Rainfall for the Great Plains, 1844–1880," *Huntington Library Quarterly*, X, 169–193 (February, 1947).

2. John W. Gregory, "What of the Desert?" *Century*, XLI, 796 (April, 1891). The pioneer discussion of the problem of settlement on the Plains is Walter P. Webb's *The Great Plains* (Boston, 1931), especially pp. 319–382.

3. Fred A. Shannon, *The Farmer's Last Frontier. Agriculture, 1860–1897* (*The Economic History of the United States*, edd. Henry David, Harold U. Faulkner, Louis M. Hacker, Curtis P. Nettels, and Fred A. Shannon, vol. V, New York, 1945), pp. 218–220.

4. Carter Goodrich and others, *Migration and Economic Opportunity* (Philadelphia, 1936), pp. 517–518; The Great Plains Committee, *The Future of the Great Plains* (Washington, 1936), pp. 2–3.

5. Ralph C. Morris, "The Notion of a Great American Desert East of the Rockies," *Mississippi Valley Historical Review*, XIII, 190–200 (September, 1926); Webb, *Great Plains*, pp. 152–160.

6. *The Expeditions of Zebulon Montgomery Pike*, ed. Elliott Coues, 3 vols. (New York, 1895), II, 525.

7. Thomas Pownall remarked in 1776: "This Globe, the Earth which we inhabit, is, in its natural State, . . . universally, wherever the Waters do not prevail, covered with Woods . . . . Except where the Land is worn to the Bone, and nothing remains on the Surface but bare Rocks, every Soil, even the poorest, hath its peculiar Cloathing of Trees or Shrubs" (*A Topographical Description of Such Parts of North America as Are Contained in the (Annexed) Map of the Middle British Colonies* [London, 1776], p. 5).

8. Henry M. Brackenridge, *Views of Louisiana: Containing Geographical, Statistical and Historical Notices of That Vast and Important Portion of America* (Baltimore, 1817), p. 72.

9. *Account of an Expedition from Pittsburgh to the Rocky Mountains Performed in the Years 1819, 1820* (1823), reprinted in Reuben G. Thwaites,

ed., *Early Western Travels, 1748–1846,* 32 vols. (Cleveland, 1904–1907), XVII, 191, 147–148.

10. *Travels in the Great Western Prairies, the Anahuac and Rocky Mountains, and in Oregon Territory* (1843), in *Early Western Travels,* XXVIII, 108–109.

11. *The California and Oregon Trail: Being Sketches of Prairie and Rocky Mountain Life* (New York, 1849), pp. 81–82.

12. *What I Saw in California: Being the Journal of a Tour by the Emigrant Route and South Pass of the Rocky Mountains, across the Continent of North America* (1848), 3d ed. (New York, 1849), p. 98.

13. For example, Benton called the southern plains Indians "Arabs of the New World" (*Thirty Years' View; or, A History of the Working of the American Government for Thirty Years, from 1820 to 1850,* 2 vols., New York, 1854–1856, I, 41). A writer in the *Port Folio* in 1817 (Fourth [Fifth] Series, III, 422) referred to the northern plains Indians as "the American Tartars." Timothy Flint spoke of the Southwestern Indians who attacked James O. Pattie as "ruthless red Tartars of the desert" (*Pattie's Personal Narrative* [1831], edited by Flint, in *Early Western Travels,* XVIII, 330). These associations gave Melville an epithet. In the chapter on dreams in *Mardi,* the Arkansas brings down his Tartar rivers from the plain (*Works,* 16 vols., London, 1922–1924, IV, 54).

14. *The Works of the Right Honorable Edmund Burke,* 12 vols. (Boston, 1866–1867), II, 131–132.

15. *Astoria, or Anecdotes of an Enterprise beyond the Rocky Mountains,* 2 vols. (Philadelphia, 1836), I, 232.

16. *Idem.* Irving was so deeply impressed with the idea of outlaw bands in the American desert that he used it again as a conclusion for his version of Captain B. L. E. Bonneville's journal, *The Rocky Mountains: or, Scenes, Incidents, and Adventures in the Far West,* 2 vols. (Philadelphia, 1837), II, 239.

17. *DeBow's Review,* I, 67 (January, 1846).

18. *Hunt's Merchants' Magazine,* XXV, 167 (August, 1851).

19. *Southern Quarterly Review,* XVI, 84 (October, 1849).

20. 35 Cong., 2 Sess. House Executive Document No. 2, in Vol. II, Part 2, pp. 641, 644.

21. Summary of the results of the surveys by Secretary of War Jefferson Davis in "Report of the Secretary of War Communicating the Several Pacific Railroad Explorations," 33 Cong., 1 Sess. House Executive Document No. 129, in Vol. XVIII, Part I, p. 7.

22. Representative Thomas M. Edwards of New Hampshire (37 Cong., 2 Sess. *Congressional Globe,* Part 2, p. 1704 [April 17, 1862]); Representative Frederick A. Pike of Maine (*ibid.,* Part 2, p. 1707 [April 17, 1862]); Representative Aaron A. Sargent of California (*ibid.,* Part 2, p. 1908 [May 1, 1862]); Senator James A. McDougall of California (*ibid.,* Part 3, p. 2804 [June 18, 1862]).

23. *Commerce of the Prairies: or the Journal of a Santa Fé Trader,* 2 vols. (New York, 1844), II, 202–203.

24. Bayard Taylor in the *Tribune,* June, 1866 (dispatch reprinted in *Colorado: A Summer Trip* [New York, 1867], pp. 41, 42, 45); Alexander K.

McClure in the *Tribune*, May, 1867 (dispatch reprinted in *Three Thousand Miles through the Rocky Mountains* [Philadelphia, 1869], pp. 112–113).

25. *Report of the Commissioner of the General Land Office for the Year 1867* (Washington, 1867), pp. 135–136.

26. *Preliminary Report of the United States Geological Survey of Wyoming and Portions of Contiguous Territories* (1871), 42 Cong., 2 Sess. House Executive Document No. 325, in Vol. XV, pp. 6–8.

27. Samuel G. Aughey and Charles Dana Wilber, *Agriculture beyond the 100th Meridian or A Review of the U. S. Public Land Commission* (Lincoln, Nebraska, 1880), pp. 3–6; Aughey, *Sketches of the Physical Geography and Geology of Nebraska* (Omaha, Nebraska, 1880), pp. 43–44.

28. Charles Dana Wilber, *The Great Valleys and Prairies of Nebraska and the Northwest* (Omaha, Nebraska, 1881), p. 69.

29. *Ibid.*, p. 70.

30. *Ibid.*, p. 355.

31. Samuel Aughey, *Sketches of the Physical Geography and Geology of Nebraska*, p. 155.

CHAPTER XVII. THE EMPIRE REDIVIVUS

1. IV, 500 (August, 1872).

2. *Our Western Empire*, p. 131.

3. *Ibid.*, p. 54.

4. *Ibid.*, pp. 206–207.

5. Joseph Nimmo, Jr., *Report on the Internal Commerce of the United States*, 48 Cong., 2 Sess. House Executive Document No. 7, Vol. XX, Part 2, p. 51. Nimmo points out how "exceedingly erroneous" had been earlier predictions concerning trade with Asia over the Pacific railways.

6. Richard M. Bucke, ed., *Notes and Fragments Left by Walt Whitman* (London, Canada, 1899), p. 48.

CHAPTER XVIII. FAILURE OF THE AGRARIAN UTOPIA

1. *New York Semi-Weekly Tribune* (May 9, 1862), quoted by Roy M. Robbins, "Horace Greeley: Land Reform and Unemployment," *Agricultural History*, VII, 41 (January, 1933).

2. *New York Semi-Weekly Tribune* (May 8, 1862), quoted by Joseph G. Rayback, "Land for the Landless. The Contemporary View," Unpublished Master's Thesis, Western Reserve University (1936), p. 89.

3. May 7, 1862, *ibid.*, p. 90.

4. May 7, 1862, *ibid.*, p. 89.

5. *New York Tribune* (February 5, 1867), quoted by Carter Goodrich and Sol Davison, "The Wage-Earner in the Westward Movement. I. The Statement of the Problem," *Political Science Quarterly*, L, 181 (June, 1935).

6. Fred A. Shannon, "The Homestead Act and the Labor Surplus," *American Historical Review*, XLI, 638 (July, 1936).

7. Fred A. Shannon, *The Farmer's Last Frontier*, pp. 125–147.

8. Paul W. Gates, "The Homestead Law in an Incongruous Land System," *American Historical Review*, XLI, 670 (July, 1936).

9. Shannon, *Farmer's Last Frontier,* Statistical Table, p. 418.

10. Representative George W. Julian, 31 Cong., 2 Sess. *Congressional Globe,* Appendix, p. 136 (January 29, 1851).

11. Helene S. Zahler, *Eastern Workingmen and National Land Policy,* pp. 34–35.

12. Henry George, *Our Land and Land Policy, National and State* (San Francisco, 1871), pp. 34–35.

13. *Atlantic Monthly,* XLIII, 328, 330 (March, 1879).

14. *Ibid.,* XLIII, 336.

15. *Other Main Travelled Roads* (1892, 1899, 1910), Sunset ed. (New York, n. d.), p. 102.

16. *The Man with the Hoe and Other Poems* (New York, 1899), p. 17.

CHAPTER XIX. THE MYTH OF THE GARDEN AND REFORM OF THE LAND SYSTEM

1. Powell's program is described in Walter P. Webb, *The Great Plains,* (New York, 1931), pp. 353–356, 419–422.

2. John Wesley Powell, *Report on the Lands of the Arid Region of the United States* (Washington, 1878), pp. 25–45.

3. Powell's proposals for reorganization of the surveys are discussed at greater length in my article, "Clarence King, John Wesley Powell, and the Establishment of the United States Geological Survey," *Mississippi Valley Historical Review,* XXXIV, 37–58 (June, 1947), and in Harold H. Dunham, *Government Handout: A Study in the Administration of the Public Lands* (New York, 1941), pp. 66–68.

4. "Geographical and Geological Surveys West of the Mississippi," 43 Cong., 1 Sess. House Report No. 612, p. 53.

5. Charles Schuchert and Clara Mae LeVene, *O. C. Marsh, Pioneer in Paleontology* (New Haven, 1940), p. 249.

6. 45 Cong., 3 Sess. House Miscellaneous Document No. 5, in Vol. I, p. 2.

7. Dunham, *Government Handout,* pp. 69–73.

8. The important and voluminous Report of the Commission is 46 Cong., 2 Sess. House Executive Document No. 46, in Vol. XXII. The fate of the Report in Congress is discussed by Dunham, *Government Handout,* pp. 83–84.

9. Delegate Martin Maginnis, 45 Cong., 3 Sess. *Congressional Record,* VIII, Part 2, p. 1202.

10. Representative Thomas M. Patterson, *ibid.,* VIII, Part 3, Appendix, p. 219.

11. *Ibid.,* VIII, Part 3, Appendix, p. 221.

12. *Ibid.,* VIII, Part 2, p. 1211.

CHAPTER XX. THE GARDEN AS SAFETY VALVE

1. Roy M. Robbins, "Horace Greeley: Land Reform and Unemployment, 1837–1862," *Agricultural History,* VII, 18 (January, 1933).

2. *Ibid.*, VII, 25. Further documentation of Greeley's agrarianism is provided by Roland Van Zandt in "Horace Greeley, Agrarian Exponent of American Idealism," *Rural Sociology*, XIII, [411]–419 (December, 1948).

3. February 18, 1854. Quoted by Carter Goodrich and Sol Davison, "The Wage-Earner in the Westward Movement. I. The Statement of the Problem," *Political Science Quarterly*, L, 179–180 (June, 1935).

4. *The Frontier in American History* (New York, 1920), p. 62.

5. *Calendar of State Papers, Colonial Series. America and West Indies, March, 1720, to December, 1721*, p. 473.

6. *Ibid.*, Volume for 1731, p. 90.

7. John Bartram, *Observations on the Inhabitants, Climate, Soil . . . and Other Matters Worthy of Notice. Made by Mr. John Bartram, in his Travels from Pensilvania to Onondago, Oswego and the Lake Ontario* (London, 1751), p. v.

8. *Writings*, ed. Albert H. Smyth, III, 65.

9. *The Writings of George Washington from the Original Manuscript Sources*, ed. John C. Fitzpatrick, 39 vols. (Washington, 1931–1944), XXVIII, 206.

10. *Writings*, ed. Andrew A. Lipscomb, 20 vols. (Washington, 1903–1904), XI, 55. To "Mr. Lithson," Washington, January 4, 1805.

11. 21 Cong., 1 Sess. *Register of Debates in Congress*, VI, 34 (January 19, 1830).

12. *Ibid.*, VI, 24 (January 18, 1830).

13. 32 Cong., 1 Sess. *Congressional Globe*, Appendix, p. 737 (April 22, 1852).

14. *Capital. A Critical Analysis of Capitalist Production*, trans. Samuel Moore and Edward Aveling (London, 1912), pp. 794–800.

15. Helene S. Zahler, *Eastern Workingmen and National Land Policy*, pp. 10, 23–24, 29, etc.

16. John R. Commons, "Horace Greeley and the Working Class Origins of the Republican Party," *Political Science Quarterly*, XXIV, 484 (September, 1909).

17. Quoted from the *New York Tribune*, November 7, 1859, in *DeBow's Review*, XXVIII, 253n. (March, 1860).

18. 36 Cong., 1 Sess. *Congressional Globe*, p. 1631 (April 10, 1860).

19. Representative recent articles: (1) *Contra* the safety-valve theory: Carter Goodrich and Sol Davison, "The Wage-Earner in the Westward Movement. I. The Statement of the Problem," *Political Science Quarterly*, L, 161–185 (June, 1935); "II. The Question and the Sources," *ibid.*, LI, 61–116 (March, 1936); Fred A. Shannon, "The Homestead Act and the Labor Surplus," *American Historical Review*, XLI, 637–651 (June, 1936); Clarence H. Danhof, "Farm-Making Costs and the 'Safety Valve': 1850–60," *Journal of Political Economy*, XLIX, 317–359 (June, 1941). (2) *Pro* the safety-valve theory: Joseph Schafer, "Some Facts Bearing on the Safety-Valve Theory," *Wisconsin Magazine of History*, XX, 216–232 (December, 1936); "Concerning the Frontier as a Safety Valve," *Political Science Quarterly*, LII, 407–420 (September, 1937); "Was the West a Safety Valve for Labor?" *Mississippi Valley Historical Review*, XXIV, 299–314 (December, 1937). Fred A. Shannon seems to me to have established the falsity of the idea in

his most recent article on the subject, "A Post Mortem on the Labor-Safety-Valve Theory," *Agricultural History*, XIX, 31–37 (January, 1945).

20. *Writings,* ed. Albert H. Smyth, III, 65.

21. Joseph J. Spengler, "Population Doctrines in the United States. I. Anti-Malthusianism," *Journal of Political Economy*, XLI, 433–467 (August, 1933); "II. Malthusianism," XLI, 639–672 (October, 1933).

22. *The Writings of Thomas Jefferson,* ed. H. A. Washington, 9 vols. (Washington, 1853–1854), II, 332.

23. "An Address, on the Influence of the Federative Republican System of Government upon Literature and the Development of Character. Prepared to be Delivered before the Historical and Philosophical Society of Virginia," *Southern Literary Messenger*, II, 277 (March, 1836).

24. *Cannibals All! or Slaves without Masters* (Richmond, 1857), p. 61.

25. "R. E. C.," "The Problem of Free Society," *Southern Literary Messenger*, XXVII, 93–94 (August, 1858).

26. Quoted in Richard C. Beatty, *Lord Macaulay, Victorian Liberal* (Norman, Oklahoma, 1938), pp. 366–369. The letter was addressed to R. S. Randall.

27. *Clarel. A Poem and Pilgrimage in the Holy Land,* 2 vols. (New York, 1876), II, 524–527. The allusion to the god Terminus is apparently a reminiscence of Benton's speech on the occupation of Oregon in 1825: ". . . the ridge of the Rocky mountains may be named without offence, as presenting a convenient, natural, and everlasting boundary. Along the back of this ridge, the western limit of this republic should be drawn, and the statue of the fabled god, Terminus, should be raised upon its highest peak, never to be thrown down" (18 Cong., 2 Sess. *Register of Debates in Congress,* I, 712. Senate, March 1, 1825).

CHAPTER XXI. THE AGRICULTURAL WEST IN LITERATURE I: COOPER AND THE STAGES OF SOCIETY

1. *The Oak Openings; or, The Bee-Hunter,* 2 vols. (New York, 1848), I, 154.

2. *Ibid.,* I, 113.

3. *Westward Ho! A Tale,* 2 vols. (New York, 1832), I, 4.

4. Bushfield had been a companion of Boone (*ibid.,* I, 70); he was a loyal retainer of Colonel Dangerfield (I, 71); he felt crowded by the advance of settlement (I, 179–181); he wished to be able to fell a tree near his house for fuel (I, 184); and finally he fled to a remote military post on the Missouri River (II, 193).

5. *The New Pastoral* (Philadelphia, 1855), p. vi.

6. *Ibid.,* p. 208.

7. *Ibid.,* pp. 215–217, 225, 233–234, 237.

8. *Little Alice; or, The Pet of the Settlement. A Story of Prairie Land* (Boston, 1863), p. iii.

9. *Ibid.,* p. 143.

10. *Ibid.,* p. 56.

11. *Ibid.,* p. 236.

12. *Ibid.,* pp. 18, 67, 28.

13. *Ibid.*, p. 45.

14. *A Sermon Preached in Boston, New-England, before the Society for Encouraging Industry, and Employing the Poor, September 20, 1758* (Boston, 1758), pp. 10–11, 13.

15. *Travels; in New-England and New-York,* 4 vols. (New Haven, 1821–1822), II, 459.

16. *Ibid.*, II, 461–462.

17. *North American Review,* XLIII, 27–28 (July, 1836).

18. *Ibid.*, LV, 511 (October, 1842).

19. The origins of the conception and its currency in the United States are traced in Charles A. and Mary Beard, *The Rise of American Civilization,* Volume IV: *The American Spirit : A Study of the Idea of Civilization in the United States* (New York, 1942).

20. Philadelphia, 1796, and Baltimore, 1802.

21. This point, for example, was frequently made by missionaries working with Western Indians (*Twenty-Sixth Annual Report of the American Board of Commissioners for Foreign Missions,* Boston, 1835, p. 99; *Twenty-Seventh Annual Report,* Boston, 1836, pp. 95–96). William Tooke, an English traveler in Asia cited by William Darby (*View of the United States,* Philadelphia, 1828, p. 321), had asserted that the transition from a migratory pastoral life to agriculture "determines the boundary between civilized and barbarous nations" (*View of the Russian Empire during the Reign of Catherine the Second,* 3 vols., London, 1799, III, 230). Volney made the same point with regard to the Bedouins of Arabia (*Travels through Egypt and Syria,* Eng. trans., 2 vols., New York, 1798, I, 231).

22. *The Emigrant's Guide to the Western and Southwestern States and Territories* (New York, 1818), pp. 61–62.

23. *Port Folio,* Fourth [Fifth] Series, XVII, 214 (March, 1824).

24. Adam Hodgson, *Letters from North America,* 2 vols. (London, 1824), I, 318–319.

25. *Writings,* ed. H. A. Washington, VII, 377–378 (Monticello, September 6, 1824).

26. *Francis Berrian; or, The Mexican Patriot,* 2 vols. (Boston, 1826), I, 39.

27. *The Prairie* (Philadelphia, 1827), I, 88.

28. *Ibid.*, I, 26, 103.

29. Cooper calls the Bush group "semi-barbarous" (*ibid.*, I, 165), which was Jefferson's word for American settlers just within the frontier, immediately above the pastoral Indians in the scale of social stages.

30. *Ibid.*, I, 16–17, 20. At I, 166 Ishmael is again compared to "a well-fed and fattened ox," and is said to be a member of "a race who lived chiefly for the indulgence of the natural wants. . . ."

31. *Ibid.*, I, 78.

32. *Ibid.*, II, 237–248.

33. *Ibid.*, I, 222.

34. *Home as Found,* 2 vols. (Philadelphia, 1838), I, 180–183.

II: FROM CAROLINE KIRKLAND TO HAMLIN GARLAND

1. Vernon L. Parrington, *The Beginnings of Critical Realism in America* (*Main Currents in American Thought,* Volume III, 1930), reprint ed. (New York, n. d.), p. 288.

2. Ludwig Lewisohn's comment greatly overstates the case, but suggests the importance of this development for American literature: "It took genuine courage, genuine independence of mind to give literary treatment to the rude peasantry that peopled the Mississippi Valley. And it is from the treatment of this peasantry that our modern literature takes its rise. . . . The germs of our period of national expression are to be found in those few writers like Edward Eggleston and E. W. Howe who, whether consenting to it or resisting it, made the collective life of the American people the substance of serious literature" (*The Story of American Literature,* New York, 1932, p. 276).

3. The fullest account of Mrs. Kirkland's life and work is Langley Carleton Keyes, "Caroline M. Kirkland. A Pioneer in American Realism," Unpublished Doctor's Dissertation, Harvard University, 1935. The social position of the Stansburys is discussed on p. 96.

4. *A New Home — Who'll Follow? or Glimpses of Western Life,* by Mrs. Mary Clavers (pseud.) (first published 1839; 4th ed., New York, 1850), p. 3.

5. *Ibid.,* pp. 7, 8.

6. *Forest Life,* 2 vols. (New York, 1842), I, 122.

7. *Ibid.,* I, 209.

8. *Ibid.,* I, 7.

9. *A New Home,* p. 9.

10. *Ibid.,* pp. 29–31.

11. *Forest Life,* I, 237–250, II, [3]–45.

12. *Ibid.,* II, 46–146.

13. *Western Clearings* (New York, 1845), pp. 66–86.

14. *Ibid.,* pp. 118–143.

15. *Alice Wilde,* p. 72.

16. *Ibid.,* p. 20.

17. *Ibid.,* pp. 77, 81.

18. Advertisement on p. [30] of Edward S. Ellis, *The Frontier Angel,* New and Old Friends, No. 7 (New York, 1873).

19. Beadle's Dime Novels, No. 10 (1860).

20. *Ibid.,* pp. [9], 11, 14.

21. *Ibid.,* p. 17.

22. *Ibid.,* p. 19.

23. *Ibid.,* p. 23.

24. *Ibid.,* p. 98.

25. Beadle's Dime Novels, No. 16 (1861), p. 103.

26. *Ibid.,* pp. 103, 119–120.

27. Beadle's Dime Novels, No. 35 (1862), pp. 9, 41.

28. *Ibid.,* pp. 58–59.

29. *Ibid.,* pp. 84–85.

30. Beadle's Dime Novels, No. 39 (1862), pp. 9, 95.

31. *The Hoosier School-Master. A Novel* (New York, 1871), p. [5].

32. *Clovernook or Recollections of Our Neighborhood in the West. Second Series* (first published 1853; New York, 1884), pp. 109–145.

33. *Ibid.*, p. 143.

34. *Ibid.*, p. 25.

35. *Ibid.*, pp. 363–364. The Preface to the First Series of Clovernook sketches (New York, 1851, reprint, 1852), pp. v–vi, makes the same point about the failure of city dwellers to sympathize with poor and humble farm people. Although Miss Cary does not consider all Westerners socially inferior (Cincinnati, for example, has an upper class), she is vividly conscious of class differences between urban and rural populations.

36. *Clovernook* (Second Series), pp. 245–280.

37. *Married, Not Mated; or, How They Lived at Woodside and Throckmorton Hall* (New York, 1856), pp. 67, 97, 266, 270.

38. Miss Cary's other fictional efforts (*Hager. A Story of To-Day*, [New York, 1852; "second edition," 1852]; *The Bishop's Son. A Novel* [New York, 1867]) show no change in the rather confused pattern of her attitudes toward Western farmers.

39. *Hoosier School-Master*, pp. 122, 125.

40. *The Circuit Rider: A Tale of the Heroic Age* (New York, 1874), p. [173].

41. *Roxy* (New York, 1878), p. 183.

42. *Ibid.*, p. 343.

43. *Hoosier School-Master*, p. 163; *The Mystery of Metropolisville* (New York, 1873), p. 93.

44. *Hoosier School-Master*, p. 29.

45. *Mystery of Metropolisville*, p. 21.

46. *Hoosier School-Master*, p. [5].

47. *The End of the World. A Love Story* (New York, 1872), p. 8.

48. Eggleston remarks of Nancy Kirtley that she had only "something which a sanguine evolutionist might hope would develop into a conscience, by some chance, in many generations" (*Roxy*, p. [346]). His interest in and eventual acceptance of Darwin's position is discussed by his biographer William P. Randel (*Edward Eggleston, Author of The Hoosier School-Master* [New York, 1946], pp. 11, 218). In *The Faith Doctor* Eggleston referred to Darwin as "the intellect that has dominated our age" (Randel, *Eggleston*, p. 196). He publicly accepted Darwin in 1887 (*ibid.*, p. 218).

49. Randel, *Eggleston*, p. 123.

50. *The Circuit Rider*, pp. 55–56.

51. Some instances: George W. Kendall, *Narrative of the Texan Santa Fé Expedition*, 2 vols. (New York, 1844), I, 216–217; Francis Parkman, *The California and Oregon Trail: Being Sketches of Prairie and Rocky Mountain Life* (New York, 1849), p. 187; Thomas B. Thorpe, *Spirit of the Times*, X, [361] (1840).

52. If the term "realism" has any use in the vocabulary of literary criticism — and until a Professor Lovejoy discriminates the half-dozen or more current senses of the word it will probably continue to confuse more things than it clarifies — it might well be made to designate precisely these aspects of Dutch pictorial method transferred to the sphere of psychological analysis.

53. *Clovernook* (Second Series), pp. 116–117, 121–122.

54. *Ibid.*, pp. 119–120.

55. In "Mrs. Wetherbe's Quilting Party" the play-party is a functional

part of the plot. The "plays" include the nonmusical "Hunting the Key" as well as "rude rhymes, sung as accompaniments to the playing." Three specimens of the rimes are quoted: "O Sister Phoebe," "Uncle Johnny's sick a-bed," and a four-line stanza announcing, "My love and I will go, / And my love and I will go, / And we'll settle on the banks / Of the pleasant O-h-*i*-ó" (*ibid.*, pp. 50–51).

56. *The Circuit Rider*, p. 22.

57. *Ibid.*, p. 21. Volney, among others, had long before compared American Indians to "the nations so much extolled of ancient Greece and Italy" — intending of course to belittle the Greeks and Romans (*A View of the Soil and Climate of the United States of America*, [1803], trans. Charles Brockden Brown [Philadelphia, 1804], p. 410). The theory that the American West exhibited all the stages of social development lent itself easily to the discovery of a "heroic" age at some point in the Mississippi Valley.

58. *The Circuit Rider*, p. 22.

59. Mrs. Wetherbe, in "Mrs. Wetherbe's Quilting Party," whom Miss Cary admires, is given a marked dialect (*Clovernook*, Second Series, pp. 18–19, etc.), but the poverty-stricken family in "Ward Henderson" do not speak in dialect (*ibid.*, pp. 346–360). The strongly sentimental atmosphere of this story has perhaps exerted a refining influence on the language of the characters.

60. Randel, *Eggleston*, p. 79.

61. *Ibid.*, p. 105.

62. *Ibid.*, p. 187. It is not clear what publication Eggleston had in mind.

63. *Hoosier School-Master*, p. 6.

64. Randel, *Eggleston*, p. 126.

65. *The English Language in America*, 2 vols. (New York, 1925), I, 229.

66. Edward Eggleston, "Folk-Speech in America," *Century Magazine*, XLVIII, 870 (October, 1894).

67. *Roxy*, pp. 426–427.

68. Eggleston remarks that if the Backwoods Philosopher in *The End of the World* had known Whitman's work, he would have assigned the poet to the "Inferno" section of his library along with Swinburne, *Don Juan*, and "some French novels" (p. 44).

69. Eggleston wrote to his wife in 1888, after meeting Mark Twain, that he was "only a good clown after all" (Randel, *Eggleston*, p. 184).

70. *The End of the World*, p. 37 and note.

71. Randel, *Eggleston*, p. 184.

72. Kirkland told Hamlin Garland he was trying to improve on Eggleston, although he did not specify in what respect (*Roadside Meetings* [New York, 1930], p. 111).

73. *Zury: The Meanest Man in Spring County. A Novel of Western Life* (Boston, 1887), pp. 80–81. I have not been able to trace this allusion.

74. *Ibid.*, pp. 348–356. Kirkland explains in a note that one of the illustrations in the speech — based on feeding a calf — is derived from a stump speech of "Representative Horr, of Michigan" (p. 352n.).

75. *The McVeys: An Episode* (Boston, 1888), p. 339.

76. *Roadside Meetings*, pp. 90–94.

77. *Ibid.*, p. 95.

78. *Ibid.*, pp. 94–95.

79. *The Story of a Country Town* (Boston, 1883), pp. 239–240.

80. *Ibid.*, p. 3.

81. *Roadside Meetings*, p. 94.

82. *Ibid.*, p. 111.

83. *A New Home*, pp. 173–176.

84. *Clovernook* (Second Series), pp. 346–360.

85. Lytle Biggs is an unscrupulous man who organizes chapters of the Alliance to make money for himself. He cynically tells the farmers how industrious, honest, and oppressed they are in order to win their favor (*Story of a Country Town*, p. 240). The character of Biggs is not sympathetic but here he seems to be voicing Howe's own views.

86. *Roadside Meetings*, p. 113.

87. *Idem.*

88. *Jason Edwards, An Average Man* (Boston, 1892), p. [v].

89. *Ibid.*, p. [vi].

90. *Ibid.*, pp. 103, 111.

91. *Ibid.*, p. 142.

92. *A Spoil of Office. A Story of the Modern West* (Boston, 1892), p. 152.

93. *Main-Travelled Roads. Six Mississippi Valley Stories* (Boston, 1891), pp. 217–240.

94. *Ibid.*, pp. 96–97.

CHAPTER XXII. THE MYTH OF THE GARDEN AND TURNER'S FRONTIER HYPOTHESIS

1. *References on the Significance of the Frontier in American History*, compiled by Everett E. Edwards (United States Department of Agriculture Library, Bibliographical Contributions, No. 25, 2nd ed. [April, 1939]. Mimeographed), lists 124 items bearing on the subject, ranging in date from Franklin's "Observations on the Peopling of Countries" (1751) to 1939. A passage from a radio address by Franklin D. Roosevelt in 1935 which Dr. Edwards quotes in his excellent Introduction illustrates the political application of Turner's ideas: "Today we can no longer escape into virgin territory. We must master our environment. . . . We have been compelled by stark necessity to unlearn the too comfortable superstition that the American soil was mystically blessed with every kind of immunity to grave economic maladjustments . . ." (p. 3).

2. "The Significance of the Frontier in American History," in *The Early Writings of Frederick Jackson Turner, with a List of All His Works Compiled by Everett E. Edwards and an Introduction by Fulmer Mood* (Madison, Wisconsin, 1938), p. 186.

3. A growing body of scholarship is being devoted to this challenging question. George W. Pierson has called attention to inconsistencies in Turner's doctrines and has inquired into the extent of their currency among historians at the present time: "The Frontier and Frontiersman of Turner's Essays: A Scrutiny of the Foundations of the Middle Western Tradition," *Pennsylvania Magazine of History and Biography*, LXIV, 449–478 (October, 1940); "The Frontier and American Institutions: A Criticism of the Turner Theory," *New England Quarterly*, XV, 224–255 (June, 1942); "American Historians and the Frontier Hypothesis in 1941," *Wisconsin Magazine of*

History, XXVI, 36–60, 170–185 (September, December, 1942). I am indebted to Professor Pierson for many ideas, especially the remark he quotes from a colleague to the effect that Turner's frontiersman closely resembles the stock eighteenth-century picture of the small farmer of Britain (*Wisconsin Magazine of History*, XXVI, 183–184) and the suggestion that Turner's "poetic interpretations" revived "the grandest ideas that had gone to make up the American legend" (*idem*).

4. James C. Malin points out that most of Turner's ideas were "in the air." He remarks that great thinkers are normally "the beneficiaries of the folk process and are probably seldom so much true creators as channels through which the folk process finds its fullest expression in explicit language . . ." ("Space and History: Reflections on the Closed-Space Doctrines of Turner and Mackinder and the Challenge of Those Ideas by the Air Age," *Agricultural History*, XVIII, 67–68, April, 1944).

5. *Early Writings*, p. 187.

6. Fulmer Mood, "The Development of Frederick Jackson Turner as a Historical Thinker," *Publications of the Colonial Society of Massachusetts*, XXXIV: *Transactions 1937–1942* (Boston, 1943), pp. 322–325.

7. Turner copied into a Commonplace Book that he kept in 1886, during his first year of teaching, a quotation ascribed to Franklin: "The boundless woods of America which are sure to afford freedom and subsistence to any man who can bait a hook or pull a trigger" (Commonplace Book [II], p. [1]. Turner Papers, Henry E. Huntington Library). The idea occurs often in Franklin but I have not been able to find these words.

8. "The Poet of the Future," delivered at the Junior Exhibition, University of Wisconsin, May 25, 1883, and reported in full in the Madison *University Press* (May 26, 1883), p. 4 (clipping in Turner Papers, Henry E. Huntington Library).

9. Commonplace Book [I], 1883, pp. [25–27]. Turner Papers, Henry E. Huntington Library.

10. *Ibid.*, pp. [49–53].

11. *Early Writings*, p. 221.

12. "The West and American Ideals," an address delivered at the University of Washington, June 17, 1914, *Washington Historical Quarterly*, V, 245 (October, 1914). When Turner revised this address for inclusion in the volume of collected papers *The Frontier in American History* in 1920, he omitted the words "stark and strong and full of life" (New York, 1920, reprint ed., 1931, p. 293). Although Turner repudiated the "germ theory" of constitutional development in his 1893 essay (*Early Writings*, p. 188), he had accepted it for a time after he left Herbert B. Adams' seminar at Johns Hopkins. Reviewing the first two volumes of Theodore Roosevelt's *The Winning of the West* in the Chicago *Dial* in August of 1889 (X, 72), he remarked that "the old Germanic 'tun'" reappeared in the "forted village" of early Kentucky and Tennessee, the "folkmoot" in popular meetings of the settlers, and the "witenagemot" in representative assemblies like the Transylvania legislature. "These facts," he added, "carry the mind back to the warrior-legislatures in the Germanic forests, and forward to those constitutional conventions now at work in our own newly-made states in the Far West; and they make us proud of our English heritage." In an undergraduate address he had asserted that "The spirit of individual liberty slumbered in

the depths of the German forest" from the time of the barbarian invasions of Rome until it burst forth in the American and French Revolutions (Madison *University Press* [May 26, 1883], p. 4). Turner's discovery of the American frontier as a force encouraging democracy may exhibit some imaginative persistence of this association between desirable political institutions and a forest.

13. A characteristic phrase is the reference to "this rebirth of American society" that has gone on, decade after decade, in the West (from an essay in the *Atlantic*, 1896, reprinted in *The Frontier in American History*, p. 205). In his undergraduate Commonplace Book Turner had jotted down, among notes for an oration, "See Emerson's preface to 'Nature' . . ." and had added part of a sentence: ". . . let us believe in the eternal genesis, the freshness & value of things present, act as though, just created, we stood looking a new world in the face and investigate for ourselves and act regardless of past ideas" (Commonplace Book [I], p. [3]). This is quite Emersonian; it might well be a paraphrase of the familiar first paragraph of Emerson's essay: "Why should not we also enjoy an original relation to the universe? Embosomed for a season in nature, whose floods of life stream around and through us, and invite us, by the powers they supply, to action proportioned to nature, why should we grope among the dry bones of the past, or put the living generation into masquerade out of its faded wardrobe?" (*Complete Works*, Volume I: *Nature, Addresses, and Lectures* [Boston, 1903], p. [3]). Turner said in 1919 that he had been impressed with Woodrow Wilson's emphasis on Walter Bagehot's idea of growth through "breaking the cake of custom" (Frederick Jackson Turner to William E. Dodd, Cambridge, Mass., October 7, 1919, copy in Turner Papers, Henry E. Huntington Library). The phrase appears in the *Atlantic* essay (*The Frontier in American History*, p. 205).

14. Address at the dedication of a new high school building at Turner's home town of Portage, Wisconsin, January 1, 1896, reported in the Portage *Weekly Democrat*, January 3, 1896 (clipping in Turner Papers, Henry E. Huntington Library).

15. *The Frontier in American History*, pp. 255, 267.

16. *Ibid.*, p. 250.

17. *Publications of the Colonial Society of Massachusetts*, XXXIV, 304–307. Mr. Mood says that the idea of applying the theory of evolution to social phenomena was the "fundamental, unifying concept" of Turner's early writings (p. 304), but adds that the *a priori* idea of a sequence of social stages "can be asserted to be, as a universal rule . . . fallacious . . . . It is one component element in Turner's [1893] essay that will not now stand the test of inspection" (p. 307n.).

18. *The Frontier in American History*, p. 121 (1908).

19. *Early Writings*, pp. 199, 285.

20. *Ibid.*, p. 222.

21. *Ibid.*, p. 285.

22. Frederick Jackson Turner to Merle E. Curti, San Marino, Cal., January 5, 1931. Copy in Turner Papers, Henry E. Huntington Library. Turner says he had not read George before writing the 1893 essay and that he had never accepted the single-tax idea.

23. Professor Malin has emphasized the fact that in his later career

Turner was "baffled by his contemporary world and had no satisfying answer to the closed-frontier formula in which he found himself involved" (*Essays on Historiography*, Lawrence, Kansas, 1946, p. 38).

24. *The Frontier in American History*, p. 285 (1910).

25. "Since the Foundation," an address delivered at Clark University, February 4, 1924, *Publications of the Clark University Library*, VII, No. 3, p. 29. After the words "dangers that menace him" Turner has indicated in his personal copy in the Henry E. Huntington Library (No. 222544) the addition of the following words: "that there are automatic adjustments in progress."

26. Charles A. Beard makes this point in what seems to me a convincing manner in "The Frontier in American History," *New Republic*, XCVII, 359–362 (February 1, 1939). Professor Malin asserts vigorously that "among other things, the frontier hypothesis is an agricultural interpretation of American history which is being applied during an industrial urban age . . ." ("Mobility and History," *Agricultural History*, XVII, 177, October, 1943).

27. Benjamin F. Wright has a similar comment in his review of *The Significance of Sections in American History*, *New England Quarterly*, VI, 631 (September, 1933). Professor Malin calls the frontier hypothesis "an isolationist interpretation in an international age" (*Agricultural History*, XVII, 177). "It seemed to confirm the Americans," he remarks elsewhere, "in their continental isolationism. Was not their United States a unique civilization; was it not superior to that of Europe and Asia?" (*ibid.*, XVIII, 67, April, 1944).

28. *The Frontier in American History*, p. 253 (1903).

29. *Ibid.*, p. 294 (1914). In the 1903 article Turner had emphasized the contrast between American democracy, which was "fundamentally the outcome of the experiences of the American people in dealing with the West," and the "modern efforts of Europe to create an artificial democratic order by legislation" (*ibid.*, p. 266). The implication is clearly that American democracy is the opposite of artificial, i.e., natural, and that this natural origin establishes its superiority.

INDEX